ANAPHORA AND CONCEPTUAL STRUCTURE

COGNITIVE THEORY OF LANGUAGE AND CULTURE

A series edited by Gilles Fauconnier, George Lakoff, and Eve Sweetser

Previously published:

Constructions: A Construction Grammar Approach to Argument Structure
Adele E. Goldberg

Spaces, Worlds, and Grammar
edited by Gilles Fauconnier and Eve Sweetser

Anaphora and Conceptual Structure

Karen van Hoek

The University of Chicago Press
Chicago and London

Karen van Hoek is assistant professor of linguistics at the University of Michigan.

The University of Chicago Press, Chicago 60637
The University of Chicago Press, Ltd., London
© 1997 by The University of Chicago
All rights reserved. Published 1997
Printed in the United States of America

06 05 04 03 02 01 00 99 98 97   1 2 3 4 5

ISBN: 0-226-84893-0   (cloth)
ISBN: 0-226-84894-9   (paper)

P299
·A5
V36
1997

Library of Congress Cataloging-in-Publication Data

Van Hoek, Karen.
    Anaphora and conceptual structure / Karen van Hoek.
        p.   cm. — (Cognitive theory of language and culture)
    Revision of the author's thesis (University of Chicago) under the
title: Paths through conceptual structure.
    Includes bibliographical references and index.
    ISBN 0-226-84893-0 (alk. paper). — ISBN 0-226-84894-9 (pbk. : alk.
paper)
    1. Anaphora (Linguistics)   2. Semantics—Psychological aspects.
3. Reference (Linguistics)   4. Connectionism.   5. Cognitive grammar.
I. Title.   II. Series.
P299.A5V36   1997
415—dc21   96-37640
                                                                          CIP

♾ The paper used in this publication meets the minimum requirements of
the American National Standard for Information Sciences—Permanence
of Paper for Printed Library Materials, ANSI Z39.48-1984.

For my family

CONTENTS

This work is a revised version of my dissertation, *Paths through Conceptual Structure: Constraints on Pronominal Anaphora,* in which I develop a model of constraints on pronominal anaphora within the framework of Cognitive Grammar. In contrast to analyses based on syntactic structural relations such as c-command, I argue that only semantically grounded notions, such as prominence and semantic connectivity, are needed to explain the coreference constraints. Cognitive Grammar provides the theoretical vocabulary needed to define these notions with some precision.

The differences between the analysis as it is presented here and as originally developed for the dissertation are both large and small. The most significant revision in my thinking is in the nature and function of semantic connectivity, particularly its relationship to the notions of prominence and point of view. While prominence and connectivity are treated separately for the sake of expository convenience, from a theoretical standpoint they are more clearly unified here than before.

In the first version of the model, point of view was presented as a peripheral factor within the model, almost an afterthought. Among the factors which define the relevant domains for the anaphora constraints, point of view was listed as a separate factor, along with prominence, semantic connectivity, and linear word order. I now understand point of view to be integral to the system of semantic domains within which coreference is determined to be acceptable or unacceptable.

"Viewing" a conception from a particular point of view means setting up a mental space (in the sense of Fauconnier 1985) which represents the imagined viewer's awareness or perceptions. The distinction between adopting a particular person's point of view or understanding a conception more or less "objectively" is a question of which mental space is taken as the primary context within which the conception is to be understood.

In the revision of the analysis, it has become more clearly apparent that the semantic domains relevant for anaphora (here termed "dominions") are mental spaces, and that they are not fundamentally different in kind from one another, whether they are established through "adoption of a point of view," or through semantic relations within argument structure, or through other means. It has also become clear that the semantic connectivity which determines the extent or scope of a dominion is fundamentally a matter of the relative prominence of mental spaces, an observation which lays the groundwork for an account of interactions between point of view and other factors. Ultimately, the constraints on anaphoric coreference rest on the relative prominence of the conceptual constructs which collectively make up the context for a nominal. The study of anaphora constraints is therefore the study of conceptual structure.

It would be impossible to acknowledge all the people who have provided support, suggestions, or inspiration for this work. A few names must be mentioned, however. I am particularly grateful to Ronald Langacker, who supervised the original research in his capacity as dissertation committee chair, and since then has generously made himself available for in-depth discussion of the issues which arose as I revised the analysis. I would like to thank series editors Gilles Fauconnier, George Lakoff, and Eve Sweetser, and senior editor Geoffrey Huck, for their assistance and support. I am indebted to the referees for the University of Chicago Press for their impressive thoroughness and numerous suggestions.

Many other colleagues have contributed directly or indirectly to this work by making insightful suggestions, by asking questions which pushed me to clarify and refine my analysis, and by sending me pertinent works. With apologies to those whom I have inadvertently omitted, I would like to thank Michel Achard, Mira Ariel, Frances Cornish, Paul Deane, Michel DeGraf, Richard Epstein, Jeffrey Heath, Michael Hegarty, Michael Israel, Ray Jackendoff, Robert Kirsner, Edward Klima, John Lawler, Scott Liddell, Linda Manney, Carl Pollard, Johanna Rubba, Nicholas Ruwet, Daniel Seely, Michael Smith, Leonard Talmy, Arie Verhagen, Gregory Ward, Yael Ziv, and Anne Zribi-Hertz.

I would like to thank my colleagues at the University of Michigan for providing a stimulating intellectual environment in which to carry out this work, and the students in my Cognitive Grammar courses for asking some of the most challenging questions. I owe a special debt of gratitude to Bonnie Dixon, Valerie Hammel, and Neil Clennan, without whose friendship, assistance, and support this project would have been far more difficult and far less enjoyable.

ONE

Introduction

In this study I propose a model of constraints on pronominal anaphora within the framework of Cognitive Grammar. Cognitive Grammar (CG) proceeds from the position that grammatical structure can be characterized and explained in terms of semantic and phonological representations without the need for autonomous syntactic structures or principles, including the tree structures commonly used in generative syntactic theories (see Langacker 1987a, 1991). I show that the constraints on anaphora can be explained in terms of semantic interactions between nominals and the contexts in which they are embedded.

1.1 THE ISSUE

Pronominal anaphora has been a major concern within syntactic theory for nearly three decades. The constraints on pronominal coreference, which are highly complex and which involve relationships between distantly separated elements within a sentence, have been seen as an important avenue for exploring the fundamental principles of linguistic structure. The c-command relationship that is used to explain why coreference is permitted in sentences like (1a, c) but prohibited in sentences like (1b, d) has become a linchpin of generative analyses of constraints on wh-question formation, quantifier scope, negative polarity, and the positioning of noun phrases within the sentence, among other things. (Italics are used here to signify coreference.)

(1) a. Near *him, John* noticed a trapdoor.
     b. *Near *John, he* noticed a trapdoor.

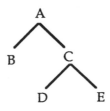

Figure 1.1

  c. *John* loves *his* mother.
  d. **He* loves *John's* mother.

Within the generative syntactic tradition, the standard explanation for the anaphora constraints is based on some version of the structural notion of c-command proposed by Reinhart (1976, 1981, 1983, 1986). In the simplest formulation of c-command, NP1 (noun phrase 1) c-commands NP2 if neither dominates the other and the first branching node dominating NP1 also dominates NP2. In the tree shown in Fig. 1.1, node B c-commands C, D, and E, while C c-commands only B, and D and E each only c-command the other.[1]

The constraint on coreference which applies to data such as (1) is that a full noun phrase (which may be either a descriptive phrase such as *the man* or a name such as *John*) cannot be c-commanded by a coreferential noun phrase of any kind. Given the structures which Reinhart argues for in sentences such as (1), the pronoun in (1b), but not in (1a), c-commands the name. The c-command analysis has since been adopted as the core of the Binding Conditions of Government-Binding theory (Chomsky 1981).

The relative success of the structurally defined anaphora constraints, and the centrality of the c-command notion to generative syntactic theory, present a significant challenge to a cognitive semantic theory of grammar such as CG, which does not utilize syntactic tree structures. At the same time, I will argue, the structural constraints have left a number of important questions unanswered in precisely the areas in which a cognitive semantic theory provides the necessary theoretical constructs to offer an analysis. I argue for the superiority of the CG account presented here on the basis that this analysis provides a semantically grounded *explanation* of the constraints (rather than just a list), as well as answers to several significant questions that have been left open by previous accounts. Some of these questions, which are discussed in more detail below, are as follows:

1. The conceptual basis for the constraints: why full noun phrases, pronouns, and reflexives have differing distribution patterns, and why the domains for determining coreference possibilities are defined the way they are.

2. Why the c-command analysis has been as successful as it has in predicting a large number of the facts. CG does not avail itself of autonomous-syntactic tree structures, and the account given here does not make use of c-command. To the extent that the alternative analysis proposed here is workable, it raises the question of why the c-command notion has seemed to account for both pronominal anaphora facts and other phenomena.

3. The nature of the relationship between the syntactic constraints and the principles which govern cross-sentential, discourse-level coreference.

4. The role of allegedly peripheral factors such as point of view and linear word order, which have either been neglected by structural accounts or have been the subject of controversy concerning their proper domain of application.

5. The proper treatment of variability in speakers' judgments of coreference, and the reason that certain construction types, although arguably permitted by the grammar, are very rare in actual usage and are frequently judged as marginal. While questions of this sort have typically been considered to be outside the domain of inquiry for a generative account, I will argue that there is no a priori reason to exclude these issues from consideration, and will show that the answers to some of these fall out naturally from the principles used here to account for the anaphora constraints (§5.1–5, §8.1.1).

These questions are briefly addressed in the following sections, in which I outline the CG analysis which will be developed more fully in subsequent chapters.

1.2 THE CONCEPTUAL BASIS OF THE CONSTRAINTS

The analysis developed here is grounded in the theory of Accessibility developed by Givón (1983b, 1985, 1989, 1994), Ariel (1988, 1990), and Gundel, Hedberg, and Zacharski (1993), among others. It is claimed that distinct nominal forms differ with respect to the degree of accessibility (roughly "retrievability" or salience) of their referents in the immediate context.[2] The constraints on coreference reflect the contextual requirements of the various nominal categories. A full noun phrase (a name such as *John* or a descriptive phrase such as *the angry baker*) indicates that its referent is currently of low accessibility, that is, not salient in the immediate context. A pronoun is used for a referent of relatively high accessibility, one which is relatively salient within the speaker's and addressee's awarenesses (typically because the referent has been recently mentioned or because the person is physically present and perceptible).

The relevance of Accessibility theory in accounting for discourse-level patterns of coreference and renaming of referents seems intuitively obvious. Applying it to the problem of sentence-internal anaphora constraints is more difficult. The major hurdle to be cleared is the question of defining the relevant notion of context within the sentence, determining which nominal conceptions are construed as accessible at any given point. Given the guiding principles of CG, defining the necessary contexts in terms of autonomous-syntactic structural notions such as c-command is ruled out.

The detailed semantic vocabulary of CG provides the tools necessary to define the relevant clause-internal semantic contexts. I develop a model in which some nominals serve as **conceptual reference points**, which function roughly as local topics. Reference points are similar to Chafe's (1979, 1987, 1991, 1994) starting points, as well as the starting points discussed by MacWhinney (1977).[3] Reference points are associated with dominions, where a dominion is defined as the conceptual domain relative to which the reference point is highly accessible and functions as a central part of the background context. Coreference is ruled out when a nominal form which signifies low accessibility is embedded in the dominion of a corresponding (i.e., coreferential) reference point; in (1b, d) above, for example, the conception signified by the name *John* is construed within the dominion of the conception designated by the pronoun *he*, and so the sentence is judged anomalous if coreference is assumed: A low accessibility marker appears in a domain in which its referent is in fact highly accessible.

The selection of reference points is determined primarily by semantic prominence. A nominal tends to be construed as a reference point to the extent that it is prominent as determined by general principles of semantic prominence developed independently in CG and discussed in §2.1 and §3.2.4. The extent of a reference point's dominion is determined primarily by semantic connectivity: Nominals which are semantically connected with the reference point (in a sense to be specified below; see §3.2.4, §3.3, and Chap. 4) are construed as belonging to its dominion.

Under this approach, the anaphora constraints are not independently stated syntactic principles, but are rather the effects of the semantic interaction of nominals with the reference point configurations in which they are embedded. The model thus makes the claim that the anaphora constraints are fundamentally semantic/pragmatic in nature.

As it draws on the details of clausal and phrasal semantics, the analysis also functions as an exploration of the cognitive semantic representation of sentences and an illustration of the explanatory power of CG. The constructs utilized here have all been independently developed and motivated within the CG literature. The semantic constructs involved are all notions which arguably must be dealt with by any comprehensive and psychologically real theory of natural language semantics: prominence, head/argument relations, point of view, and conceptual connectivity (the extent to which elements are understood to belong to a single semantic unit of some kind).

It may be asked whether the analysis developed here is a notational variant of the traditional c-command analysis. Semantic prominence, for example, might be argued to be essentially a renaming of structural superiority. Even if there were no independent evidence for the fundamentally semantic nature of the anaphora constraints, the analysis would still be motivated on the grounds of theoretical austerity: The CG account explains the facts using only independently needed semantic constructs without appeal to the additional mechanism of autonomous-syntactic tree structures.

There is, however, direct evidence for the conceptual-semantic basis of the analysis. The model incorporates domains of data for which c-command offers no account, such as coreference patterns at the discourse level and point-of-view effects. The claims made here are also indirectly supported by other research in cognitive linguistics, functional linguistics, and discourse analysis. The claim that the subject of the clause is a kind of local topic or starting point in relation to the predicate, a claim which is motivated here by considerations internal to CG, is also familiar from the work of Givón (1976, 1989, 1994), Chafe (1987, 1991, 1994), and others. The import of semantic connectivity is supported by an array of studies in discourse and narrative analysis, some of which are cited in Chapter 5. The overall claim that the relevant contexts for the anaphora constraints are fundamentally conceptual-semantic is supported by evidence showing the effects of point-of-view shifts in cases where an analysis in terms of autonomous syntax would predict point of view should have no effect (see §3.4, Chap. 8).

1.3 THE NATURE AND LIMITATIONS OF C-COMMAND

An important question which any alternative to c-command must address is why the c-command restrictions on anaphora work as well as they do. Before I answer this question, let me first point out a few empirical shortcomings of the c-command model. The c-command restrictions in some cases require questionable modifications of tree structure to obtain the right result, as in (2). In each of these sentences, the pronoun does not c-command the full noun phrase unless we assume that the PP (prepositional phrase) node immediately dominating the pronominal noun phrase is somehow "transparent" and does not count as the first branching node (see Reinhart 1983:54).

(2)   a.   *I spoke to *him* about finances in *Ben*'s office.
        b.   *John gave a book to *her* for *Sally*'s birthday.

In (3a), which involves point-of-view effects, enabling the pronoun to c-command the full noun phrase would require significant modifications of the tree structure or a major revision of the definition of c-command. Note that whatever reformulation we might come up with would have to be prevented from applying to (3b), which is structurally identical to (3a) (in all of the relevant respects) but which permits co-reference.

(3)   a.   *Her* wish is that *Sally* will become a physicist.
        b.   *Her* mother is *Sally*'s best friend.

While it is unarguable that the c-command analysis has been remarkably successful, it should also be pointed out that the appearance of near-complete success is augmented by the fact that certain classes of data have been excluded from consideration. If we broaden our horizons somewhat to include data traditionally considered extrasyntactic, it becomes apparent that the c-command analysis covers only a portion of the domain of pronominal anaphora facts. In some cases the justification for assigning certain data to an extrasyntactic domain of inquiry is not immediately clear.

Linear word order, for example, has frequently been argued to be irrelevant to the syntactic anaphora constraints, though it is accorded relevance at the discourse level.[4] (4c–d) would not be ruled ungrammatical owing to any violation of c-command principles, as the pronoun in each case does not c-command the full noun phrase.

(4) a. *Peter* went home, and then *he* took a nap.
     b. Sally visited *Peter* and reassured *him*.
     c. **He* went home, and then *Peter* took a nap.
     d. **Sally visited *him* and reassured *Peter*.

It seems clear that the problem with (4c–d) pertains to the linear word order: The pronoun precedes the full noun phrase (see Langacker 1969). Reinhart (1983:54–55) proposes that these data be explained by a discourse-level principle of linear order rather than by a syntactic constraint. Essentially, speakers prefer to introduce a referent into the discourse with a full noun phrase and then "refer back" with a pronoun rather than the other way around. Reinhart's proposal means that the ungrammaticality of (4c–d) is explained in the same way as (5b), where coreference seems equally unacceptable. (The # symbol is used to indicate that the sentence, while grammatical, is anomalous in the discourse context.)

(5) a. *John* went into the study. *He* picked up the phone.
     b. *He* went into the study. #*John* picked up the phone.

There are at least two weaknesses in Reinhart's specific account, though the general idea seems at least partially correct. The discourse principle has not been developed in any detail, and so it is unclear why, for example, sentences such as *Near him, John noticed a trapdoor* would not also be rejected by the discourse linear order rule. There is also little (if any) independent basis for deciding which phenomena should be attributed to syntax or discourse. Lasnik (1989) points out that violations of discourse principles typically produce less robust judgments of grammaticality than syntactic violations, but this is not a reliable guide. Many speakers judge the sentences in (4c–d) and (5b), for example, to be fully unacceptable.

A different problem with the extrasyntactic status of linear word order is that linear order clearly affects speakers' judgments, even in cases where c-command makes an unequivocal prediction of (un)grammaticality. If the c-command restriction applies within the syntactic component to flag a sentence as ungrammatical, discourse-level principles should not be able to undo or ameliorate that judgment. But in fact, speakers frequently hesitate before judging a sentence such as *Near Dan, he saw a snake* ungrammatical, and a small number accept it under the coreferential reading.

This is not a difficulty for Reinhart's analysis of (4c–d), which assumes that a sentence which has passed the c-command filter may be judged awkward at the discourse level, but it is problematic in general to claim that a construction which should be clearly ungrammatical under the c-command analysis may be partially saved by linear order considerations in a different, extrasyntactic module. The implication is that linear word order interacts with other factors to a greater extent than implied under most applications of c-command.

Point-of-view phenomena, as in (3a) above and in (6), have also been excluded from consideration under most versions of the c-command analysis. This has been tacitly justified by the observation that the judgments involving point of view are frequently less reliable and robust than the judgments involving syntactic principles (the % symbol is used in [6] to indicate variable judgments). The effect, however, has been to exclude a large domain of data from consideration (see Kuno 1987). In §3.4 and Chapter 8 I argue that point-of-view considerations interact with the "purely syntactic" anaphora phenomena to a greater extent than previously acknowledged; as with linear word order, the decision to relegate point of view to a separate domain of inquiry is questionable.

(6)   a. %The idea that *John* might have AIDS worried *him*.
        b. %That *Sally* could lose the election was unthinkable to *her*.

Overall, the c-command model has been quite successful, but it has some clear shortcomings, including simply not covering certain domains of data. The conceptual basis or motivation for c-command also remains an open question (unless we accept that it is simply given innately as part of Universal Grammar [Grodzinsky and Reinhart 1993]).

Reinhart (1983, 1986) proposes a partial, pragmatic motivation for the anaphora constraints, but it is flawed both empirically and conceptually. She proposes that the syntactic constraints on anaphora be reduced in essence to a single constraint on bound anaphora. The constraints on coreference between a pronoun and full noun phrase would then be explained by a pragmatic principle which states essentially that one should use a bound pronoun wherever one is possible, and that if a speaker avoids using a bound pronoun where one would have been allowed, the addressee will infer that coreference could not have been intended—since if it had been, a bound pronoun would have been a less ambiguous way of expressing the coreference relation.

Reinhart's proposal is based on the observation that there is, by and large, an isomorphic relationship between the structures which allow for bound anaphoric readings of pronouns and the structures which—if a full noun phrase is inserted—give a judgment of obligatory non-coreference. For example, (7a–b) allow for bound anaphoric readings; (7c–d) illustrate that, if the quantifier phrase is replaced with a pronoun and a full noun phrase is inserted in the slot which in (7a–b) was occupied by the bound pronoun, coreference is unacceptable.

(7) a. Everyone loves his mother.
    b. Sandy gave each boy his own crayons.
    c. *He loves John's mother.
    d. *Sandy gave him Bill's crayons.

Reinhart generalizes the notion of bound anaphora to include not only constructions in which a pronoun is anteceded by a quantifier phrase but also constructions in which a pronoun is anteceded by a c-commanding nominal of any kind, including definite nominals. She notes that "bound anaphora is the most explicit way available in the language to express coreference, as it involves direct dependency of the pronoun upon its antecedent for its interpretation" (Reinhart 1986:143). Reinhart therefore proposes that speakers and hearers follow a strategy based on a Gricean maxim of manner, as developed by Kasher (1976), which is that speakers should be as explicit as circumstances permit. As Reinhart (1983:166) notes, "In a rational linguistic exchange we would expect that if a speaker has the means to express a certain idea clearly and directly, he would not arbitrarily choose a less-clear way to express it."

It is empirically incorrect to maintain that the structures allowing bound anaphora and the structures determining obligatory non-coreference are one and the same. There is, however, a very large overlap between the two categories, which is explained under the CG analysis by the claim that the structures in which bound anaphora are possible are defined by the same notions of semantic prominence and connectivity which define the configurations for obligatory non-coreference (the analysis of bound anaphora is presented in Chap. 6). Essentially, antecedents for bound anaphora must be prominent within the construction and conceptually strongly connected with the pronoun, and so they are usually complements of the main verb, most typically the subject (the subject is, in CG, considered a complement of the verb).

There are however certain nominals within the clause which are sufficiently salient to function as antecedents for bound anaphora, although they are not complements of the main-clause verb. These include possessive nominals and nominals embedded in relative clauses, as exemplified in (8a–b). As (8c–d) illustrate, coreference is not ruled out in the analogous configurations involving full noun phrases—as predicted by the reference point model (see §3.3.6). (The c-command model also predicts that coreference is acceptable in [8c–d], but has some difficulty in accounting for the possibility of bound anaphora in [8a–b] [but see Reinhart 1987].)

(8) a. Everyone's mother loves him.
     b. Everyone who owns a donkey feeds it.
     c. *His* mother loves *John*.
     d. Everyone who knows *him* admires *John*.

The attempt to reduce the c-command restriction to a restriction on bound anaphora plus pragmatic principles is therefore not entirely successful. Even if it were, it would leave open the question of why c-command itself is relevant, why this particular structural relation plays such an important role. I will claim in this study that c-command works as well as it does because the tree structures on which it is defined capture a certain amount of *semantic* information. I argue that tree structures, though they are not generally thought of in this way, are rough sketches of conceptual structure. To the extent that the tree structures and the c-command relation fail to capture significant conceptual-semantic relationships, they are inadequate to explain anaphora facts which depend on those relationships.

Anticipating the discussion somewhat, I claim that the organization of reference points and their dominions depends largely on semantic prominence (as well as semantic connectivity, as defined below). More-prominent nominals function as reference points, with less-prominent nominals in their dominions. Prominence is defined in accordance with general principles of CG (see Langacker 1987a, 1991, and references there). Roughly speaking, prominence is defined by the familiar grammatical relations hierarchy SU > DO > IO > OBL (Keenan and Comrie 1977; Bresnan 1982; Perlmutter and Postal 1983; Perlmutter and Rosen 1984; Dalrymple 1993), and by the distinction between complements and modifiers, where complements of a head are more prominent than modifiers or elements contained within modifiers.

Notice that in the standard generative tree structures, the subject c-commands most of the clause, and complements of the verb c-command larger portions of the tree than do elements within modifying phrases. In (1a–b) above, the subject nominal in each sentence c-commands the rest of the clause, but the object of the preposition *near* c-commands only that preposition, nothing more. C-command indirectly reflects what the CG analysis terms an asymmetry of prominence: The subject is the most prominent nominal in both of those sentences; the object of the preposition, the least prominent. This kind of correlation between semantic relationships and tree structure holds fairly generally; it fails primarily with respect to phenomena such as point-of-view effects, where the semantic connection between viewer and viewed may be given no representation in tree structure.[5]

1.4 THE RELATIONSHIP BETWEEN SYNTAX AND DISCOURSE

The c-command analysis does not provide a unified account of the relationship between syntactic constraints on coreference and the principles which govern coreference at the cross-sentential discourse level. The two sets of principles are assumed to be distinct, involving different theoretical notions and applying to different domains (e.g., Reinhart 1983; Lasnik 1989). While such a split might, of necessity, be motivated on theory-internal grounds, it seems rather unsatisfying to have to posit that nominal coreference within the sentence is governed by one set of principles, while coreference across sentences, involving exactly the same morphological forms—pronouns, full noun phrases, and so on—is treated as an entirely different phenomenon.

I will argue that a unified account is more consistent with the facts of usage, which indicate that there is no sharp split between syntactic and discourse-level anaphora phenomena. Rather there is a continuum from syntax to discourse, involving degrees of conceptual-semantic connectivity. The seemingly vast difference between the sharp syntactic constraints and the fuzzier, more variable "discourse tendencies" is explained by semantic connectivity as well. In other words, not only are both domains covered by the same general principles, but the explanation for the apparent difference between them lies in those principles as well (see §5.6).

As a general principle, a nominal tends to be construed as belonging to the dominion of a reference point to the extent that it is semantically connected with that reference point. Semantic connectivity is defined as a continuum, ranging from strong connectivity (defined by explicitly coded relational interconnections, such as those provided by a verb), to weaker connectivity (defined by co-occurrence within a larger linguistic unit, such as a sentence, without direct interconnection), to weakest connectivity (defined by conceptual junctures or discontinuities, such as changes in scene, topic, conceptual paragraph boundaries, etc. [see Fox 1987a, 1987b; Tomlin 1987b]). Here I will briefly illustrate the points on the continuum; Chapters 4 and 5 provide more detailed discussion.

Where the strongest connectivity obtains, a less-prominent nominal is unequivocally assigned to the dominion of a more-prominent reference point, as in (9a) below. This is frequently the case with sentences which would traditionally be analyzed as involving a c-command relationship. Where there is weaker connectivity, linear word order plays a significant role: A less-prominent nominal is assigned to the dominion of a reference point which precedes it in the linear string without a clear conceptual break, as in (9b). A conceptual disjuncture, as in the shift from an assertion to a comment on the background circumstances in (9c) (from Bosch 1983), makes it possible for a nominal to "escape" the dominion of the preceding reference point; a full nominal may therefore be used.

(9)   a.   *He loves John's mother.
       b.   *He went home, and then Peter took a nap.
       c.   He betrayed me—and John was my friend!

The extreme end on the continuum of connectivity is represented by larger conceptual disjunctures at the discourse level. A number of researchers, particularly Fox (1987a, 1987b) and Tomlin (1987b), have found that speakers and writers tend to reidentify referents after certain kinds of discourse unit boundaries, even where the use of a pronoun would have been entirely unambiguous. In the following example, cited by Fox (1987b:169), Leia is the only female character in the scene. A pronoun could have been substituted for the name Leia with no loss of clarity. The appearance of the name is conditioned by what Fox terms a **development structure boundary**, which is a point in a narrative in which a character takes action. Fox has argued that writers tend to reidentify characters at such boundaries regardless of whether the names are needed to avoid ambiguity. In the terms of the model presented here, a development structure boundary is a semantic discontinuity which motivates closure of the preceding reference point's dominion, resulting in the re-use of the character's name.

(10)   That did it for the Ewok. He jumped up, grabbed a four-foot-long spear, and held it defensively in her direction. Warily he circled, poking the pointed javelin at her, clearly more fearful than aggressive.
"Hey, cut that out," Leia brushed the weapon away with annoyance. (*Return of the Jedi*, p. 94)

There is an obvious difference in the strength of the judgments in (9a) and (10). (9a) is clearly ungrammatical under coreference, while (10) would almost certainly allow for the use of a pronoun in place of the name. Similar observations could be made concerning other examples of discourse-level coreference patterns, which do not generally involve sharp, strong judgments of the kind found with sentence-internal anaphora constraints (see Lasnik 1989). This difference could be taken as evidence that we are dealing with different systems rather than a single unified set of principles.

I claim in this study not that the difference indicates a fundamental split between the two domains of anaphora principles, syntax and discourse, but rather that it reflects the difference between overtly coded versus implicit semantic interconnections. The strongest connectivity, involving head/complement relations within clauses, gives rise to the most unequivocal judgments because there is little or no flexibility in the construal of the relationships between the nominals. In multisentential discourse, there is more room for alternate construals. A speaker could potentially ignore the development structure boundary in (10) and construe the last sentence as a continuation of a single scene and hence a single discourse unit. The distinction between explicitly coded and implicit semantic connectivity will be shown to be a consistent and significant factor throughout the reference point model.

Chapter 2 gives a brief overview of the theory of CG, focusing on just the theoretical notions which will play a critical role in the reference point model. The second half of Chapter 2 discusses the semantic distinctions between pronouns and full nominals which motivate the analysis, drawing extensively on Accessibility theory (Givón 1983b, 1985, 1989, 1994; Ariel 1988, 1990; Gundel, Hedberg, and Zacharski 1993 et al.). In Chapter 3 I develop the model of reference point organization within sentences and address some of the better-known examples of obligatory non-coreference.

Chapter 4 discusses gradations of semantic connectivity involving modifiers, offering a semantic analysis of the distinction between VP-modifiers and S-modifiers. The role of linear order in the reference point model is illustrated through the analysis of preposed-modifier constructions. Chapter 5 explores two domains of data typically excluded from consideration in generative syntactic accounts of the anaphora constraints, backwards anaphora and coreference patterns in discourse and narrative. Analyzing a collected corpus of backwards anaphora examples, I argue that the relative frequency of different types of backwards anaphora constructions is explained if we assume that speakers tend to use constructions in which the intended antecedent is most clearly qualified to function as a reference point. The section on discourse interprets several published studies (by various researchers) in terms of the reference point model, arguing that the principles of connectivity which apply within sentences explain an array of reported facts about cross-sentential coreference as well.

Chapter 6 presents an account of constraints on bound anaphora involving quantifiers. Chapter 7 addresses reflexives and the pronoun-reflexive distinction. The distinction between reflexive constructions such as (11a) and (11b) is analyzed; the obligatory status of the reflexive in constructions analogous to (11a) and the optionality of the reflexive pronoun in (11b) and a range of related constructions are explained in terms of degrees of connectivity.

(11)   a.   John loves himself.
       b.   Somebody such as yourself might enjoy this.

Chapter 8 discusses point-of-view effects, arguing that the distinction between explicitly coded and implicit semantic interconnections plays a critical role in explaining the relative variability of judgments involving point of view. The larger implications of the reference point model and its potential applicability to other domains of inquiry are briefly discussed in Chapter 9.

The most significant claim of the analysis presented here is that data which have perhaps most strongly exemplified the need for autonomous syntactic tree structures and the c-command relation are in fact explicable entirely in terms of conceptual-semantic relationships. To the extent that this claim is borne out, it argues for a fundamental reevaluation of the arguments for autonomous syntax.

Theoretical Foundations

In this chapter I first introduce the theory of Cognitive Grammar, in which the analysis of the anaphora constraints has been developed. (This is a necessarily brief introduction; for further details, see Langacker 1982, 1986a, 1987a, 1991.)[1] The second half of the chapter discusses the view of nominal semantics which motivates the constraints on anaphora, drawing primarily on Accessibility theory as it has been developed by Givón (1983b, 1985, 1989, 1994), Ariel (1988, 1990), and others.

2.1 INTRODUCTION TO COGNITIVE GRAMMAR

In contrast to generative theories such as the Extended Standard theory and Government-Binding, CG does not posit an autonomous syntactic component, nor does it posit distinct components or modules for morphology, phonology, syntax, and semantics. CG takes the position that syntax is inseparable from semantics, and forms a continuum with morphology and discourse structure. CG addresses syntactic issues, but it does so without appealing to the constructs of *autonomous* syntax, such as tree structures conceived as purely syntactic entities, syntactic diacritics (such as indices) which are understood to have no inherent semantic content, or grammatical relations considered as syntactic primitives. CG posits only three types of linguistic units: **semantic, phonological**, and **symbolic**. A symbolic unit is a bipolar entity consisting of a semantic unit paired with a phonological unit. Lexicon, morphology, and syntax are fully describable by means of these three kinds of units.[2]

While CG does not assume an autonomous syntax, neither does it make the claim that grammar can be predicted from meaning. Rather, the grammar of a language is a matter of **conventional symbolization**. Speakers must learn the conventional units of their language, including the conventional patterns of phrase structure and sentence structure. Nevertheless, these syntactic conventions can be analyzed as patterns characterized in terms of semantic, phonological, and symbolic units.[3]

In CG, a speaker's knowledge of a language is characterized as a structured inventory of conventional units (Langacker 1987a). These units include morphemes, words, and phrases. They also include **schemas** which describe the conventional grammatical patterns of the language, and which are used for the creation of novel phrases and sentences. A schema is acquired through exposure to actually occurring expressions which instantiate it. The schematic pattern becomes entrenched through repeated activation. To the extent that a schema is entrenched, it is well established and potentially available to guide the construction of novel expressions. In this conception of grammar, grammatical constructions (schematically represented) are linguistic units in their own right (an insight developed in detail in Construction Grammar; see Fillmore and Kay 1993; Goldberg 1995).

Schemas are utilized in comprehension as well as production of novel expressions. A specific expression is judged well formed to the extent that it conforms with the relevant established schemas (on the assumption that only certain schemas are activated by a particular expression; the principles of schema selection are discussed in §2.4).

CG assumes a conceptual, rather than truth-conditional, semantics: The meaning of an expression is equated with the conceptions it activates in a speaker's mind. An expression may activate any number of knowledge systems, beliefs, images (visual and otherwise), and so forth. Particularly critical to explaining grammatical patterns is the notion of **construal**, which refers to a conceptualizer's ability to portray a conceived situation in various ways. Many grammatical constructs such as the subject/object asymmetry and the head/complement/modifier distinction pertain to aspects of construal such as the relative prominence of substructures within a conception, the degree of schematicity or specificity with which the conception is portrayed, and the vantage point which the conceptualizer assumes.

Two facets of construal are particularly significant for the CG analysis of grammatical patterns: profiling and figure/ground asymmetry (Langacker 1987a). Both are understood to involve prominence asym-

Figure 2.1   Profile and base

metries, but they are treated as distinct notions within current formulations of CG (the question of whether they will ultimately reduce to a single cognitive process remains open). Profiling is central to the CG definitions of syntactic categories (nouns, verbs, etc.), as well as the notions head, complement, and modifier; figure / ground asymmetry is the basis for the CG definitions of grammatical relations.

2.1.1 Profile and Base

The notion that a linguistic expression designates or 'refers to' something (in an intuitive rather than formal sense) is captured in CG in terms of the relationship between a profile and a base (Langacker 1987a: 183–89).[4] A linguistic expression invokes or activates some set of conceptions, termed its base. The word *knuckle* invokes as its base the conception of a finger, while the base for the expression *timing belt* is the knowledge of automobile engine structure. Within the base, the expression designates or profiles some subpart.[5] The profile is hypothesized to be more prominent or more highly activated than the base (Langacker 1987a:187), and is accordingly represented in CG notation with bold lines (see Fig. 2.1). The noun *Friday* invokes as its base the conception of a week, and profiles one day within that cycle. Given a particular context, the expressions *handle* and *rim* both invoke as their base the conception of a cup, but profile different subparts of that conception.[6] Although the profile is what the expression designates, the base is a critical part of the meaning of the expression.

The CG definitions of grammatical categories (noun, verb, adjective, etc.) are stated in terms of the nature of their profiles. (In this section I will only summarize the CG definitions; see Langacker 1987a, 1987b.)

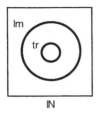 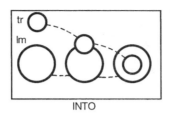 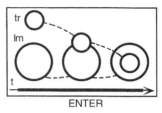

Figure 2.2   *In, into,* and *enter*

A noun profiles a **thing**, which is defined as a set of interconnected
entities (**entity** refers to any kind of conception). The definition encompasses both typical things, such as the conception of physical objects,
and abstractions, such as the concepts designated by the expressions
intermission, democracy, assassination. Each of these abstract conceptions
is characterized as a region made up of interconnected entities.

Verbs, adjectives, and prepositions profile different kinds of **relations**, which are defined as interconnections between entities (Langacker 1987a:214–17). Relations which involve only one configuration
are termed simple relations; an example would be the profile of *in* which
is characterized as a configuration in which one entity is located within
the boundaries of another (Fig. 2.2; the notations "tr" and "lm" are
explained below). Complex relations involve multiple configurations,
as in the case of *into*, in which an entity (labeled tr) moves from a position outside another entity to a position inside. The dotted lines, termed
correspondence lines, indicate that the mover is the same from one configuration to the next, and the entity into which it moves is the same
throughout as well (in other words, the diagram does not represent six
different entities). (Fig. 2.2 is based on an example given by Langacker
[1988a, his fig. 6].)

Verbs are a special class of complex relations in that they profile
processes, complex relations whose component configurations are arranged sequentially in conceived time (indicated in Fig. 2.2 by the arrow
labeled t). Langacker (1987a, 1987b) further proposes that verbs are accessed differently from nouns and nonprocessual relations in that processes are sequentially scanned, which is to say that the components of
the verbal conception are accessed in sequence, similar to watching a
movie. Things and nonprocessual relations are summary scanned; all
the component configurations are active simultaneously. (I include
these definitions only for completeness; the summary / sequential scan-

ning distinction is not directly relevant to the analysis of anaphora constraints, and so I will not discuss it in detail.)

One detail which should be highlighted is the claim that relations profile not only the interconnections between entities but also the interconnected entities themselves. Conceiving of a relation such as the profile of a verb or a preposition necessarily includes conceiving of the interconnected participants, which are therefore included within the profile.

2.1.2 Trajector and Landmark

The profile/base distinction is one prominence asymmetry which plays a critical role in the CG characterization of grammatical constructs. Relations involve an additional prominence asymmetry, characterized as figure/ground alignment. One of the entities involved in the relation stands out as the figure within the relation (Langacker 1987a:217–18); it is termed the **trajector**, abbreviated as tr. The choice of the term **trajector** is motivated by the fact that, for verbs of motion, the thing most easily picked out as figure on perceptual grounds—the thing which moves along a trajectory—is typically selected as the subject (Langacker 1987a:217).

The less-prominent entity in the relation is termed the **landmark**, abbreviated lm. Relations profile both a trajector and a landmark (or landmarks), never a trajector by itself. In some cases the landmark is abstract and is not conventionally expressed with an overt nominal. The relation profiled by *red*, for example, profiles an association between its trajector (specifically, the visual sensation evoked by the trajector) and a particular region in the domain of color (see Langacker 1987a:231–43). Both the trajector and the landmark(s) in a relation are profiled, as the trajector/landmark asymmetry is distinct from the profile/base distinction.[7]

The choice of trajector and landmark in a particular case is not automatically determined by the objective properties of the situation being described, but is rather a matter of the construal which the speaker imposes on the conceived situation. For example, the prepositions *on* and *under* may be used to describe the same configuration (two objects located in vertical space, one higher than the other, with physical contact between the two [in one sense of *under*]). They differ in the choice of trajector and landmark. For *on*, the higher object is the trajector, while *under* selects the lower object as trajector (Fig. 2.3).

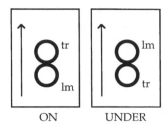

Figure 2.3   *On* and *under*

The trajector/landmark distinction is the basis for the CG definitions of grammatical relations. The subject is the trajector of the process
profiled by a clause, while the direct object is a landmark (some verbs
profile two landmarks). The evidence for equating the subject/object
distinction with conceptual figure/ground alignment is necessarily indirect. Langacker (1987a:231–34) gives several examples of the relevant
type of evidence. Where there is a clear perceptual motivation for pick-
ing out one entity as the figure within a scene, active-voice verbs tend
strongly to pick out the perceptual figure as the entity to be coded as
the subject (this appears to be true cross-linguistically, though my focus
here is on English). Verbs of motion, for example, almost invariably
take as their subject (in the active or unmarked voice) the element which
moves rather than the stationary background; the moving entity is more
naturally perceived as figure than the background.

Langacker points out that English has a number of pairs of prepositions such as *in front of/behind, above/below, on top of/under.* Speakers
generally feel that the first one in each pair here is unmarked or neutral
as compared with the other member of the pair. The unmarked choice
in each case picks out as trajector (as in *The chair is in front of the table*)
the thing which is likely to be closer to the viewer (under typical circumstances) and more easily perceptible, that is, the thing which is more
likely to stand out as the visual figure.

The equation of subjects with clausal figures is also supported by
the well-known association of subjects and topicality at the discourse
level (e.g., Givón 1976, 1979a, 1983b, 1989, 1994; Chafe 1976, 1987, 1991,
1994; Tomlin 1983; Kuno 1987), including the tendency for the subject
of a sentence to refer to the person the speaker thinks of as the topic
or the main character of a narrative (Karmiloff-Smith 1981). Although
the notion subject is not defined as discourse topic (or vice versa), the

ON (the) MAT

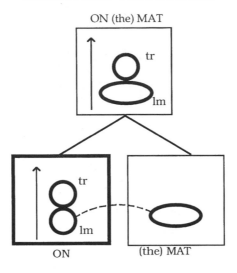

Figure 2.4   *On the mat*

subject's prominence as figure within the clausal conception gives it a natural affinity with the discourse topic, the figure which is conceptually tracked through the discourse.

2.1.3 Complex Expressions

Assembling complex expressions, such as multiword phrases, requires conceptual integration of elements. Figure 2.4 illustrates the assembly of the semantic pole of the expression *on the mat*. If we focus first on the bottom row of boxes, the preposition *on* is represented as a relationship between two things which are arranged in vertically oriented space, with contact between the two (the darker box for *on* indicates that it is the head; the CG definition of head is given in §2.1.4). The dotted line connecting the landmark of *on* and the profile of *mat* indicates **correspondence** between the two. Intuitively speaking, the profile of *mat* and the landmark of *on* are construed as two conceptions of the same entity. At the next level of conceptual organization, represented by the top box, the corresponding elements are conceptually superimposed, producing the composite conception which is the profile of the entire phrase *on the mat* (the diagram is simplified by omission of any indication of defi-

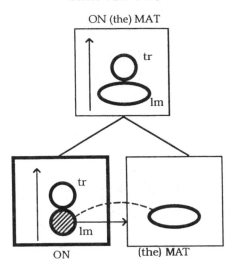

Figure 2.5　*On the mat* (revised)

niteness, though that could be included as well; see below and Langacker 1991:96–107).

The diagram in Figure 2.4 leaves out one significant detail, however. Although the landmark of *on* and the profile of *mat* are in some
sense conceived as the same entity, the two expressions do not contribute equally to the overall conception. The profile of *mat* serves to flesh
out the landmark of *on*, which is much more **schematic** (i.e., much less
specified). The technical term for fleshing out a conception in this way
is **elaboration,** and the schematic conception to be fleshed out is termed
an **elaboration site,** usually abbreviated as **e-site.** In the diagram above,
the cross-hatched region is the e-site; the arrow points to the conception
which elaborates it.

Figures 2.4 and 2.5 have shown only the assembly of the semantic
pole of the expression. The phrase is of course bipolar; that is, it has a
phonological representation as well. Figure 2.6 very schematically
shows the assembly of the phonological pole of the expression. The
word *on* has a phonological form (represented here by orthography
rather than phonetic transcription); its status as a phonological word is
indicated by the label W. Part of a speaker's knowledge of the word *on* is
that it may combine with another word, which follows it in the temporal
sequence (indicated by the arrow labeled t). I am assuming, for sim-

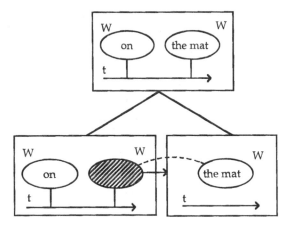

Figure 2.6   Phonological pole for *on the mat*

plicity's sake, that we can analyze the definite article as phonologically cliticized to the noun *mat*, so that the phrase *the mat* functions as a phonological word for purposes of elaborating the schematic conception invoked by the word *on*. The two words combine to form a single phrase at the higher level of organization. (This representation is of course highly simplified; there is no indication of phrasal stress, intonation, etc. This brief illustration is intended simply as an overview of the assembly of complex expressions at semantic and phonological poles.)

Included in a speaker's knowledge of the expression *on the mat* (though not represented in the figures presented here) are symbolic links between the semantic and phonological components of the expression. The phonological pole of each word (*on*, *mat*, etc.) individually symbolizes the semantic pole for that word, and the entire phonological phrase symbolizes the composite semantic conception.

2.1.4 Heads, Complements, and Modifiers

When two conceptions are combined to form a composite conception, typically the composite will have the same profile as only one of the two components. In the combination of the relation *on* with its landmark *mat*, the composite profiles a spatial relation, not a thing. The relation *on* contributes its profile to the integrated conception, and so is termed the **profile determinant.** The profile determinant at each level of organization is the head. Notationally, profile determinance is represented by the use of heavy lines for the box representing the profile determinant.

The definition of complements and modifiers depends on profile determinance and elaborative relations, specifically the distinction between autonomy and dependence. Where one conception elaborates a salient subpart of another, as in the semantic combination of *on* with *mat*, the conception containing the e-site is **dependent** on the elaborating conception, in the sense given in the definition in (1) (Langacker 1987a:300).

(1)   One structure, *D*, is dependent on the other, *A*, to the extent that *A* constitutes an elaboration of a salient substructure within *D*.[8]

The opposite of dependence is autonomy. A conception is autonomous if it is not elaborated by another conception. In the combination of *on* with *mat*, the conception profiled by *mat* is autonomous, as it is not elaborated by the relation profiled by *on*. The definitions of complement and modifier are stated in terms of dependence in combination with profile determinance, as in (2).

(2)   i.   When the profile determinant (head) at a given level of organization is dependent, the entity elaborating it is a complement.
       ii.   When the profile determinant (head) at a given level of organization is autonomous but elaborates some other entity, the dependent entity is a modifier.

Complements and modifiers behave very differently in their relationship to the composite conception. Since a complement elaborates part of the profile of the head, the composite conception includes the profile of the complement within the composite profile. (For example, the composite conception profiled by *on the mat* includes the profile of *mat* as part of the profiled relation.) In contrast, a modifier does not elaborate a salient subpart of the conception profiled by the head, but is rather elaborated by the head. The composite conception produced by combining a head and modifier profiles only the head, while the modifier, although included semantically within the composite conception, is not profiled; instead it becomes part of the unprofiled base. The semantic pole of the phrase *the cat on the mat* will serve as illustration (see Fig. 2.7).

In assembling the semantic pole of the expression *the cat on the mat*, the conception corresponding to *cat* is the profile determinant (as the

CAT ON (the) MAT

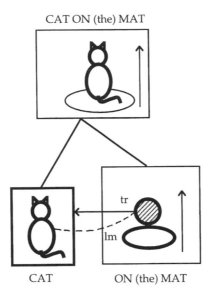

Figure 2.7 *Cat on the mat*

composite conception designates a cat, not a spatial relationship). The profile determinant is autonomous and elaborates the trajector of the relation profiled by *on the mat*, which is dependent and therefore a modifier. The modifying relation becomes an unprofiled part of the base in the composite. Although it is still part of the meaning of the expression, it is less prominent than the profile, which is solely the nominal conception contributed by *cat*. This is a general characteristic of head / modifier constructions. Complements and modifiers thus differ significantly in their prominence within the composite conception, as complements remain profiled in the composite, while modifiers become unprofiled. This observation will be shown to have significant ramifications for coreference possibilities. Figure 2.8 schematically illustrates the characterization of head / complement and head / modifier configurations in CG.

One additional comment must be made about the difference between correspondence and elaboration. Observe that the elaboration arrow in each case goes from the schematic participant conception, the e-site, to the edge of the box representing the nominal that elaborates it. The arrow does not point directly to the profile of the elaborating conception. In contrast, the correspondence line indicates precisely which subparts of each conception correspond. The elaboration arrow

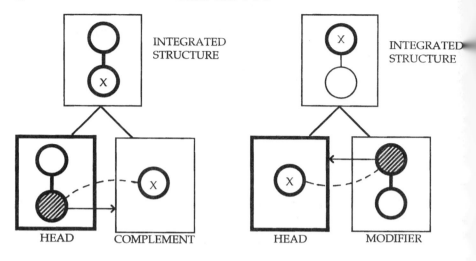

Figure 2.8   Heads, complements, and modifiers

indicates that the entire conceptual assembly designated by an expression, not just a subpart, elaborates the schematic e-site.

The general import of this distinction can be made clear by example. If we change the expression *the cat on the mat* to specify the color of the mat, for example, *the cat on the blue mat*, we can assemble the expression as in Figure 2.9. The relation *blue* profiles a relationship between an object and a particular color sensation, indicated abstractly here by the oval labeled B and the arrow representing an assessment of similarity between the color and some facet of the object. The profile of *mat* elaborates the trajector of *blue*. As *mat* is the profile determinant and the conception *blue* is dependent, *blue* is a modifier and becomes an unprofiled part of the base.

The article *the* is termed a **grounding predication** (Langacker 1991); it indicates a relationship between the nominal conception and the current discourse context, specifically that the speaker believes the addressee can make mental contact with the unique instance of the nominal type (mental contact is defined as "singling something out for individual conscious awareness" [Langacker 1991:550]). The grounding predication profiles the grounded entity, not the relationship to the ground; it is represented here as the profile of a thing connected with the ground, indicated by the circle labeled G. The profile of *the* corresponds to the profile of *blue mat*, but the entire conception expressed

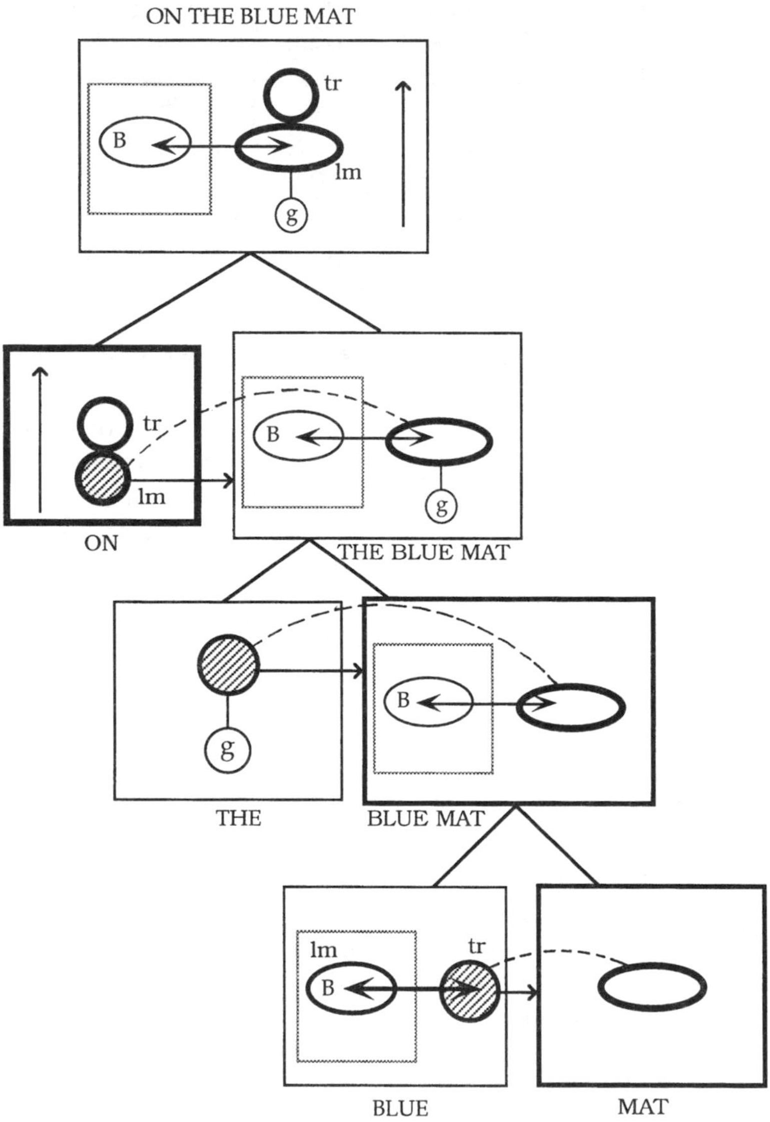

Figure 2.9   *On the blue mat*

as *blue mat* elaborates the profile of *the*. In other words, the entire conceptual assembly coded as *blue mat* is combined with the meaning of *the*, but only the profiled conception of the mat itself corresponds with the profile of *the*.

The same principle applies when the conception expressed by *the blue mat* elaborates the landmark of *on*. Only the profile of *mat* corresponds to the landmark, but the entire conception expressed as *the blue mat* is integrated with the profile of *on*. The unprofiled elements in the conception *the blue mat* are retained as part of the base through successive levels of conceptual organization. At each level, however, the specific correspondences between subparts of each conception are indicated by the exact placement of the correspondence lines.

This distinction between correspondence and elaboration is significant at several points in the analysis of anaphora constraints. One of the central factors in the organization of reference points and dominions is conceptual connectivity, determined by correspondences between entities. Elements which directly correspond to a subpart of a relation are somewhat more strongly connected with that relation than elements which are merely associated with such a correspondent. The distinction is too subtle to have a noticeable impact in many cases, but there are some construction types in which its contribution becomes apparent (see §4.3.4, §8.4).

For completeness, I will show the assembly of one complete sentence, involving a number of levels of conceptual organization. We can use *The cat is on the mat*, illustrated in Figure 2.10. The assembly of the conception described by *on the mat* is familiar by now; I am omitting the steps by which the grounding predications (articles and tense) are added in. The verb *be* profiles a highly schematic processual conception, essentially specifying only that some relation extends through conceived time and is accessed conceptually as a verb.[9] *Be* functions as the head, while the composite conception *on the mat* is a complement; present tense is here abbreviated as grounding. The integrated conception has the same content as the relation profiled by *on the mat*, now construed as a process. Its trajector is then elaborated by the conception expressed by *the cat*. Since the semantic pole of *the cat* elaborates a salient subpart of the process, it is a complement. (In CG, the subject of a clause is by definition a complement of the verb.) The composite conception includes the profiles of *cat*, *mat*, the relation *on*, and the processual construal contributed by *be*.

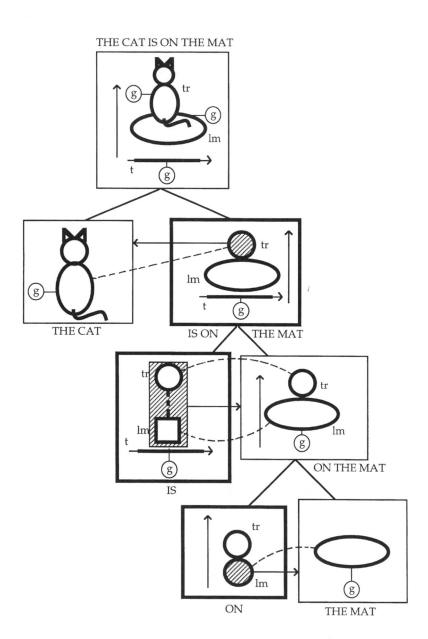

Figure 2.10 *The cat is on the mat.*

2.2 DESIDERATA FOR A MODEL
OF ANAPHORA CONSTRAINTS

The underlying principles of CG strictly limit the kinds of linguistic units and principles which an analysis can appeal to. One of the central principles it embodies is the Content Requirement, given in (3) (from Langacker 1987a:488).

(3)   The Content Requirement

> The only structures permitted in the grammar of a language are:
> i.   phonological, semantic, or symbolic structures that actually occur in linguistic expressions;
> ii. schemas for such structures;
> iii. categorizing relationships involving the elements in (i) and (ii)

In essence, the Content Requirement states that one cannot posit any rules or structures which do not correspond to conceptual or phonological forms which actually occur in the language. Overtly occurring expressions consist of only three types of units: semantic units, phonological units, and symbolic units (bipolar structures consisting of a semantic unit paired with a phonological unit).

Categorizing relationships, which also play a central role in explaining grammaticality judgments, are of two kinds, **schematicity** and **extension**. An element A is schematic for element B if B is fully compatible with the specifications of A but B is characterized in greater detail. An element B is an *extension* from A if A is partially schematic for B but B conflicts with A in some of its specifications. A speaker's inventory of linguistic units is structured by these categorizing relationships, as some linguistic units are represented as schematizations or extensions relative to others.

Most of the standard syntactic accounts of the constraints on pronominal anaphora would not be permitted by the Content Requirement, as they assume that speakers' knowledge of their language includes a set of syntactic principles, not stated in semantic or phonological terms, which are applied as filters to rule out certain configurations. The Binding Conditions of GB theory (Chomsky 1981), for example, appeal to syntactic constructs with neither semantic nor phonological import, and they are formulated as a list of negative conditions or filters, which are not fully stable in terms of constructions which speakers have been exposed to.[10] If the Binding Conditions are taken as merely descriptive generalizations, there is of course no problem. But insofar as they are put forth as formalizations of speakers' internalized knowledge of English syntax, they are in conflict with the basic principles underlying CG theory.

If the goal of our analysis is to explain the restrictions on coreference rather than merely to list them, the observed restrictions should be motivated by some fundamental difference between pronouns and full noun phrases, and should provide a unified model of the distribution of pronouns and full noun phrases both within clauses and cross-sententially. Ideally, the analysis would account for the extremely tight restrictions on first- and second-person referring forms, and unify those facts with the explanation of the constraints on third-person reference.

Drawing on work in Accessibility theory (e.g., Ariel 1988, 1990; Givón 1983a, 1983b, 1985, 1989, 1994; Ward, Sproat, and McKoon 1991; Gundel, Hedberg, and Zacharski 1993), I propose the intuitive notion that pronouns and full noun phrases differ with respect to the 'recoverability' of their referents in the immediate context. A pronoun portrays its referent as something which is already part of the immediate context, while a full noun phrase portrays the referent as something relatively new to that context. This distinction correlates with an additional distinction in the degree of conceptual closeness (roughly, but not exactly, akin to 'empathy') implied by a pronoun or a full noun phrase, discussed below. These very simple notions, combined with an appropriate semantic characterization of clause structure (developed in the following chapters), make it possible to explain 'anaphora constraint violations' as instances of semantic and pragmatic anomaly. We therefore do not need to posit that the grammar of English includes explicit anaphora constraints formulated as syntactic filters.[11]

2.3 NOMINAL SEMANTICS

Fundamental to the analysis presented here is the claim that (nonpronominal) nouns and pronouns differ in their portrayal of the relationship between the referent and the discourse context. I am assuming the model of nominal semantics developed in Langacker (1991), briefly summarized here. A complete nominal expression (equivalent to an NP rather than an N) profiles (i.e., designates) an **instance** of a nominal **type,** and carries some information about its relationship to the discourse context (such as definiteness). The most basic notion in a nominal conception is the type conception. For example, the noun *cat* invokes the conception of the type *cat*; the noun *thin black cat* (a noun is defined in CG as an expression which profiles a thing, and so it may be a word or a multiword phrase) invokes a more specific type conception.

A full nominal (what would be termed a full NP in some theories) profiles an *instance* of a type. Instances are distinguished by having unique locations in a conceived domain such as physical space (e.g., two occurrences of the type *pencil* are conceived as distinct instances if they occupy different physical locations at the same time).

Grounding pertains to the relationship between the nominal instance and the ground, which is the conception of the speech event itself, including the speaker and addressee and their current state of awareness (Langacker 1978, 1985).[12] The definite/indefinite contrast indicates whether the speaker believes that the addressee can make mental contact with the unique intended nominal instance (i.e., single it out for individual, conscious awareness), given the current discourse context (see Hawkins 1978; Langacker 1991:98; this is essentially the same claim as the Familiarity Condition of Heim 1982). The definite nominal *the cat* presupposes that the addressee can identify the unique instance of cat intended—typically because of prior mention in the discourse, or because of shared background knowledge.

Proper names and pronouns, which will be to some extent the focus of this study (reflexives are discussed in Chap. 7), have different structures from the canonical descriptive noun phrase structure. In Langacker's analysis, proper names such as *Regina Hartley* and *Bob Waters* invoke an idealized cognitive model in which each human has a unique name. The name itself is therefore sufficient to specify type, instance, and grounding. The name invokes a type conception of which the particular referent is conceived as the unique instance, making the use of articles superfluous.

Pronouns also depart from the canonical nominal structure. A pronoun profiles some referent which is recoverable from the discourse context. In contrast to nouns, which may specify the type conceptions of their referents at any level of detail, a pronoun specifies only person, number, and (for third-person singular only) animateness and gender. The base for a pronoun (i.e., the conceptual structure which it crucially invokes for its meaning) is the conception of the speech event, including the speaker and addressee, their surroundings, and the conceptions which are currently in their awarenesses (such as elements that have been introduced in the preceding discourse). Within that base, the pronoun profiles a conception that is salient in the awarenesses of both speaker and addressee—such as the conception of the speaker or addressee, or, in the case of third-person pronouns, the conception of some other referent that is active in the discourse context.

2.3.1 Accessibility Theory

The largest hurdle to be faced by any semantic analysis of the anaphora constraints is that at first glance, it appears that pronouns and full noun phrases, when they refer to the same person, essentially mean the same thing. This could be taken to imply that speakers should be able to use full noun phrases at any point, risking only redundancy. The fact that speakers judge sentences with an inappropriate full noun phrase to be not merely too specific, but fully unacceptable, suggests that we are dealing with a more significant problem.

Given the CG characterization of meaning as conceptualization, it is possible to argue that there are systematic semantic distinctions between pronouns and full noun phrases (even when they refer to the same person), and that distinct nominal forms used to refer to the same referent are not identical in meaning. The analysis developed here is based in large part on Givón's (1983b, 1985, 1989, 1994) and Ariel's (1988, 1990) work in Accessibility theory, which also draws on the Relevance theory of Sperber and Wilson (1986) (and see also Ward, Sproat, and McKoon 1991; Gundel, Hedberg, and Zacharski 1993). Accessibility theory holds that different nominal forms, ranging from null pronouns (phonologically empty pronominal elements) to full noun phrases, are arrayed on a continuum reflecting the relative accessibility of a referent within a given context. Accessibility can be thought of as a description of the amount of processing effort that the conceptualizer must expend to make mental contact with a referent.

Accessibility theory, and the model of anaphora constraints developed here, have some elements in common with the theory of Discourse Representations proposed by Kamp (1984) and further articulated by Roberts (1987); these assume a level of discourse representation which in some way includes the entities or referents introduced into the discourse, as well as representations of the coreference relations between nominals.[13] Kamp, however, does not develop the concept of varying degrees of prominence within the discourse, nor does he attempt to replace the c-command constraint on coreference. A certain amount of similarity between my work and that of Roberts (1987) is apparent in Chapter 6, which addresses bound anaphora. Roberts, however, defines some critical notions in her model in terms of the c-command relation, whereas I argue that c-command can be replaced with notions of prominence and semantic connectivity.

The notion of a discourse context within which referents may be more or less Accessible also bears a clear resemblance to Heim's (1982) File Change Semantics theory. In Heim's terminology, a discourse referent (not to be confused with a real-world referent) is described as a **file card** which is introduced into a file (i.e., a representation of the immediate discourse context); subsequent reference to the same entity can be thought of as updating the information on the file card. Indefinite noun phrases introduce new file cards, while pronouns and definite noun phrases access file cards already present. Heim (1982:386) notes in passing that discourse prominence is significant, and that anaphoric pronouns seem to require more prominent antecedents, or file cards, than do definite NPs (this is stated in terms of her Prominence Condition on pronominal reference). However, her observation is not articulated in sufficient detail to permit one to predict where full noun phrases, as opposed to pronouns, would be ruled out. She does not address this issue, but comments only on the question of when a discourse referent is insufficiently prominent to facilitate the use of a pronoun. Her work, like those cited above, is not intended to replace the standard c-command condition on coreference.

It is generally accepted within the Accessibility literature that the relative accessibility of a conceived referent is determined by a number of factors, such as the number of competing referents in the context, the amount of material intervening between current and previous mentions of the referent, and the degree of conceptual connectivity between the current context and the context containing the previous mention(s) of the referent (Ariel 1988, 1990). Ariel (1990) draws data from written texts, in a variety of languages, to argue that pronouns are relatively high accessibility markers, while full noun phrases are relatively low accessibility markers (the precise degree of accessibility associated with each varies across languages, but their relative positioning on the scale remains constant). In other words, pronouns are appropriate when the referent is highly recoverable within the context, and full noun phrases are appropriate when the referent either cannot be recovered from the context or can be recovered only with relatively greater difficulty.[14]

A pronoun invokes the conception of the discourse context (or some more specific subcontext within it), and picks out as its profiled referent some entity which is salient within that context—the speaker, the addressee, or some third-person referent that is recoverable within the context. A name or descriptive noun phrase, in contrast, invokes a more fully specified type conception, which is expected to be relevant to the context either by introducing a new referent or by calling attention to some specific characterization of the referent. A full noun phrase thus contrasts with a pronoun in that it conventionally draws attention to some relatively new conception, whereas a pronoun characterizes its referent as a continuation of some conception which is already part of the context. The subtle semantic distinction between nouns and pronouns can be seen in contexts in which a full noun phrase is used, not to avoid ambiguity of reference, but to highlight a particular conception of the referent.

A name may be used to highlight a conception of the referent as he is overall, by his nature. (Bolinger 1972, 1979). A name, like a descriptive noun phrase, thus draws attention to something relatively new in the context by focusing attention on a particular conception of the referent (the referent as he inherently is) which is distinct from the conception that would be invoked by a pronoun. The psychological reality of this distinction is borne out by the observation that a name is frequently used in contexts where a pronoun would have been completely unambiguous but where the speaker wants to invoke the conception of the person as he inherently is, by his nature.

The examples in (4), both taken from actual conversations, illustrate this point. In both cases, the preceding context was such that pronominal reference would have been completely unambiguous. Nevertheless, the speaker renamed the referent. It seems intuitively clear that the use of the full nominal in each case invokes a conception of the referent's inherent or general nature, and thus serves a different semantic function than a pronoun would have served in the same context.

(4) a.   It's hard to imagine *Jim* in any kind of sexual context.
     b.   So then she—you know Carol, how she's so funny. . . .

The same pattern is found in written usage as well. In the following example, taken from a novel, "he" refers to the character Mayland Long:

(5). He hit a pothole, skidded across the lane and recovered automatically.
      His conviction that Martha was alive was not a feeling like his anger,
      which he could test and find durable. It was rather a gift from outside,
      and Long had never trusted gifts. (R. A. MacAvoy, *Tea with the Black
      Dragon*, p. 86)

Here again, although a pronoun would be fully unambiguous, a full noun phrase is used in a sentence which relates something about what the character is like overall, outside the immediate context. This usage is not strictly required—speakers would not judge the construction unacceptable if a pronoun were substituted for the name—but it is motivated by the semantic difference between pronouns and names. Pronouns and full noun phrases, including names, do not "index referents" in the sense of accessing identical semantic representations, but rather invoke subtly different conceptions of referents and of the relationship between the referent and the context.

Additional support for this claim may be found in studies of written English, particularly research by Barbara Fox (1987a), who argues that the use of a pronoun or full noun phrase carries information about how the writer construes the relationship between the referent and the context. When the referent has previously been accessible in the immediately preceding context, a full noun phrase can serve as a signal of a discontinuity or juncture in the evolving context. In the terms of Ariel's theory, a speaker may use a low-accessibility marker to indicate that the immediate context is partly discontinuous from the preceding context, in which the referent was highly accessible.

As mentioned in §1.4, Fox (1987a, 1987b) argues that the use of full noun phrases in written text, in contexts where pronouns would have been unambiguous, indicates textual boundaries. This notion manifests in different ways in different kinds of texts (e.g., popular fiction versus expository prose of various kinds). One such boundary is the development structure, which begins when a character takes action in response to preceding events. A number of Fox's examples are discussed in §5.6.3.5; (6) is my own example, taken from a novel:

(6)   Marina lay in bed, starving and staring at the ceiling. She didn't know what she was supposed to do. So she just stayed there, under the covers, waiting for Roger to make a sound.
          After what seemed a very long time, the doorbell rang and a moment later there was a lot of sharp, happy noise coming from the kitchen. Marina jumped into her jeans and tee shirt. (Ann Druyan, *A Famous Broken Heart*, p. 40)

In this example, a pronoun could have been used unambiguously in place of the name *Marina*. The appearance of the name is therefore not sufficiently motivated merely by a desire to avoid ambiguity or by the notion that the referent was not recoverable; rather it must be explained by some notion such as Fox's development structure boundary.

Fox claims that the appearance of full nominals in such contexts contributes to signaling textual unit boundaries and discontinuities within the text. Another way of putting it is that the full noun phrase is expected to introduce something which is relatively new or inaccessible within the context. When a full nominal appears in a position in which a pronoun would have been unambiguous, one way of resolving the potential conflict is to infer that there has been a discontinuity in the evolving context, so that the immediate context of the full noun phrase is less closely connected with the previous mention of the referent than would otherwise be the case. We can assume that different written genres and discourse styles would then exploit this potential in various ways, giving rise to conventionalized uses of full noun phrases at different kinds of unit boundaries (this point is explored further in §5.6.3).

These observations support the claim that the difference between pronouns and full noun phrases does not reduce to rules for obligatory non-coreference and strategies for avoiding ambiguity. Rather there is a fundamental difference between pronouns and full noun phrases in terms of the accessibility of their referents. Unacceptable coreference within a sentence may be characterized as a configuration in which a full noun phrase, indicating low accessibility of the referent, is embedded in a context in which the referent is in fact highly accessible. This assumes, of course, that we have an adequate definition of the relevant notion of context, and an explanation of why certain units (e.g., clauses) must be construed as defining a single uninterrupted context for purposes of anaphora—why speakers do not simply infer that there is some sort of unit boundary between the pronoun and the full nominal, as with Fox's development structures.

More specifically, an account based on accessibility must distinguish between the situation in which a referent is merely recoverable from the discourse context (in which case either a pronoun or a full noun phrase may be acceptable) and the situation in which a referent is so extremely accessible relative to a certain nominal (i.e., so prominent and so closely connected, conceptually, with the nominal in question) that the appearance of a full noun phrase rather than a pronoun is judged anomalous. Before developing the necessary notion of context, I will first sketch one other way of thinking about the semantic motivation for the restrictions on coreference.

2.3.2 Conceptual Distance and Subjectivity

As a corollary to the Accessibility distinction between pronouns and full noun phrases, there is a sense in which a pronoun portrays its referent as conceptually closer to the speaker and addressee than a full noun phrase. By "conceptually closer," I have in mind a conception similar, but not identical, to the idea of empathy (Kuno 1987).

The relevant notions can be made clear in the terms of Langacker's (1985) **stage model,** a cognitive model of the way in which the speech event participants (the speaker and addressee) relate to the discourse. The participants engaging in the speech event are analogous to an audience watching a play, while the conceptions invoked by the speaker's utterances are what is "put onstage," that is, brought into the focus of attention. The conceived real-world context in which the discourse unfolds, including the speaker and addressee, can be termed the "offstage region."

Recall that every linguistic expression invokes some conceptual content, called its **base,** within which it profiles (i.e., designates) a subpart. The base for the notion invoked by a pronoun is the conception of the discourse context, including the offstage region, within which the pronoun profiles some salient thing (in the technical sense, i.e., a nominal conception). First-person pronouns profile the conception of the speaker, and second-person pronouns, the addressee. A third-person pronoun profiles a conceived referent with which the speaker and addressee have pre-existing mental contact either because of previous mention or because the person or thing is physically present and perceptible.

The profile of a pronoun thus corresponds to something which is already in the awareness of both the speaker and the addressee and, therefore, in a sense, conceptually close to them. A full noun phrase portrays its referent as something relatively new to the context, and hence more distant (metaphorically speaking) from the speaker and addressee. It is fully (or almost fully) onstage rather than residing partially within the offstage region comprising the speaker and addressee and the contextual knowledge they share.

The distinction between the onstage and offstage region is described by Langacker (1985, 1987a, 1990) in terms of the notions **subjectivity** and **objectivity** (here defined in a specific way). As a first pass, the subjective/objective distinction can be described as the difference between the viewer and that which is viewed. A conception is objective to the extent that the viewer focuses attention on it and makes it the center of his conscious awareness. A conception is subjective to the extent that it is outside conscious awareness, but functions as part of the offstage, background conceptual structure which the conceptualizer uses to interpret what is in the onstage region.

The viewer himself is maximally subjective when his attention is completely focused on the onstage region, so that he loses awareness of himself. The element which is onstage, that is, in the focus of awareness, is then maximally objective—it is fully in the center of awareness and distinct from the viewer. To the extent that an element is characterized as part of the offstage region, it is subjective. Pronouns are semantically more dependent than full noun phrases on the conception of the offstage context, and therefore invoke a more subjective construal of the referent than a full noun phrase does. A pronoun puts a nominal conception onstage (making it somewhat objective), but that conception is characterized by correspondence with an offstage conception. In essence, a pronoun blurs the distinction between the onstage and offstage regions. Full noun phrases, in contrast, invoke a construal in which the referent is construed as fully onstage.[15]

The distinction is particularly clear with first-person reference. The pronoun *I* puts the conception of the speaker onstage; however, the onstage conception is characterized via its correspondence to an offstage conceptualizer, the speaker. Thinking of oneself as "I" is not the same as calling oneself by name, which would imply seeing oneself from an outside vantage point, as if looking at another person. The same remarks apply to the use of the second-person pronoun. Although the pronoun *you* puts the conception of a person onstage, that conception is semantically dependent upon its correspondence with the conception of the offstage addressee. First- and second-person pronouns blur the distinction between the viewer and that which is viewed.

Third-person pronouns also portray their referents somewhat more subjectively than do full noun phrases. The profile of a pronoun is characterized via correspondence with an entity which is salient in the awareness of the speaker and addressee; it is thereby construed somewhat more subjectively than it would be if a full noun phrase were used. A third-person pronoun thus conveys a subtle sense of conceptual proximity, as compared with a full noun phrase.

This distinction is reflected by the use of full noun phrases to invoke the conception of the referent as an object of viewing or of scrutiny. The example in (7) is taken from a novel. In this scene there are only two characters, one male and one female. Pronouns could be used un-ambiguously throughout the passage, but instead the author uses a full noun phrase at a development structure boundary, when the focus shifts from the female character's dialogue to the male character's ac-tion. The crucial detail here is the use of a full noun phrase in the last sentence, where the author describes how one of the characters ap-peared from the other's point of view.

(7) Liz took the stuff of the drape in one hand. She leaned against the wall, head drooping.
       "And I designed a really good piece of software. Nobody could have broken it. Except me."
       One dark hand snaked out; Mayland Long turned on a lamp. In the soft yellow light Liz Macnamara looked lovely. (R. A. MacAvoy, *Tea with the Black Dragon*, p. 68)

The use of the name *Liz Macnamara* is motivated by the shift to Long's viewpoint, so that Liz Macnamara is described as she is seen from his perspective, that is, objectively. To put it from a different angle, the use of the full noun phrase makes it clear that an objective view of Liz Macnamara is being invoked, and this underscores the shift to Mayland Long's viewpoint.

Barbara Fox, in her study of pronominal anaphora in spoken dis-course (1987a), has made several observations which provide support for this analysis. She notes that there are certain conditions under which a full nominal may be used in discourse even though the preceding context would lead one to expect a pronoun. She comments that "a speaker's attitude towards characters can be displayed through the ana-phoric devices chosen to refer to those characters" (1987a:66). She gives as an illustration of this the observation that there is a tendency to use a full noun phrase in making negative assessments, as in the following examples (Fox gives these examples in semiphonetic transcription; I have chosen to use standard orthography):

(8) a. Just think what good training it is. Besides Bill Steffie lives under-neath them. Pay a hundred and fifty and live over Bill Steffie, huh.
      b. . . . whenever I do anything not for my wife, my wife wants to know why I did it.

Fox comments, "It is not clear to me why assessments should 'induce' the use of full NPs. Nonetheless, there seems to be a demonstrable pat-tern of this association in the data I have examined" (1987a:66). I have found similar examples of the use of full names in negative assessments within written texts. (9) is from a humor column, (10) is from a novel.

(9)   Also we have Woody Allen, whose humor has become so sophisticated that nobody gets it anymore except Mia Farrow. All those who think Mia Farrow should go back to making movies where the devil makes her pregnant and Woody Allen should go back to dressing up as a human sperm, please raise your hands. (Dave Barry, *Dave Barry's Greatest Hits*, p. 2)

(10)   And Threve? Thinking about Threve, Liz clutched her pillow spasmodically, hiding her face in white cotton. Threve was the devil himself. (R. A. MacAvoy, *Tea with the Black Dragon*, p. 102)

This pattern can be explained by the semantic distinction I am positing between pronouns and full noun phrases. The pronoun portrays the referent as part of the offstage conception shared between speaker and addressee, while the full noun phrase places the referent fully onstage and downplays any connection between the referent and the ground. The full noun phrase is therefore better suited for contexts in which one wishes to distance oneself from the referent and place it onstage as the focus of (unfavorable) attention. This distancing effect may involve the conception of the ground, or the conception of another viewpoint (such as a character's viewpoint in narrative) which is adopted as a **surrogate ground** in the sense of Langacker (1985). In (10) above, the distancing involves the conception of a character's viewpoint—the conception of Threve is distanced from Liz's viewpoint, which functions as a surrogate ground from which the scene is viewed.

Fox (1987a) points out an additional set of data which may combine both the conceptual distance distinction and the use of full noun phrases as noncontinuity markers. She notes that there is a tendency, in discourse, for the speaker to use a full noun phrase if he disagrees with the statement made by the previous speaker. The following example is from Fox (1987a:62):

(11)   R.   Those are Alex's tanks, aren't they?
       V.   Pardon me?
       R.   Weren't—didn't they belong to Alex?
       V.   No—Alex has no tanks; Alex is trying to buy my tank.

Fox does not offer an explanation for this pattern (which she illustrates with a number of examples), but it seems to reflect both of the general claims I am making about noun phrases as noncontinuity markers and as indicators of conceptual distance. By not using a pronoun, the second speaker subtly avoids portraying his statement as a mere continuation of the conception set up by the first speaker, instead highlighting the discontinuity engendered by the fact that he is contradicting the first speaker's statement. In addition, by using a full noun phrase, the second speaker maintains a certain distance from the conception offered by the first speaker, leaving the referent fully onstage rather than accepting it as part of the updated offstage context.

The subjectivity distinction between pronouns and full noun phrases is part of a larger conception of the range of nominal forms. Langacker (1985) notes that there is an iconic correlation between the phonological content of an expression and the degree of objectification of its referent. A larger amount of phonological content generally correlates with putting more conceptual material onstage. So-called zero marking would represent the most subjective construal of the referent, while full noun phrases represent a more fully objective construal, and pronouns fall somewhere in between. In Chapter 7 I argue that reflexives (*herself*, *himself*, etc.) also provide a semisubjective construal of their referents, but differ from pronouns with respect to the choice of conceived vantage point.

The Subjectivity Scale is essentially the same as the Accessibility Scale proposed by Givón (1983b, 1989) and Ariel (1988, 1990), among others. Givón points out that phonological content correlates inversely with the retrievability of the referent. Low phonological content typically indicates that the referent is easily accessed, while greater phonological content (as with full noun phrases) indicates that accessing the referent requires somewhat more effort (presumably, it represents more of a processing load). Languages differ in their specific conventions for use of various referring forms, but low-phonological-content forms quite generally correlate with greater accessibility. Thus full noun phrases indicate relatively lower accessibility, and a relatively more objective or "distant" portrayal of the referent, while pronouns indicate relatively high accessibility and a relatively more subjective portrayal of the referent.

The correlation between subjectivity and accessibility is, of course, no accident. A referent is accessible to the extent that it is part of the conceptual structure shared by the offstage viewers, the speaker and addressee. Low phonological content typically indicates that the referent is conceived as an active part of the speaker's and addressee's awarenesses. If the referent is portrayed or characterized as part of the offstage viewers' awareness, it is construed somewhat subjectively. A full noun phrase, which indicates low accessibility, also invokes a more fully objective construal of the referent, as it portrays the referent as more fully distinct from (i.e., not yet part of) the speaker's and addressee's awarenesses. This observation has been made in other terms by Ariel (1990), who notes in passing that high accessibility correlates with empathy (in the sense of Kuno [1987]), which is a notion closely related to (though not identical to) Langacker's concept of subjectivity. Subjectivity and accessibility are essentially two sides of the same coin. Awareness of the close connection between the two facilitates explaining the prevalence of point-of-view effects in the anaphora constraints.

Conceptual closeness offers another way of discussing the motivation for the anaphora constraints. A simple illustration of this is the well-known difference between reference to the speaker via the pronoun *I* as compared with the use of a name. Notice how the sentences in (12), if they are understood to be spoken by Lisa herself, give very different impressions of Lisa's conception of herself.

(12)   a.   I can sit and draw for hours.
        b.   Lisa can sit and draw for hours.

(12a) illustrates typical first-person reference. The first-person pronoun invokes as the base of its semantic pole the conception of the discourse context. Within that base, it profiles a thing (in the technical sense— i.e., a nominal conception) corresponding to the offstage speaker. (12b) is anomalous because the name portrays Lisa fully objectively, as if she could stand outside herself and look at herself in the same way that she could look at another person. The semantic specifications of the nominal form conflict with the context in which the nominal appears (in this case, the conception of the actual speech situation).

Restrictions on third-person reference can be analyzed in terms of avoidance of just this kind of semantic conflict. It may be semantically incongruous for the speaker to use a pronoun, thereby portraying the referent as conceptually proximal, in combination with a full nominal which portrays the referent as more distant. To give a concrete example, the pronoun in (13) implies that the speaker conceives of the referent as part of the offstage region. The full noun phrase *Dan* which is 'viewed' from that position implies a greater conceptual distance between the speaker and the referent; it portrays the referent as fully objective and onstage. Metaphorically speaking, the effect would be like looking over someone's shoulder and simultaneously seeing that same person face-on and at some distance away.

(13)   *He saw a snake near Dan.

If it is true that nouns and pronouns differ subtly in their portrayal of the referent, in terms of subjectivity or conceptual distance, then the restrictions on coreference between pronouns and full nominals can be captured and explained in terms of the principle that speakers do not tolerate contradictory portrayals of referents. This would be entirely analogous to observing that it is bizarre for the speaker to refer to herself by name, portraying herself as if she were viewed fully objectively, when she is the viewer. Sentences like (13) would be considered anomalous because they are semantically incoherent. This analysis depends, of course, on developing a model of clause structure which will determine the requirements for maintaining this kind of semantic coherence. This is the subject of the next chapter.

2.4 ANAPHORA CONSTRAINTS AND GRAMMATICALITY JUDGMENTS

It was mentioned above that grammaticality judgments are characterized in CG as categorizing judgments in which the construction in question is characterized as either an instantiation of a particular schema or an extension from that schema. To say that the construction is judged to be an instantiation of the schema means that the construction is fully compatible with the schema in all of its specifications, and the construction is sanctioned as a well-formed instance of the conventionally established pattern described by the schema. If the construction is an extension from the schema, it conflicts in some of its specifications with the specifications of the schema. With a small amount of conflict, the construction may be felt to be an acceptable innovation, but a significant conflict will cause speakers to judge the construction to be anomalous, that is, ungrammatical.

The schema used to categorize the construction is selected by competition among all the schemas activated by the construction (here I am taking a listener-oriented perspective on the process, assuming that we are talking about how conceptualizers react to sentences they hear or read).[16] The factors determining the extent of activation of a schema are conceptual overlap and entrenchment (Langacker 1987a:428–33). A schema tends to be activated to the extent that salient specifications of the construction in question accord with the specifications of the schema; the greater the degree of "fit" between the two (and the more salient the overlapping characteristics are, within the schema and/or within the construction), the greater the activation of the schema. A schema also tends to be activated to the extent that it is entrenched, that is, well established as a pattern to which speakers have had frequent exposure. The schemas which are initially activated compete for activation in an interactive-activation model (see Elman and McClelland 1984) in which each schema contributes to suppressing the activation of competing schemas. The schema emerging from this competition as the most highly activated is the one which is used to make the categorizing judgment and to judge the construction well formed or deviant.

With respect to the anaphora constraints, this means that judgments of obligatory non-coreference (i.e., ungrammaticality with coreference) may be explained in terms of the schemas activated by the nominal form in question, and in terms of the schemas activated by the context in which it is embedded. I have spoken in terms of semantic and pragmatic compatibility (or incompatibility) between a nominal form (a pronoun or full noun phrase) and the context in which it is embedded—where context is defined in terms of reference points and dominions. The specific mechanism which would produce grammaticality judgments is comparison between the constructions themselves and the schemas activated by different nominal forms (nouns, pronouns, and reflexives) and by the coreference configurations within the constructions.

Suppose a full noun phrase appears in the dominion of a corresponding (i.e., coreferential) reference point, as in *He loves John's mother* (under a coreferential reading). We can posit that the appearance of a full noun phrase activates a schematic conception of the kind of context in which full noun phrases are felicitous—a context in which the referent is of low accessibility. The schema activated by the full noun phrase, if it is selected as the categorizing schema, would be used to judge that the construction is deviant, as the actual context does not match the schema.

At the same time, if the speaker conceives the pronoun and the possessor to be coreferential, the correspondence between the reference point (the subject pronoun) and the nominal conception in its dominion (the possessor) will strongly activate a schema which would sanction the use of a possessive pronoun. Such a schema would categorize the construction as deviant in that a full noun phrase appears where a pronoun is expected. In short, the schemas activated by the overall coreference configuration and by the full noun phrase itself both conflict with the actual specifications of the construction, and so the sentence would be judged deviant. (Alternatively, the speaker could judge the pronoun and full noun phrase to be noncoreferential, in which case the sentence would be fully sanctioned.)

In many respects the schema-competition model is not yet fully developed. We do not always know with any certainty what the degree of salience is for different factors in the constructions to be categorized or in the schemas themselves (in other words, how much weight to give them). We can safely assume, however, that the central prominence relations of profiling and figure / ground organization play a major role.

In this study I do not focus specifically on competition between schemas, but instead address (in)compatibility between a nominal (either pronoun or full noun phrase) and the context in which it is embedded, assuming that it is understood that the mechanism underlying the grammaticality judgments is categorization by the most highly activated schema. Chapter 5 however develops the network of constructional schemas for backward anaphora in some detail, while Chapter 7 describes the inventory of schemas sanctioning reflexives. §9.3 offers some additional discussion of the schema competition model.

THREE

Reference Points and the Complement Chain

Drawing on the semantic characterization of nominals developed in the preceding chapter, I analyze obligatory non-coreference as an instance of semantic conflict between a nominal and its immediate context. The central goal of this analysis is to provide an appropriate characterization of the relevant semantic contexts. It is clear from numerous examples which are well known in the literature that linear order alone is not adequate to define the relevant contexts. I propose instead a model of **reference points** (similar to Chafe's [1987, 1994] starting points), which are roughly analogous to local topics, and which are selected on the basis of interaction of a number of factors, primarily prominence and conceptual-semantic connectivity.

3.1 DEFINING THE RELEVANT CONTEXTS

The anaphora constraints are not defined here as a set of independent syntactic principles. Rather, the constraints are based on the same semantic/pragmatic principles underlying restrictions on first- and second-person reference in discourse. The use of a full noun phrase for reference to the speaker is almost always felt to be anomalous, yet it is clear that the anomaly has nothing to do with illicit coreference between nominals, as there may be no coreferential nominal in the sentence. It seems essentially that speakers do not refer to themselves by name because they are already present in the discourse context and so should be conceptually accessible.

Restrictions on third-person reference appear, at first glance, very different from restrictions on first- and second-person reference, since the use of a third-person full noun phrase is not felt to be anomalous when its referent has already been introduced into the discourse context. While reference to first and second person is typically restricted to pronominal forms only, third-person reference may be accomplished via full noun phrases even when the referent has already been mentioned or is physically present.

The apparent difference between first- and second-person, as opposed to third-person, reference reflects the fact that the speaker and addressee are not merely present in the discourse context but also are participants or co-conceptualizers of the discourse. In terms of the stage model, they are the viewers of the onstage conception. The direct conceptual interconnection between these offstage participants and the onstage conception is the reason that first- and second-person referents are obligatorily accessed via pronouns (with certain exceptions, described below). In explaining the constraints on third-person reference and co-reference, I will argue that a slightly different version of direct conceptual interconnection is a strong factor in determining which nominal form(s) are appropriate.

The restrictions on full-nominal reference to first-, second-, and third-person referents can be broken down rather neatly according to each one's function as a participant or nonparticipant in the construal of the onstage predication. A full exploration of these facts would require a much larger study, but here I will outline what seem to be the basic conventions for first-, second-, and third-person reference, focusing just on the facts which pertain to their different roles in the discourse (without yet addressing the facts concerning coreference within sentences).

3.1.1 First Person

The speaker is always a conceptualizer or viewer of the onstage conception, and first-person reference by full name is almost always anomalous, as explained above. This is not only because the speaker is part of the discourse context but also more specifically because the speaker is conceptually connected with the onstage region by virtue of the speaker's role. Reference via a full noun phrase is significantly more acceptable if the speaker specifically wishes to portray himself as viewed by someone else, that is, objectively. The examples in (1) are taken from actual usage; (1a) is a quotation from Oliver North, (1b) is from a column by Dave Barry, in which "he" refers to his son and "his father" is Dave Barry.

(1)   a.   "While reporters were talking about how Ollie North sodomized
            goats on the South Lawn of the White House, or how Ollie North
            was selling White House china to fund the Contras. . . ." (Oliver
            North interview in *TV Guide* 12/28/91)
      b.   Sometimes he can't believe what an idiot his father is. (Dave
           Barry, *Dave Barry's Greatest Hits*, p. 74)

In (1a), the name *Ollie North* indicates that we are seeing Oliver North
from the reporters' perspective (as portrayed sarcastically by Oliver
North himself), not his own perspective. (1b) is taken from a column
in which Barry had already referred to himself a number of times, using
first-person pronouns; in this sentence, however, the use of the nominal
his father signals that the sentence describes his son's thoughts.

These same sentences, with first-person pronouns in place of the
full noun phrases, could more easily be mistaken for representations of
the speaker's conceived reality than the original sentences in (1) could
be. A phrase such as "how I sodomized goats" in the context of (1a)
could still be understood as a description of the reporters' perspective,
but might also be mistaken for a description of Oliver North's view of
reality more easily than (1a). The fact that speakers use full-nominal
reference to the speaker to signal an intended *de dicto* reading is further
evidence for the association of pronouns and full noun phrases with
different points of view, and specifically the claim that the full noun
phrase signals a more objective portrayal of the referent (in these cases,
the referent as objectively perceived through someone else's eyes).

3.1.2 Second Person

The addressee is a co-conceptualizer of the onstage conception, and
therefore must almost invariably be referred to by a pronoun rather
than a full noun phrase. The few contexts in which it is appropriate to
refer to the addressee by name provide further support for this claim.
A name is most commonly used to get the addressee's attention when
the speaker presumably construes the addressee as not yet a viewer of
the onstage predication—otherwise the speaker would not need to get
his or her attention.

Address by name may also be used to offer reassurance of the
speaker's sincerity and attentiveness to the addressee—for example, *I
know how you feel, Bob.* This usage seems to include an appeal to the
addressee to pay close attention to the rest of the predication, so again
we have the notion that the addressee is not conceived as being fully

engaged as a viewer of the onstage predication. The use of a name in offering reassurance warrants detailed analysis, but I would tentatively suggest that in portraying the addressee objectively (through the use of a name rather than a pronoun), the speaker is invoking the conception of his own point of view, implying that the addressee is in the center of his (the speaker's) focused awareness. If something along these lines is correct, it would explain why repetition of the addressee's name is a conventional way of drawing the addressee's attention to the predication, and simultaneously assuring the addressee that he has the speaker's sincere and focused attention.[1]

3.1.3 Third Person

A third-person referent is not a co-conceptualizer or viewer of the onstage predication. If coreference restrictions depend on some notion akin to viewing, then the mere presence of a person other than the speaker or addressee in the real-world discourse context should not rule out the use of a full noun phrase for reference to that person. This is in fact the case: The physical presence of someone who is not the speaker or addressee does not make it entirely unacceptable to refer to such a person by name, although repeated reference by name may seem redundant. By the same token, the fact that a referent has been mentioned previously in the discourse, and is still a topic of discussion, does not make it entirely unacceptable to refer to that person by name.

Nevertheless, third-person reference is at times influenced by point-of-view considerations. The data here are typically quite variable, possibly reflecting dialect variation, but certain trends have been noted which indicate that the conception of a viewer is significant. Ross (1970), Bolinger (1977), Kuno (1987), and van Hoek (1993) have discussed restrictions on anaphora which seem to depend on the notion of a third-person viewer.[2] The following example is from Kuno (1987), who credits personal communication from John Goldsmith.

(2)   a.   Mary spoke to the school doctor about her ever-worsening depression. He gave her some excellent advice; that she/*Mary might consider a different major was perhaps his most important suggestion.

      b.   Mary's mother talked to the school doctor about her daughter's ever-worsening depression. He gave her some excellent advice; that she/Mary might consider a different major was perhaps his most important suggestion.

Reported speech events (or reported cognitive events—e.g., reporting someone's thoughts) imply the presence of a surrogate ground, which is a conception of the discourse context of the reported speech event— including the vantage points of the speaker and addressee (Langacker 1978, 1985). The surrogate ground serves as a vantage point for "viewing" the reported material. For many speakers, there is a tendency to construe the second clause in (2a) from Mary's vantage point, since she was a participant in the reported speech event. In other words, the conception of Mary's vantage point is an important part of the context through which one apprehends the embedded clauses. The judgments here illustrate that essentially the same principle applies here as in the examples with first-person reference discussed in §2.3.2: Use of a full nominal, *when it corefers with part of the conceptual structure through which one "views" that nominal*, is semantically anomalous. The use of a full noun phrase is acceptable in (2b) because Mary's vantage point is not a part of the conception of the reported speech event. This is essentially the analysis proposed by Ross (1970) and by Kuno (1987), albeit in slightly different theoretical terms.

As noted above, judgments are variable for this kind of construction. Some speakers (including myself) judge (2a) anomalous, while others report that it is perfectly acceptable. Variability is also found for sentences such as (3a–b) (variable judgments are indicated by the % symbol).

(3) a. %The idea that *Jim* might have AIDS frightened *him*.
     b. %In *his* opinion, *Dan* is a nice guy.
     c. In *his* ex's opinion, *Dan* is a nice guy.

Of the eight native English speakers I consulted, four rejected (3a), and five rejected (3b) (all of the speakers who rejected [a] also rejected [b], so the difference between the two was due to one speaker who accepted [a] only). The variability in judgment between speakers may be a reflection of the tenuousness of the implicit third-person viewpoint conception, which may be rather easily encouraged or discouraged by subtle semantic factors. It is possible, in fact, that the speakers who accept (3a–b) take the presence of the full noun phrase itself as a cue that the construction is not to be construed as being "within the scope" of the third-person viewpoint. (3c) provides further evidence that in (3b) it is precisely Dan's role as a *viewer* of the clausal conception that makes it anomalous (for some speakers) to use the full noun phrase inside the clause; if Dan is mentioned in essentially the same position (in terms of linear word order), yet not identified as the 'viewer' of the clause, speakers agree that coreference is fully acceptable.

Despite the variability of judgments, the point remains that for many speakers, the conception of a viewer—even an implicit viewer who is not a participant in the current discourse—may have a significant effect in determining the possibility for reference via a full nominal. The variable data involving implied third-person viewers echo the more clear-cut restrictions, which all (or almost all) speakers seem to observe, on reference to first and second person. We can assume that there is variability because the viewing relation is merely implicit, not actually part of the current discourse situation (in that the conceived viewer is not currently a participant in the discourse) nor explicitly coded within the clause (van Hoek 1993, and see §8.2–3).

Third-person point-of-view phenomena, like the restrictions on first- and second-person reference, are usually excluded from consideration in studies of the constraints on intrasentential coreference. Presumably they are considered irrelevant to the problem of formulating the syntactic constraints. I suggest, though, that these facts provide significant clues to the conceptual-semantic motivations for the anaphora constraints.

The overall generalization is that a pronominal, rather than full-nominal, form is required when its referent is conceived as a viewer of the conception of which it is a part. This is consistent with both the Accessibility and the subjectivity accounts of the difference between pronouns and full noun phrases. The viewers of a conception are conceived as directly interconnected with it, and therefore highly accessible. At the same time, it is semantically incoherent to use a form which portrays the referent as fully objective, that is, distinct from its viewers, when the referent is one of the viewers.

In the next section, I suggest that viewer or point-of-view is not precisely the right notion to define the constraints on coreference between third-person pronouns and full noun phrases, but that what is needed is essentially a schematization of that notion. I propose the more abstract notion **reference point** as a basis on which to define the relevant contexts for the anaphora constraints.

3.2 REFERENCE POINTS AND DOMINIONS

A conceived viewer or point of view (POV) sets up a **mental space,** in the sense of Fauconnier (1985).[3] Elements construed within that mental space are understood to be the thoughts or perceptions of the person whose POV is adopted. Several subcomponents of this conception can be identified, separate from the notion of empathy, or "seeing through the eyes" of another person. First, the POV is a central part of the background context within which the referent of the full noun phrase is construed. Second, the POV is subjectively construed, meaning that it is not itself within the focus of awareness, but rather functions solely as part of the background conceptual structure which contributes to construing the material that is within the focus of awareness. Third, it is closely connected, conceptually, with the material which is construed as viewed from that POV.

In short, everything within the mental space set up by a POV is construed *in relation to* the POV, and the POV is a central part of the subjective background context which shapes the construal of the viewed material. In these respects, the conceived viewing configuration is very similar to certain conceptual structures which Langacker (1991, 1993) has described in terms of **reference points** and **dominions.** In the remainder of this chapter, I develop a model of sentential conceptual structure in terms of reference points and dominions, and thereby define the contexts in which coreference is possible. Here I first explain the basic notions involved.

3.2.1 The Reference Point Model

The notion of reference points was introduced in Langacker's (1991) analysis of possessive constructions. A possessor functions as a reference point via which one can make mental contact with the possessum. "Making mental contact" is defined as "singling something out for individual conscious awareness" (Langacker 1991:97). Through the relationship with the possessor, one can single out a particular instance of a nominal type for awareness. For example, the nominal *the boy's knife* uses the conception of *the boy* as a reference point for locating a particular instance of the nominal type *knife*—the instance associated with the boy. The conceptualizer makes mental contact with the profile of *the boy*, and can then make mental contact with the intended instance of *knife*.

A reference point anchors a conceptual structure, which Langacker terms a *dominion*. The dominion includes the conceptual entities which can be located via the reference point. The dominion of X is the conceptual structure with which one makes mental contact through first making contact with *X*. In the case of a possessive construction, the head noun is contained in the dominion of the possessor.

Langacker presents a number of arguments to support the claim that the reference point function is fundamental to the meaning of the possessive construction. The minimal requirement for the use of a possessive form seems to be merely the reference point relationship itself, as the possessive construction does not necessarily indicate that there is any ownership relation. For example, the driver of a car could say to the passenger, "The buzzer's going off; one of the doors must not be closed—is it my door or yours?" There is no implication that the passenger owns part of the car; rather the driver uses the conceptions of the passenger and of himself as reference points to identify the doors.

Langacker also points out that possessive constructions are more felicitous when the possessor is a good choice for a reference point on perceptual grounds—for example, *the car's steering wheel*, where the conception of the car serves to locate the steering wheel, but not **the steering wheel's car*. Additional support for the model can be found in the observation that possessors tend to be 'topical', or in Givón's (1984) terms, 'high continuity' noun phrases (Riddle 1984; Deane 1987; Taylor 1994a, 1994b).

Langacker (1991, 1993) extends the reference point/dominion configuration to apply to the familiar relationship between a discourse topic and the clauses which are understood to be linked to that topic. A topic functions as a reference point within the discourse; clauses which are linked to it are construed within the context (the dominion) set up by the topic. A topic may be established by explicit mention, as in "The final exam is next week." Subsequent clauses may then be construed as being located within the dominion of the topic. If the speaker continues, for example, "The room will be different, and I think we'll need three hours," these statements are understood as pertaining only to the circumstances of the final exam, not to any other possible context. The topic functions as a central part of the subjective background context used to construe the material in its dominion.

3.2.2 Schematic Characterization of Reference Points

In this study I explore the proposal that reference points are ubiquitous in linguistically coded conceptions, and that the organization of reference points and dominions in linguistic conceptual structure defines the relevant contexts for the anaphora constraints. I propose the following description as a schematic characterization of the reference point/dominion configuration.

The referent point is salient within the overall reference point/dominion configuration. In relation to the material in its dominion, however, the reference point is a subjective part of the background—not in the objective focus of awareness. In other words, the reference point/dominion configuration can be thought of as having a dynamic character (see Langacker 1993). There is one level of conceptual structure at which the reference point is a highly salient entity, as the conceptualizer makes mental contact with it (singles it out for individual conscious awareness). There is another level of the conception at which the reference point is not in the center of awareness, but remains as a highly active or central, yet subjective, part of the background.[4]

Another crucial characteristic is that, relative to the material in its dominion, the reference point is not merely "part of the background" in the sense of something that is merely recoverable in the larger context and that can optionally be taken into consideration. The material in the dominion is construed *in relation to* the reference point. The reference point is a salient part of the subjective background conception through which the material in the dominion is construed, in the same way that the conception of the speaker is a central element in the subjective background conception through which any discourse is construed. I take this as the central characteristic of the reference point/dominion configuration, and propose that we can consider the following as a rough definition of the notion dominion: The dominion of a reference point consists of the conceptual structures that are construed in relation to the reference point; the reference point functions as a part of the subjective background context through which one makes mental contact with those conceptions, and which shapes their construal.

This characterization of the relationship between a reference point and its dominion schematically encompasses the configurations involving empathy with a POV, described earlier. The POV functions as a reference point inasmuch as the conceptualizer makes mental contact with it, and then construes another conception—that is, makes mental contact with it—through the relationship with the POV. The conception which is viewed is contained within the dominion of the POV in that the POV is conceived as a central part of the subjective background context which shapes the construal of the viewed material. Adopting a POV may frequently include semantic notions that are not present in every reference point/dominion configuration (such as the idea that one is seeing what the viewer sees), but at a schematic level, the reference point/dominion notion describes the conceptual configurations involved with "adopting a point of view." Configurations involving empathy with a conceived viewer can therefore be considered as a special, more specific case of the schematic reference point configuration. One consequence of this conception of the nature of reference points is that it suggests that conceived POVs may play a more central role in determining anaphoric coreference possibilities than is often assumed (see §3.4 and Chap. 8).

3.2.3 Reference Points within the Clause

Anticipating the discussion somewhat, the anaphora constraints are formulated in terms of a model of clausal conceptual structure which involves layering multiple reference point/dominion configurations. The subject of a clause is the primary reference point within the clause, with all other nominals in the clause in its dominion. The direct object is the secondary clausal figure (see Givon 1984; Langacker 1991) and is therefore a secondary reference point; it is construed within the subject's dominion, and other nominals in the clause are in its dominion. Successive nesting of reference point/dominion configurations describes a conceptual path which leads from one nominal to the next within the clause, and from higher-level clauses to embedded clauses. This conceptual path defines the relevant contexts for the anaphora constraints. The conceptual path produces an effect as if the subject preceded all other nominals within the clause, so that the other nominals are integrated into the context set up by the subject. The direct object, in turn, behaves as if it preceded all other nominals except for the subject, and it too sets up a dominion within which the other nominals in the clause are construed, and so on.

   This is in some respects not a new proposal. It bears a particularly clear resemblance to the Information Flow Model and the notion of **starting points** put forth by Chafe (1987, 1994). The key difference between this study and Chafe's work is the present focus on clause-internal and phrase-internal reference point organization, which Chafe does not address in detail. I arrive at some of the same conclusions as Chafe (such as the identification of the subject as a starting/reference point for the clause) through a bottom-up analysis based on CG principles of clausal semantics, while Chafe's work takes a top-down, discourse-oriented approach. The convergence between the models is therefore all the more striking.

The reference point notion is also quite similar to MacWhinney's (1977) notion of starting points. MacWhinney has claimed that the conceptualizer needs to be able to "get inside the clause" in order to comprehend it. I believe that his intuitive notion of getting inside is captured by the dynamic conception of mental contact proceeding from a reference point to its dominion. The conceptualizer makes mental contact with each distinct element within the relation (i.e., singles out each element for individual conscious awareness) rather than construing the integrated relation as an undifferentiated conceptual unity, but each distinct instance of mental contact is made within the dominions established by the preceding elements rather than within a conceptual vacuum. The element with which one first makes mental contact becomes subjective, relative to the next element—as if, in a sense, one adopted the first element as a vantage point from which to view the second. This process of successive mental contacts, with subjectification of each element in turn, seems to capture MacWhinney's sense of getting inside the clause.[5]

The effect of reference point/dominion organization is that the conceptualizer makes mental contact with each nominal within the context defined by the relation, including nominals previously encountered on the conceptual path. These relations define the contexts which are relevant for pronominal anaphora. The possibilities for coreference between nouns and pronouns can be described (not defined) as follows:

(4) i.   A full nominal cannot appear in the dominion of a reference point which it corresponds to.

     ii. The antecedent for a pronoun must be sufficiently salient (i.e., distinct and prominent) within the context in which the pronoun appears that it can plausibly be construed as a reference point with the pronoun in its dominion.

It should be emphasized that these are not independent or free-standing syntactic principles. Rather, they are an abbreviated description of the **semantic and pragmatic effects** that occur when different kinds of nominals are integrated into different conceptual structures. The anaphora facts arise from the interaction of these semantic and pragmatic notions, not from applying these constraints as filters to rule out certain constructions.

It should also be noted that reference point status is a matter of degree. Different nominal forms are associated with different degrees of accessibility for their referents, indicating that we are dealing with more than a binary distinction (see Givón 1983b; Ariel 1988, 1990; and references cited above). For purposes of this study, in which the central issue is the admissibility of a low accessibility marker (a full noun phrase) in particular contexts, it is convenient to speak as if we needed only a two-way distinction.

3.2.4 Factors Determining the Selection of Reference Points

Turning the general notion of a reference point into a specific, explanatory model requires answering two distinct questions. First is the question of the general factors which motivate selecting one entity as a reference point in relation to other entities. Second is the question of which specific reference point/dominion configurations have become entrenched within established constructional schemas of English. These well-established configurations are particularly important to describing the anaphora facts which involve robust grammaticality judgments (the kinds of data typically addressed in the literature on the pronominal anaphora constraints). Three general considerations underlie the reference point patterns which the model of anaphora constraints appeals to. They are as follows.

Prominence. X is likely to be taken as a reference point relative to Y if X is prominent in the context which includes Y. This reflects the basic nature of a reference point as something which is selected on the basis of salience and used as a starting point from which to make mental contact with other, less salient entities. The importance of salience or prominence as a factor in anaphoric coreference has of course long been noted (e.g., Givón 1983b, 1985, 1989; Sproat and Ward 1987; Ariel 1990; Ziv 1994). Within CG, there are two particularly important notions of prominence: profiling and figure/ground organization. These same two notions are central to defining reference points within linguistic predications. An element is significantly more likely to be selected as a reference point within a conception if it is profiled within that conception than if it is not. It is also significantly more likely to be selected as a reference point within a conception if it is the trajector of a relation within that conception.

Linear Word Order. Other things being equal, X is more likely to be taken as a reference point in relation to Y if X is introduced into the conceptualizer's awareness before Y is. As with prominence, the role of linear order is motivated by the very conception of a reference point as something which is identifiable and available to the conceptualizer before the conceptualizer makes mental contact with the things in the reference point's dominion. The effects of linear order are somewhat weak, however, and do not outweigh the combination of prominence and conceptual connectivity.

Conceptual Connectivity. The extent of a reference point's dominion is determined by the interaction of conceptual (semantic) connectivity and linear word order. Connectivity between two nominals is determined by the relations in which they participate. Nominals are strongly interconnected when they participate in (i.e., elaborate) an explicit interconnecting relation, as in the complement chain. Nominals are more weakly interconnected when they merely co-occur within a single linguistic unit of some kind, such as a sentence or a conceptual paragraph (see Hinds 1979; Longacre 1979). In this chapter I will be concerned mostly with the situation in which X and Y are part of the same head/complement structure, hence strongly interconnected. In Chapters 4–5 I address the gradations of connectivity in more detail.

In van Hoek (1992), POV was listed as an additional factor determining reference point selection, along with prominence, connectivity, and linear order. This was an oversimplification, and was in some ways misleading. A POV is a kind of reference point, by its nature, but the speaker's choice of POV is not a fourth factor on a par with the three listed above. Clarifying this distinction may also allow us to clarify the limited sense in which the other three factors can be said to determine the organization of reference points.

A POV is a reference point (by definition), but its status as such is frequently determined entirely by the speaker's (or hearer's) construal, not by any combination of other factors. If the speaker construes a conception from a particular POV, the construal itself is sufficient to establish the reference-point/dominion configuration regardless of whether the POV is associated with a nominal that is topical or otherwise prominent (though there is a natural association between POV choice and factors such as salience). In the case of a sentence like the second clause in (2) above, repeated here as (5), the discourse promotes the adoption of a particular POV, but ultimately the perspective from which each clause is viewed is a matter of the speaker's construal and is not determined in a mechanistic way by a set of objectively identifiable factors.

(5)   Mary talked to the school doctor about her daughter's ever-worsening depression. He gave her some excellent advice; that she/*Mary might consider a different major was perhaps his most important suggestion.

Such a POV configuration illustrates the underlying principle that reference point organization is itself a matter of construal and is not determined mechanistically by adding up factors. There is of course a certain sense in which the factors listed in (4) above can be said to determine reference point construal. Once the speaker has made certain choices with respect to describing a conceived situation, such as determining which referents to mention explicitly and which verb(s) to employ, the prominence asymmetries and semantic interconnections among elements will largely determine the organization of reference points. The choices of nominals, verbs, and so on are, however, matters of construal, that is, how the speaker chooses to portray the situation. Even where those construal decisions strongly promote a particular conception of reference point relationships, reference point organization itself remains to some extent independent of those considerations.

One implication of this view of reference point organization is the expectation that construal will be to some extent flexible even in the 'core' cases, that is, even in the kinds of data traditionally covered by structural constraints such as those based on c-command. Purely subjective considerations such as POV may interact with objectively identifiable factors to a much greater extent than is usually recognized in analyses of the anaphora constraints. In §3.4 below I discuss examples in which POV considerations produce judgments different from what would be predicted by the three factors in (4) alone or by an analysis based on c-command.

3.2.5 A Note on Intonation

In addition to the factors listed above, it should be mentioned that intonational cues, including both pitch accent and pauses, have significant import for coreference possibilities. In many of the examples to be discussed in this study, the construal of both prominence and connectivity is a matter of degree. Intonational cues may be used by a speaker to signal particular intentions about construal, and may override (to some extent) the contribution of other factors. In this study I will not attempt to do justice to the complexities involved here, but will briefly summarize what appear to be the key observations concerning intonational factors, leaving the details as a project for future research.

3.2.5.1 Pauses and Intonation Breaks

Bolinger (1977, 1979) demonstrates that intonation breaks, or the absence of such breaks, is highly relevant to coreference possibilities. In his work on "repeat identification" (configurations in which a referent is already under discussion in the discourse, and is nevertheless referred to via a name or descriptive noun phrase), he points out that it is much easier to rename a referent following a pronominal reference if a pause or intonation break separates the name from the preceding coreferential pronoun(s). The examples in (6) are from Bolinger (1979: 298).

(6)　a.　*He* choked when *John* swallowed the bone.
　　　b.　*He* choked (when *John* swallowed the bone, that is).

On the assumption that intonational units in some sense correspond to conceptual units (Chafe 1994), the significance of intonation breaks is straightforwardly described, at least in rough outline.[6] A critical notion in the reference point model is conceptual connectivity, defined as the extent to which two elements are conceived as participating together in a larger conceptual unit (such as a verb-argument structure, a sentence, or a paragraph). An element is more likely to be construed within the dominion of a reference point to the extent that it is conceptually connected with it, while intervening conceptual discontinuities make it easier for an element to "escape" the dominion of a reference point. An intonation break reflects a conceptual discontinuity of some kind, such as the speaker's sense that the material after the intonation break constitutes an afterthought or comment on the previous material.

The intonation break may also be associated with a contrast in the foreground/background or prominence status of the material before and after the break. In Chapter 5 I argue that backwards anaphora involving parenthetical expressions, as in (7), relies crucially on semantic backgrounding of the conception represented by the parenthetical. Parenthetical expressions in speech are set off by distinctive intonation, represented in writing by commas or dashes.

(7)　It was 6:10 p.m.—almost time for her break—when Claudia Hawkins pulled her airport shuttle into Lot C. (*Los Angeles Times* 2/2/91)

3.2.5.2 *Pitch Accent*

The role of pitch accent (construed as contrastive or emphatic stress) is difficult to pin down, and again I will make only a few preliminary observations. Lakoff (1971) notes that contrastive stress on a pronoun seems to signal that the speaker intends a nondefault reading of the pronoun. In conjoined clause constructions, in which a parallel interpretation of the clauses would typically be expected (i.e., coreference between the subjects of the two clauses [See Grober, Beardsley, and Caramazza 1978]), stress serves as a signal that the less-likely (nonparallel) reading of the pronouns is the intended one. A typical example would be something like (8), where underlining is used to indicate pitch accent.

(8)   Sally complained to Betty, and then *she* got mad at *her* (i.e., Betty got mad at Sally).

Hirschberg and Ward (1991), in a study of "sloppy identity," found that a pitch accent on the pronoun seems to encourage speakers to select the reading which would be less likely under neutral stress (i.e., the opposite of the reading which they would be more likely to choose when the sentence is presented in writing, where they presumably apply unmarked stress patterns). In other words, a pitch accent seems to signal that the speaker intends the otherwise less-likely interpretation of the pronoun.

Stress on a nominal also raises the salience of the nominal conception, with consequences for the likelihood that that nominal will be construed as a reference point in relation to other material. As Bolinger (1977, 1979), Roberts (1987), and others have pointed out, backwards anaphora or repeat identification of a referent is more likely when the pronoun which precedes the name is unstressed. Roberts (1987:85) notes that (9) is acceptable with coreference only where the pronoun and name are unstressed. The context in which such a sentence might occur is one in which the concept of John is already salient in the discourse, so the unstressed pronoun is appropriate. Stress on the pronoun would foreground the pronominal referent, making the following full noun phrase inappropriate (see Chap. 5 for discussion of the importance of backgrounding the pronominally encoded conception in backwards anaphora and repeat identification). Stress on the name would indicate that the referent is not in fact salient in the discourse, thereby undermining the construal of the pronoun as representing "given" information.

(9)   His mother loves John.

Clearly, there are many subtle distinctions not covered by this brief discussion. In particular, the relationship between specific intonation patterns and the foregrounding or backgrounding of conceptions remains to be explored in detail. In this study I am assuming that examples are pronounced with neutral or unmarked stress except as otherwise indicated, and that there are no marked intonation breaks except as indicated. Some of the examples cited in this study may receive differing judgments under different stress and intonation patterns.

3.3 THE COMPLEMENT CHAIN

The notions described above are the basic factors which underlie the selection of reference points. We can assume that, in producing or comprehending linguistic material, speakers do not choose reference points entirely *de novo*, drawing directly on these very general and schematic notions. Rather it is much more plausible that the conventionalized grammatical structures of the language include reference point / dominion configurations which have become entrenched, established configurations. Within the clause, head / complement structure and the prominence asymmetries of profiling and figure / ground organization (including grammatical relations) define a series of reference point / dominion configurations which I term the **complement chain**.

The separate label "complement chain" is only for expository convenience, and it should be understood that the complement chain is not a special entity separate from the rest of the reference point / dominion model, but is simply a particular facet of the conventionally established organization of reference points. The complement chain arises from the general conceptual considerations outlined above: that (i) the trajector of a relation is always a reference point in relation to any landmark(s) of that relation; (ii) an element which is profiled is significantly more likely to be selected as a reference point than one which is not; (iii) strong connectivity as defined by elaboration of the same relational conception determines which elements are obligatorily construed as part of the dominion of a reference point. Here I describe some of the basic links in the complement chain, beginning with the conception of the speech event itself (the ground), and continuing down into the clause structure.

3.3.1 The Ground

The entire predication is in the dominions of any elements conceived as reference points within the ground. The conceptions of discourse participants—the speaker and addressee—are reference points relative to which the entire predication is evaluated. It is therefore anomalous (except under specific circumstances, as explained in §3.1.1) for the speaker to refer to himself or herself or to the addressee by the use of a full noun phrase. Referents (other than the speaker and addressee) which have been introduced into the preceding discourse can *optionally* be construed as reference points within the ground as well. The speaker and addressee are always construed as reference points in relation to the predication (except under the special conditions noted in §3.1.1), as they are the viewers of the onstage predication, and viewers are always reference points.

3.3.2 The Composite Profile

At the highest level of organization, the composite conception which is formed by integrating the components of the predication can be described in terms of a composite profile and an unprofiled base (elements such as modifiers are unprofiled in the composite conception; see §2.1.4). Let us assume for now that we are typically dealing with complete sentences. At the highest level, a complete sentence profiles a process (the process profiled by the main-clause verb), including the participants in the process. We can think of the profile as a sort of window of prominence (Langacker 1991, 1996; Talmy 1995), containing within it a number of subcomponents—nominals and relations—which are viewed within that profile as if within a frame. Some of those complements may be clauses which set up their own windows of prominence.

   Complements elaborate salient subparts of the head (Langacker 1987a:306–10). The complements do not add anything entirely new to the overall semantic structure, but rather flesh out conceptions which are prefigured by the head. Conceptually accessing the head thus automatically invokes the conception of the complements on which it is dependent (in Langacker's [1987a:300] sense of autonomy/dependence; i.e., the complements are an intrinsic part of the process conception). The elaborative relation (the construal of one element as an elaboration of the other) thus leads directly from the head to its complements. The heads and complements form a hierarchical semantic structure, as the chain of elaborative relations leads from one head to its complements, and thence to its complements. At each level, the complements are ordered by prominence, with the trajector preceding the landmark(s), and the primary landmark preceding the secondary landmark (if there is one). Complements of a higher-level profile precede the complements of a subordinate profile (such as an embedded clause).

Topicalizing a nominal makes it a reference point in relation to the entire clause (as this is the definition of topichood). It is therefore anomalous for a pronominal topic to correspond with any full nominals in the clause, as in (10).

(10)   *Him, John's* wife can't stand.

3.3.3 The Subject

The subject of the clause is the nominal corresponding to the trajector of the clausal relation (Langacker 1987a:231–36). As the clausal trajector, it is a reference point, with any landmarks of the clausal relation in its dominion.[7] I assume that all the elements which make up a nominal are construed within the context in which the entire nominal is construed, in this case, the dominion of the subject. This explains the data in (11). The nominal *John's mother* elaborates the landmark of the verb *like*, and so the semantic poles of both of the component nominals *John* and *mother* are construed within the dominion of the trajector *he*. If the semantic poles of *he* and *John* correspond, the construction is anomalous, as a full noun phrase is juxtaposed against a corresponding pronominal conception.

(11)   *He* likes *John's* mother.

Additional properties associated with reference points tend to be associated with the subject. It is the most likely vantage point from which to view the clause conceptually (DeLancey 1981). The subject also tends to be old information, that is, already in the conceptualizer's awareness and hence suitable to serve as a reference point (e.g., Givón 1979a, 1983b, 1984, 1985, 1994; Chafe 1987, 1991, 1994; Tomlin 1984).

The relationship between a subject and the rest of the clause is similar to the relationship between a possessor and the nominal it grounds. The conceptualizer makes mental contact with the grounded nominal instance through the possessor, which functions as a starting point for the nominal in the same way that the subject is the starting point for the clause. Unlike a possessor, the subject of a clause is not a grounding predication, and the conceptualizer need not identify the other nominals in the clause through the relationship with the subject (e.g., the direct object may be an independently grounded nominal such as *John* or *the man*, whereas the nominal instance profiled by a possessum is picked out through its relationship with the possessor, as in *John's book* or *the boy's knife*). The conceptualizer nevertheless makes mental contact with the objects and other nominals within the dominion of the subject in the sense that the subject is a central part of the subjective context within which the conceptualizer singles out the object and other nominals for individual conscious awareness.

Because the subject is a reference point with the rest of the clause in its dominion, a pronominal subject cannot correspond with a full nominal elsewhere in the clause, whether or not the pronoun precedes the nominal in the linear string. This accounts for data such as (12). (Below and in Chap. 4 I will spell out more fully what I mean by "the rest of the clause," i.e., which elements are construed as being closely enough connected with the clause that they are obligatorily considered to be within the dominion of the subject. For the moment we can assume that "the rest of the clause" is any complement of the verb, as well as any complement of a complement of the verb, etc.)

(12) a. **He* saw a skunk near *Ralph.*
      b. **Near *Ralph, he* saw a skunk.

Even when the locative phrase is preposed, as in (12b), it is conceptually included in the dominion of the subject, because it elaborates the location which the subject sees, the location of the landmark, and is therefore conceptually connected with the processual conception of which the subject is the figure. Conceptual connectivity is more significant than linear order in determining which elements will be construed as belonging to the dominion of a reference point. Word order, as noted above, can function as a cue influencing the construal of a construction; word-order effects are most obvious when the components of a conception are not strongly interconnected conceptually (see §4.3).

3.3.4 The Landmark

The landmark within the clause (specifically, the primary landmark when there is more than one landmark) is the secondary figure, the second most prominent nominal in the clause (Givón 1984; Langacker 1987a, 1991). Any other complements of the verb, besides the subject, are in the dominion of the primary landmark (some modifiers are as well; see §4.2.2). This explains the following data:

(13) a.   I told *Sam* about *his* mother.
      b.   *I told *him* about *Sam*'s mother.

The double object construction makes the recipient or beneficiary the primary landmark (see Langacker 1991), with the result that it becomes a reference point with the other nominal, the theme, in its dominion. This explains the data in (14).

(14) a.   I gave *Sam his* book.
      b.   *I gave *him* *Sam*'s book.

The entire model developed here can be seen as essentially an extension of the stage model. The ground is the platform from which one conceptually views the clause, and the ordering of the other nominals as reference points defines a metaphorical 'line of sight' which extends into the clause (see Langacker 1995). This model of clausal conceptual structure is very much in the spirit of observations by Givón (1984), Chafe (1987, 1991, 1994), and others who have pointed out that there is an intuitive sense in which speaker and addressee "build out" from the conception of the ground as they apprehend new information, integrating successive predications into the evolving context.

The model of the complement chain draws on the familiar grammatical relations hierarchy (Keenan and Comrie 1977; Perlmutter and Postal 1983; Perlmutter and Rosen 1984; Bresnan 1982; Dalrymple 1993), but here it is claimed that this hierarchy is determined by semantic notions of prominence, specifically figure/ground organization (see Givón 1976, 1989, 1994; Langacker 1987a, 1987c, 1991). It should also be noted that the grammatical relations hierarchy captures only part of the overall model of reference points. So, for example, the claim that the subject of a clause is a reference point with the rest of the clause in its dominion is not a special claim about clausal subjects. Rather it reflects the general notion that the trajector of a relation is a reference point in relation to the landmark(s) in that relation.

3.3.5 Embedded Clauses

The composite conception defined by the complement chain is an integrated profile. Reference points within that profile function as reference points in relation to conceptions that are more deeply embedded in the processual conception, in other words, that are subordinate to the matrix verb.[8] The matrix-clause verb sets up the frame within which subordinate clauses are construed, as it determines the profile at the highest level of organization. Arguments of the matrix verb 'precede' any less-prominent embedded clauses on the complement chain. This explains the data in (15–16).

(15) a. *Ralph* said that Mary wanted to hire *him*.
      b. **He* said that Mary wanted to hire *Ralph*.
      c. **He* never knew that Mary wanted to hire *Ralph*.

(16) a. *Mary told *him* that *John* should find a better job.
      b. *I convinced *him* that *Roger* should do his thesis on cats.
      c. *We recently informed *her* that *Sally* was being considered for the position.

A somewhat different situation obtains regarding the relationship between a nominal within an embedded clause and a nominal within the main clause. Reference point relationships are determined by the relative prominence of nominals within an integrated conception; the fact that a nominal is prominent at one level (i.e., functions as a reference point at that level) does not mean it will necessarily continue to function as a reference point relative to nominals with which it combines at a higher level of organization. For example, the embedded-clause subject nominals in (16) above do not function as reference points in relation to the nominals in the main clause. To take a different example, the subject of a sentential subject, as in (17), need not be construed as a reference point in relation to elements in the main clause.

(17) a. That *he* has never been to college is a surprising fact about *Jim*.
      b. The idea that *he* might have AIDS made *John* very nervous.

Though the pronoun in each case is a reference point in relation to other complements of the embedded-clause verb, this has no bearing on its prominence within the larger sentence. The subject of the main clause in each case is the integrated conception profiled by the entire sentential subject; the individual elements within that subject do not have separate roles within the main-clause profile, and so need not be construed as reference points in relation to other complements of the same verb. (The speaker may, of course, choose to rely on linear word order to determine reference point relations, just as in multiclausal discourse, and so may choose to name the referents in the sentential subject; e.g., *That Jim has never been to college is a surprising fact about him.*)

It may at first appear contradictory to claim, on the one hand, that embedded clauses functioning as the landmark of a main-clause verb are construed in the dominion of the main-clause subject and, on the other hand, that elements within an embedded clause are not given prominence within the main clause. From a certain point of view, it may seem as if we have said that the reference point relationship is sometimes transitive and sometimes intransitive. In fact, it is not transitive at all, and nothing in the principles of reference point organization stated above should lead us to expect transitivity. The fact that an element is a reference point in relation to other nominals at one level of conceptual organization has no bearing on whether it will function as a reference point in relation to other nominals which are combined with it at a higher level of conceptual organization, where the erstwhile reference point has lost its prominence.

The seeming transitivity of the reference point relationship illustrated by (15–16) above is not transitivity at all. It would be misleading to think that the reference point status of the matrix subject is somehow translated into reference point status reaching into the embedded clause. It is more accurate to say that the entire embedded clause, including the nominals within it, is construed within the context set up by the matrix-clause subject. No notion of transitivity need be inferred.

3.3.6 Profiled and Unprofiled Elements

It has been claimed that prominence is a central notion influencing the selection of reference points. The discussion so far has focused on one kind of prominence—the distinction between trajectors, landmarks, and secondary landmarks. Another central prominence relation in CG is profiling. Profiling also plays a large role in defining reference point/ dominion structures.

CG draws a semantic distinction between complements, which serve as part of the profile of an integrated structure, and modifiers, which are not profiled within the structures defined by their heads (see §2.1.4). When a head and a modifier are integrated, the composite structure profiles only the head; the modifier becomes an unprofiled part of the base. This distinction provides the basis for explaining differences in the behavior of complements versus modifiers with respect to the anaphora facts. The profiled structure into which a nominal is integrated includes everything which precedes it and which is *profiled* within the complement chain. Modifiers of nominals within the clause have only a limited, local salience, since they are not part of the integrated profile, and therefore need not be construed as reference points in relation to the rest of the clause.[9]

A pronoun in a modifier can therefore correspond with a full nominal elsewhere in the sentence even if the pronoun is attached to a nominal which is prominent in the complement chain. This explains the judgments in (18).

(18) a.   *John*'s mother loves *him*.
      b.   *His* mother loves *John*.

In (18a), the pronoun which elaborates the landmark does not precede the nominal *John* on the complement chain, so coreference is acceptable. In (18b), the pronoun is attached to the subject nominal, which does precede the full nominal on the complement chain, but the pronoun itself is not part of the integrated profile of the clause, and so is not salient within the structure which includes the direct object nominal. The principles of reference point organization described above do not predict that reference point relationships will be transitive; that is, the fact that the possessive pronoun is a reference point in relationship to the head noun *mother* does not mean that it must be construed as a reference point in relationship to nominals elsewhere in the sentence, such as the direct object. Coreference between the possessor and the full nominal is not ruled out.[10]

In (18b), simple coreference (in which the referent has previously been established in the discourse, and is only being renamed by the full noun phrase) is not ruled out, but a genuine backwards anaphora reading (in which the full nominal functions as the antecedent for the pronoun) may be a bit more difficult to get. It is well known that sentences of this kind are not always accepted by native speakers when they are presented in isolation.[11] In §5.3 I argue that these constructions are extremely non-prototypical examples of backwards anaphora, and that they are not frequently found in actual usage. Backwards anaphora requires that the full nominal be prominent enough to function as a reference point in relation to the preceding pronoun. While there is an asymmetry of prominence between the profiled full noun phrase and the nonprofiled pronoun, it is not as pronounced as in the more typical backwards anaphora examples (see §5.2). The atypicality of these constructions would explain speakers' variable judgments. With sufficient motivation, this configuration seems fully acceptable—as in *His wife's opinion of John is that he's a weasel*, where the placement of the full noun phrase is motivated by the desire to invoke a highly objective, in-focus conception of John, that is, John as represented in his wife's opinion.

This profile/base distinction also accounts for an important difference between possessive nominals and subjects. The main-clause subject is a reference point in relation to an embedded clause. This explains facts such as (19a–d).

(19) a. *John* wanted Mary to phone *him*.
      b. **He* wanted Mary to phone *John*.
      c. *Sally* thought Ralph said *she* was a genius.
      d. **She* thought Ralph said *Sally* was a genius.

Possessive constructions involving multiple embedded nominals work differently than embedded clauses owing to a crucial difference in the profiling pattern. As explained above, Langacker (1991) analyzes possessive constructions as an example of reference point/dominion organization. Since the possessed head noun is in the dominion of the possessor, correspondence between a pronominal possessor and a nominal attached to the head noun is anomalous, as in (20).

(20) **his* picture of *John*

Since the possessor is not *profiled* in the integrated structure (the possessive relation is a modifying relation, and the integrated structure profiles only the head noun, not the modifier), and the reference point relation is not transitive, the possessor need not be construed as salient in relation to anything other than the head noun and the conceptual structures which directly contribute to characterizing the type conception for the head noun. In double possessive constructions, such as (21) below, the first possessor is a reference point only in relation to the second possessor—not in relation to the entire nominal. This is because the first possessor (in [21], *his*) is not directly connected with the nouns inside the dominion of the second possessor (i.e., *sister's*), nor is it part of the profiled structure into which those nouns are integrated. (21) is therefore acceptable.

(21) *his* sister's picture of *John*

From Reinhart (1983), (22) provides additional illustration of the significance of the profiled/unprofiled distinction. This invented example is grammatical with coreference, though it seems likely that the pronoun would have an antecedent elsewhere in the discourse; as an example of genuine backwards anaphora (in which the full noun phrase functions as the antecedent for the pronoun), it seems atypical (see Chap. 5).

(22) a.   The people who work with *Lola* admire *her*.
      b.   The people who work with *her* admire *Lola*.

The modifier in (22b) is contained within a relative clause, which is a modifier of the head noun *people* (see Langacker 1991:430–35 for a CG analysis of relative clause structure). The profile of the subject nominal is the profile of the noun *people*, while the contents of the relative clause are not part of the profile of the main clause. The pronoun in the relative clause does not contribute to the profile into which the full nominal is integrated, and so the full nominal is therefore not necessarily construed within its dominion. Constructions of this kind are in fact found in actual usage, though they do not seem to be very common, as determined by examination of a corpus of backwards anaphora constructions collected from written texts (see §5.1). (23) is the sole example of this construction from the corpus. The relevant clause is *underlined*.

(23) Being told you consider all my friends who post here non-nice makes me almost hope *everyone who has it will send you a copy of "Cindy's Torment."* . . .[12]

As explained above, when there is more than one landmark, the primary landmark precedes all the other landmarks on the complement chain. It is, however, possible for a nominal within a modifier (such as a pronominal possessor), attached to the direct object, to correspond with a full nominal elsewhere in the clause. Examples such as (24) are frequently judged marginal, but not fully unacceptable.

(24) a.   I gave *John's* book to *him*.
      b.   ?I gave *his* book to *John*.

(24b) is not fully sanctioned for the same reason that many speakers reject (18b) above (when it is presented out of context): The asymmetry in prominence between (the semantic poles of) the pronoun and the full noun phrase is not sufficiently pronounced to motivate construing the full nominal conception as a reference point in relation to the pronominal conception. While the indirect object is more prominent than the possessive modifier (the indirect object is a complement of the verb, hence profiled at the highest level of organization), the difference in prominence is not so great as to motivate construing the indirect object as a reference point with the possessive modifier in its dominion. In the backwards anaphora corpus mentioned above, I found just a single example of this kind of construction, which is given here in (25). I have underlined the coreferring nominals.

(25)   "But this is a fascinating project," he said, recounting scenes in which aides brought news of *his* political death knell to *Richard Nixon*. (*TV Guide* 10/28/89)

The subject pronoun *he* refers to the director of a movie about Nixon, but *his* refers to Nixon. Without the full noun phrase which follows it, the pronoun would be taken as also referring to the movie director.

One last illustration of the profiled/unprofiled distinction is the observation that a modifier of the entire clause is not profiled at the highest level of organization, and so a pronominal conception within the modifier is not necessarily construed as a reference point in relation to nominals within the clause. Coreference between the referent of such a pronoun and a full noun phrase in the clause is therefore acceptable, as in (26). (I am assuming Langacker's [1991] analysis of constructions involving modifiers such as *before* and *after*, in which the composite conception profiles only the main clause, while the subordinate clause functions as a modifier and is unprofiled.)

(26)   a.   After *it* fell off the table, *the ball* rolled across the floor.
       b.   When *he* got back from the store, *John* took a nap.

In this section I have focused on one aspect of the complement/modifier distinction: the differing behavior of complements and modifiers as reference points within the clause or sentence. The central claim here has been that complements, which are profiled as part of the composite conceptual structure profiled by the verb, are so salient within that structure that they are obligatorily construed as reference points in relation to conceptions "downstream" on the complement chain. Nominals contained within modifiers, which are not profiled within the composite clausal structure, are only optionally construed as reference points in relation to nominals elsewhere in that conception. The coreference possibilities involving pronouns in modifiers are accordingly much freer than when the pronoun elaborates a complement of the process.

3.4 POV SHIFTS AND THE COMPLEMENT CHAIN

I am arguing that the complement chain described here is not merely a notational variant of the familiar c-command relation, and that it is not an autonomous syntactic construct of any kind; rather it is defined purely in terms of semantic notions. Supporting evidence comes from semantic effects on the complement chain itself. If the complement chain were simply a notational variant of the autonomous syntactic relations posited in generative grammar, it should be insulated from the effects of semantic factors such as POV choice.[13] As data below illustrate, it is not. Rather the construal of reference point relationships, even within the complement chain, is to some extent sensitive to unquestionably semantic considerations. This supports the contention that the complement chain is itself a conceptual-semantic construct.

Dominions are mental spaces, in the sense of Fauconnier (1985), Dinsmore (1991), Fauconnier and Sweetser (1996). As explained above, a POV also sets up a mental space, the conception of the viewer's perceptions or thoughts. A nominal description which would be inappropriate from one POV may be appropriate when a different POV is adopted. For example, it is anomalous for the speaker to refer to him/herself by name, but s/he may do so if implicitly adopting a different POV (cf. §3.1.1). A dominion within the complement chain is like the dominion set up by a POV; although a full nominal is inappropriate within the dominion of a corresponding reference point, a full nominal may appear in a position which would otherwise seem anomalous, provided that a different POV is adopted, which creates a different dominion in which the nominal may be construed.

It is not standard to think of the anaphora constraints as a matter of adopting a POV, but I am claiming that this is essentially what is involved. The complement chain is a series of reference points, akin to a series of vantage points, defining what Langacker (1995) terms a "line of sight" into the clause. One dominion is nested inside another in the sense that each reference point has all the succeeding dominions in its own dominion. Where an outside POV intervenes and sets up a different dominion, outside this chain of reference points, it opens the possibility of a full nominal appearing where it would otherwise not be expected.

This potential manifests itself, so to speak, at the edges of the complement chain. As noted above, modifiers are construed within the same dominions as the heads they modify. They are not, however, directly connected conceptually with the other complements of the clause in the same way that the head is (cf. §2.1.4). This distinction is often too subtle to make an appreciable difference, but it does matter with respect to POV effects, where the claim that POV shift may affect anaphora possibilities is most easily demonstrated with nominals in modifiers.

The pairs in (27) and (28) illustrate the basic point. While most of the speakers I have consulted agree with the judgments here, even those who do not entirely accept the (b) sentence in each pair agree that it is improved relative to the (a) sentence.

(27) a. *She* joined a new organization, which paid *Sally* a lot more money.
      b. *She* joined a new organization, whose members all found *Sally* to be absolutely delightful.

(28) a. *He* found an insurance company that promised *Mark* excellent benefits.
      b. ?*He* married a woman who thought *Mark* was the greatest guy on earth.

Coreference is unacceptable in each of the (a) sentences because the relative clause modifier is construed within the same larger context as its head, that is, the dominion of the main-clause subject. The (b) sentences differ primarily in the introduction of a POV in the relative clause. The dominion set up by the POV can serve as the mental space within which the full nominal is construed.

One additional detail remains to be explicated here. In each of the (b) sentences above, it seems intuitively that the contents of the relative clause are not accessible to the subject of the main clause. If the relative clause POV and its thoughts were part of the main-clause subject's conception of the situation, then the contents of the relative clause would be viewed from that POV and would therefore be included in its dominion. The paraphases in (29) emphasize the relevant contrast. Only in (c) is the relative clause construed as entirely external to the main clause subject's conception of the situation; (b) is particularly interesting in that Sally's POV is not explicitly reintroduced, but the information in the subordinate clause is presented as her reason for joining, implying that clause is to be construed from her POV.

(29) a. *She* joined a new organization, whose members, *she* knew, all found *Sally* to be absolutely delightful.
      b. *She* joined a new organization because its members all found *Sally* to be absolutely delightful.
      c. *She* joined a new organization, whose members apparently all found *Sally* to be absolutely delightful.

Similar effects can be produced when the POV introduced is that of the speaker. Again, speakers do not unanimously agree that (30b) is fully acceptable, but they do seem to agree that (30b) is noticeably improved relative to (30a).

(30) a. *He ran into some people who had a grudge against Jim's dad.
      b. He ran into some people who I guess have a grudge against Jim's dad.

In (b), the phrase I guess invokes the conception of the speaker's own perspective, making the following clause a description from the speaker's POV. In a sense, of course, the entire sentence is construed from the perspective of the ground, which includes the POVs of both speaker and addressee, but there is a critical difference. The elements which elaborate the main-clause head are only indirectly viewed from the ground. Interjecting a reference to the speaker's POV explicitly sets up a mental space representing the speaker's current conception, distinct from the conceived event profiled by the clause. The relative clause is construed as an assessment from the speaker's current vantage point (underscored by the use of present tense on guess), rather than as an internal part of the process profiled by the main clause (though this is no doubt a matter of degree, and to some extent the clause is construed within both spaces).

Again, there is little or no effect of introducing a new POV when the material in the relative clause is clearly intended to be construed from the POV of the main-clause subject, as in (31). In (31a) the new POV is introduced at a higher point in the clause, and the relative clause is included in material that is clearly intended to be part of the reported speech. (31b) is more closely parallel to the examples above, but is still unacceptable. The interjection of I guess in this context seems to signify that the speaker is unsure whether the reported speech was accurate or whether she is reporting it correctly; it does not imply that the relative clause is entirely the speaker's assessment of the situation.

(31) a. *He was saying, I guess, that the people who sued Jim were unfair.
      b. *He was saying that these people who I guess sued Jim were unfair.

Malone (1993) has pointed out closely related phenomena, and has collected a number of examples of violation of anaphora constraints, which he analyzes in terms of POV effects. His (32b) is given here as (32).

(32) *She* had signed a promotional contract with a giant chain of freezer-food centres whose advertising agent, Mr. Hal Valance, told *Allie* during a power breakfast. . . .

Malone analyzes *Mr. Hal Valance* as a subject-of-consciousness (i.e., a POV), and argues that since the awareness of that subject-of-consciousness cannot reach into the upper clause, the full nominal *Allie* has no accessible antecedent from that perspective. In intuitive terms, from the POV of Mr. Hal Valance, Allie is an entirely new referent. This is no doubt correct, but it leaves open the question of why the subject of the main clause is not construed as a reference point or POV in relation to the material in the relative clause. It is not the case that any new POV acts as a sort of barrier, making previous POVs or reference points irrelevant; such an analysis would incorrectly predict (33) to be acceptable.

(33)   **He* thinks that the people who work with *John* like *him*.

The distinction again is that the relative clause in (32) is not presented as part of the main-clause subject's awareness during the event described by the main clause. (The most likely reading of [32], in fact, is one in which the relative clause describes an event subsequent to the main-clause event.) In (33), the relative clause describes part of the thoughts of the main clause subject, and so is included within that subject's dominion.

Although there is a general correlation between subjecthood and POV status (DeLancey 1981; Kuno 1987), it should be emphasized that the reference point status of subjects is not to be attributed entirely to their construal as POVs. Such an analysis would incorrectly predict that coreference should be very free when the subject is inanimate and hence not a possible POV, as in (34).

(34) a. **It* fell down and crushed some people who had never been inside *the building* before.
      b. **They* fell down on some people who were under *the archways*.
      c. **It* always impresses people who have never seen *the Taj Mahal* before.

In Chapter 8 I analyze POV effects and the interaction of POV shift and the complement chain in more detail. The point to be emphasized here is that the anaphora constraints are not analyzed here in terms of autonomous syntactic constructs, but are rather explained by conceptual semantic notions. This approach is supported by the demonstration that considerations which are unquestionably semantic, such as POV shift, have an impact on anaphora possibilities even in cases where generative syntactic analyses such as c-command accounts would make a clear prediction otherwise.

3.5 SUMMARY

I have argued first of all that there are a number of semantic and pragmatic differences between pronouns and full nominals which can motivate the constraints on pronominal anaphora. It is semantically and pragmatically anomalous to embed a full nominal in a context in which a coreferent pronoun is a salient part of the subjective background against, and through, which that full nominal must be construed. The most significant difficulty with developing a model of anaphora constraints based on this principle is that it requires a notion of context which does not depend exclusively or even primarily upon the linear order of words in the string. In the reference point model developed here, linear order is one factor which determines the selection of reference points, but it is only one factor (linear order is discussed in Chaps. 4 and 5). Prominence and conceptual connectivity play a more central role in defining the reference point/dominion structures which make up the complement chain.

Chapter 4 examines the conceptual connectivity factors which determine whether a modifier is (inevitably) construed as belonging to the dominion of a nominal within the clause. Connectivity is argued to be a matter of degree, ranging from the most strongly interconnected structures (head/complement structures as discussed in this chapter) to more weakly connected structures (modifiers of clauses and preposed structures). Chapter 5 further explores the anaphora patterns within more weakly connected structures through examination of backwards anaphora and anaphora patterns in discourse.

CONCEPTUAL CONNECTIVITY

The complement chain described in Chapter 3 is only part of the reference point model. The prominence and relatively strong interconnection of elements within the complement chain combine to define particularly clear and salient reference point relations, which produce robust, clear judgments of the possibilities for coreference. Nevertheless, there is no sharp dividing line between the complement chain and other facets of reference point/dominion organization. The strongly interconnected head/complement structures are part of a continuum which includes more weakly interconnected structures such as those found in discourse. This chapter explores part of the continuum of conceptual connectivity, focusing first on additional aspects of reference point organization within the complement chain, and then turning to the more loosely connected structures involving modifiers.

4.1 CONCEPTUAL CONNECTIVITY

The extent of a reference point's dominion depends on both the relative prominence of the reference point as compared with other entities, and the conceptual interconnections between the reference point and those other entities. Weaker interconnections facilitate construing a given nominal as external to the dominion of the reference point.

Connectivity between two nominals is determined by the relations in which they participate. Nominals are strongly interconnected when they participate in (i.e., elaborate) an explicit interconnecting relation, as in the complement chain. Nominals are more weakly interconnected when they merely co-occur within a single linguistic unit of some kind, such as a sentence or a conceptual paragraph (see Hinds 1979; Longacre 1979).[1] This weaker degree of connectivity is frequently observed in constructions involving clausal modifiers, discussed in §4.2.1 below.

The weakest connectivity (which could also be termed lack of connectivity) is observed when the nominals are separated by a conceptual break, such as a scene change or paragraph boundary (see Fox 1987a; and §5.6.3). Such conceptual breaks frequently bring about "closure" of a previously established dominion such that discourse referents which were previously referred to via pronouns are reintroduced via full noun phrases. Although it is convenient to speak of connectivity as if there were only these three degrees of strength (strong, weak, and weakest connectivity), it should be emphasized that we are dealing with a continuum.

4.1.1 Linear Order

The role of linear order in this model is straightforwardly described: Other things being equal, a nominal tends to be construed as a reference point in relation to elements which follow it in the linear string, and is less likely to be construed as a reference point in relation to elements which precede it. This factor is somewhat weaker than the combined effects of prominence and strong connectivity, and so it is not easily observed in constructions such as *Near him, Dan saw a snake.*[2] Its effects can be more readily seen at the discourse level and in constructions involving weaker connectivity between elements.

Once the conceptualizer has made mental contact with a reference point, it tends to be construed as a reference point in relation to material which is less prominent and which follows it in the linear string, provided there is no conceptual break or discontinuity in the flow of discourse. Consider a configuration in which the subject of one sentence is intended to corefer with a nominal in the following sentence, as in (1). (The # symbol is used to indicate significant awkwardness.)

(1) a. *John* checked the mailbox. There was a package for *him.*
  b. *He* checked the mailbox. #There was a package for *John.*

As CG does not assume a sharp division between syntax and discourse, it is expected that the subject of a sentence—the element which stands out as figure within the clausal profile—will be prominent in relation to the extrasentential context and not only in relation to nominals within the same sentence. The subject of the first sentence in both (a) and (b) is therefore construed as a reference point in relation to material in the second sentence, and coreference in (b) is unacceptable.

When there is no detectable discontinuity between sentences (e.g., a change of scene or a change in focus), and no independent motivation for the use of a full noun phrase in the second sentence (such as making a statement about the referent's inherent nature or "John qua John," as Bolinger [1977] puts it), the use of a full noun phrase deviates from the norm. Constructions such as that in (1b) may not seem quite so deviant as a sentence such as *He saw a snake near Dan* (with coreference), but the difference is only a matter of degree. When the pronoun and the full noun phrase are in two different sentences, the conceptual juxtaposition between them is not so extreme as when they are bound together as complements (or quasi-complements) of the same verb. It is also generally easier to infer a conceptual discontinuity between two sentences than to infer a conceptual discontinuity within a single clause.

This same principle explains the linear precedence restriction on coreference within conjoined clauses (the data in [2] are from Langacker [1969]).[3]

(2)   a.   *Peter* has a lot of talent and *he* should go far.
      b.   **He* has a lot of talent and *Peter* should go far.

Reinhart (1983:55) proposes capturing coreference restrictions within conjoined clauses via a discourse-level ordering constraint equivalent to that proposed here. Reinhart's analysis is a modular account which distinguishes between a syntactic level, governed by the c-command condition, and the discourse level, at which linear order is a factor. Under Reinhart's proposal, coreference in (1b) and (2b) would not be ruled out by *syntactic* principles, but would be considered anomalous at the discourse level.[4] This analysis provides no clear criteria for differentiating syntactic phenomena from discourse phenomena, as principles which apply across sentences may also apply within a single sentence. Although it appears that violations of discourse principles produce less-robust judgments of unacceptability than syntactic violations (Lasnik 1989), this is not a reliable guide; many speakers judge the sentences in (1b) and (2b), for example, to be fully unacceptable with coreference.

In the model developed here, linear order is relevant both within and across sentences. Its import is however in inverse proportion to the strength of connectivity between nominals. Within the complement chain, where nominals are interconnected by the relation(s) profiled by the head(s), linear order has little observable effect. In configurations involving weaker connectivity, discussed below, linear order is a more influential factor.

4.2 MODIFIERS INSIDE AND OUTSIDE
THE PROCESS CONCEPTION

The continuum of conceptual connectivity includes the notion that the most closely interconnected elements are those which are bound together by virtue of elaborating a single, salient relational conception, as in the complement chain. Complements, by definition, correspond to and elaborate a salient subpart of the conception invoked by the head (Langacker 1987a:309). Modifiers differ from complements in that they do not elaborate a *salient* (i.e., profiled) subpart of the conception profiled by the head, but rather are elaborated by the head (Langacker 1987a:309). A modifier may nevertheless elaborate a nonsalient conception which is invoked or prefigured, however peripherally, by the head.

In this section I will propose a distinction between two types of modifiers, exemplified by (3). This is essentially the familiar distinction between VP-modifiers and S-modifiers (Bartsch and Vennemann 1972; Cooper 1974; Thomason and Stalnaker 1973, et al.), for which I will propose a specific semantic characterization. I will argue that the differing behavior of these modifiers vis-à-vis anaphora follows from their semantic relationship to other elements in the clause, and that therefore a tree-structural characterization is unnecessary.

(3) a. *Mary will see *him* in *John*'s office.
     b.   Mary will see *him* if *John* asks her to.

It is significant that the modifier in (3a) describes the spatial setting for the event, while the modifier in (3b) describes the surrounding hypothetical circumstances. We can assume that the conception of an event implies a schematic conception of a spatial and temporal setting which is not coded via profiled arguments, but which may optionally be described by means of modifiers. We can say therefore that the conception of the setting is an intrinsic, albeit nonprofiled and peripheral, part of the conception invoked by the verb.

The modifier in (3b) contributes a purely extrinsic notion, one which is not intrinsically part of the event conception or prefigured by the verbal head. Modifiers like that in (3b) can therefore be termed process external, as opposed to modifiers like that in (3a), which will be termed process internal. The distinction between internal and external modifiers, like the complement/modifier distinction, is a matter of degree, as it depends on the extent to which a particular conception is an intrinsic part of the meaning of the head.[5] The sentences in (4), which do not involve anaphora, provide further illustration of the distinction.

(4) a. Charles is being crowned king *in his fantasy.*
     b. Charles is being crowned king *in London.*

The modifier in (4a) functions as a mental space builder in the sense of Fauconnier (1985): It introduces the conception of a fantasy as a conceptual context within which the entire proposition is embedded. The process profiled by the clause is embedded within that mental space, and is not construed as pertaining directly to conceived reality, but is rather confined to the mental space set up by the modifier. The modifier is process external in that it does not elaborate any internal part of the conception invoked by the verb and its arguments. The process-internal modifier in (4b) does not set up a "conceptual address" for the proposition, but rather describes an internal part of the scene described by the clause, as it elaborates the spatial setting for the process. These modifiers would traditionally be characterized as an S-modifier and a VP-modifier, respectively, and would be represented as having different tree-structural positions; here I am claiming that the distinction is fundamentally semantic.

Process-internal modifiers are somewhat more like complements than are process-external modifiers. A complement of a head is defined as a predication which elaborates a salient subpart of the conception invoked by the head, while a modifier does not elaborate a salient subpart of that conception. Process-internal modifiers elaborate a nonsalient subpart of the conception invoked by the head, and so are somewhat closer to the complement end of the complement/modifier continuum than are the process-external modifiers, which are closer to "pure" modifiers.[6] The internal/external distinction between modifiers is not fundamentally different from the complement/modifier distinction. It can legitimately be thought of as merely a terminological convenience which is useful for bringing into focus distinctions within a certain range of the complement/modifier continuum.

Reinhart (1983) provides a number of tests for the status of modifiers to determine whether, in her terms, they are attached to the syntactic tree at the S or VP level. One of her tests distinguishes specifically the S-modifiers which function as mental space builders from the VP-modifiers which function to elaborate internal parts of the processual conception (though Reinhart does not, of course, state her analysis in those terms). Reinhart credits Bartsch and Vennemann (1972) and Cooper (1974) with the observation that an affirmative sentence with a VP-modifier has the same entailment as the same sentence without the modifier, while an affirmative sentence with an S-modifier has no such entailment. The contrast is illustrated by the examples in (5).

(5)   a.   Rosa found a scratch in Ben's picture. →Rosa found a scratch.
       b.   The gangsters killed Hoffa in Detroit. →The gangsters killed Hoffa.
       c.   Rosa is riding a horse in Ben's picture. ⇾Rosa is riding a horse.
       d.   Kathleen Turner fell in love with Tom Cruise in her new movie. ⇾Kathleen Turner fell in love with Tom Cruise.

The difference in entailments is explained directly by the mental spaces analysis. The modifiers in (5a–b) function as internal parts of the processual conception, not as space builders demarcating mental spaces distinct from reality. The profiled processes in (5a–b) are therefore construed within the mental space functioning as the primary or default context at that point in the discourse (typically this would be the conception of reality). In (5c–d), the modifiers set up mental spaces distinct from conceived reality (or from whatever the previous conceived context was), and the profiled processes are understood to reside in those mental spaces rather than in conceived reality. The difference in entailments is essentially a restatement of the difference in mental space organization.

(6–7) list some of the typical kinds of process-internal and -external modifiers. It should be emphasized, however, that the distinction is a matter of degree, and that these are only partial lists.

(6)   Some typical process-internal modifiers

    i.   Modifiers which introduce participants not coded as direct arguments of the verb, such as instruments, goals, sources;
    ii.   Modifiers describing the setting, both spatial and temporal;
    iii.   Modifiers further characterizing the participants (e.g., describing the mental state of the agent)

(7)   Some typical process-external modifiers

    i.   Mental space builders (Fauconnier 1985): modifiers which set up a "conceptual context" for the clause;
    ii.   Modifiers which relate the clause as a whole to the larger discourse;

iii. "Afterthoughts" (Bolinger 1979): modifiers which follow the clause and serve as comments on the clause as a whole

§4.2.1 discusses process-external modifiers, and §4.2.2 addresses process-internal modifiers. Constructions in which the modifier precedes the clause (so-called preposed modifier constructions) illustrate the effects of the linear order principle given above; these effects are addressed in a separate section, §4.3.

4.2.1 Process-External Modifiers

Process-external modifiers are relatively weakly connected with other elements in the process conception, as compared with complements. In terms of the continuum of conceptual connectivity described in §4.1, they occupy some point along the middle range in that they are part of the same sentence as the verb and its arguments, but they are not strongly connected with those elements via elaboration of an explicitly coded relation.

In their relationship to the subject, process-external modifiers exemplify the principle of linear order effects discussed in §4.1.1 above: Once the conceptualizer has made mental contact with a reference point, less-prominent material which follows in the linear string is construed within the dominion of the reference point unless there is an obvious conceptual break intervening. Process-external modifiers are therefore construed within the dominion of the subject so long as they follow the clause in the linear string without a significant conceptual break or intonation break. For example:

(8)   a. *Kathleen Turner* falls in love with Tom Cruise in *her* latest movie.
      b. *She falls in love with Tom Cruise in *Kathleen Turner*'s latest movie.

The modifier *in her latest movie* is a mental space builder; it describes the conceptual space in which the proposition is to be understood rather than the actual spatial locations of the participants Kathleen Turner and Tom Cruise. It is not an internal part of the process described by the verb, and so it is only weakly connected with the subject. Nevertheless, the modifier combines with the clause (which functions as its head) to form a single conceptual unit, and so the modifier is construed within the subject's dominion.

The basis for this construal is somewhat weak, however. It is based on the notion that the modifier is conceptually juxtaposed against the clausal profile, which is the head of the construction and hence more prominent than the modifier. In this kind of configuration, word order plays a crucial role in influencing the construal of reference point / dominion organization (just as it does in coreference across sentences, discussed above). The assignment of the modifier to the subject's dominion can be made nonobligatory by preposing the modifier. Correspondence between a pronominal subject and a full nominal in the modifier then becomes acceptable, as in (9). Preposing is discussed in more detail in §4.3.

(9)   In *Kathleen Turner*'s latest movie, *she* falls in love with Tom Cruise.

The tendency for the process-external modifier to be construed as part of the subject's dominion is somewhat delicate, as noted, since there is no strong conceptual connection between the subject and the modifier. When the modifier is conceptually more separate from the clause, it becomes possible to construe the modifier as external to the subject's dominion. Bolinger (1979) provides a number of examples of modifiers which he calls "afterthoughts," which are sufficiently discontinuous from the clause so that coreference between a pronominal subject and a nominal in the modifier is (more or less) acceptable. The examples in (10) are from Bolinger, and the judgments given are his.

(10)   a.   *He* lied to me—something that *John* was rather fond of doing.
       b.   *He* was quite a guy, if *John* doesn't mind my saying so.

Bolinger also notes a contrast between an afterthought and a modifier which describes the temporal setting for the clause. Temporal modifiers are discussed in §4.3.2; essentially, I claim that they are typically construed as internal to the process, since the conception of a temporal setting is an intrinsic part of a process conception. Bolinger gives (11b) a question mark, but several speakers I have consulted report that coreference is fully unacceptable.

(11)   a.   *She* could pass for my sister, though *June* wasn't related to me at all.
       b.   ?*She* could pass for my sister, before *June* had her facelift.

A somewhat similar pair, also from Bolinger (1979), is given in (12). The modifier *as John stood there* in (12a) elaborates the event conception profiled by the main clause, as it describes what the subject of the main clause was doing contemporaneously with the main-clause process. In (12b), the modifier *as John always did* does not describe an internal part of the event conception, but rather gives the speaker's opinion on the typicality of John's behavior. (Bolinger also notes that [12b] involves "characterization" of the referent, which enhances the acceptability of the full nominal, as it serves to signal accessing of a more general conception of the referent than that which is currently active in the immediate discourse context.)

(12) a. *He looked at me, as John stood there, with a seraphic smile.
      b. He looked at me, as John always did, with a seraphic smile.

Coordinate clauses vary in the extent to which they are construed as unified or separate with respect to reference point/dominion organization. When both conjuncts are full clauses, the construal of their relationship depends on whether they are conceived as describing two parts of a single event conception or whether there is an asymmetry between them, such as the notion that one describes an event and the other gives a comment on that event. An example of conjoined clauses forming a unified conception was given in (2), above, from Langacker (1969). Bosch (1983) gives the examples in (13). (13a) is a description of one event with two parts—it could be paraphrased as "John lied to me and betrayed me." (13b) is quite different, as it is a description of an event, followed by a comment about the circumstances surrounding the event. The second conjunct is thus much more external to the first clause, in (13b), than is the case in (13a). Note that (13b) also involves characterization, which, as Bolinger has pointed out, increases the acceptability of the use of the full nominal.

(13) a. *He lied to me and John betrayed me.
      b. He lied to me, and John was my friend.

Ariel (1990) addresses a similar set of data, and proposes that they be explained in terms of differences in degree of **unity,** which seems to be equivalent to part of my continuum of conceptual connectivity, which I have termed weaker connectivity (see §4.1 and §5.6.3.1). She cites the examples in (14), from McCray (1980), to illustrate the effects of differences in degree of unity.

(14) a. *She's almost 65, and Mary won't be hired by anyone.
      b. She's almost 65, and therefore Mary won't be hired by anyone.

The two conjuncts in (14a) are roughly equal in informativeness or givenness, but in (14b), the first conjunct provides the background for the main point, which is that Mary won't be hired by anyone. The differing functions of the two conjuncts in (14b), and the focus on the second

conjunct as the point of the statement, produce a slightly greater conceptual separation than in (14a), facilitating the construal of the second
conjunct as external to the dominion of the pronominal subject.

The elements which stand out as prominent in relationship to a
modifier (and to the nominals in it) are those which are prominent
within the conception with which the nominal combines. In the case of a
process-external modifier, the complete clausal conception (the profiled
process, along with the subject and object, if any) corresponds to and
elaborates the trajector of the modifying relation—in other words, the
modifier combines with the process as a whole. Within the process conception, the subject stands out as figure; the direct object, if there is
one, is part of the process which functions as ground and is therefore
somewhat less prominent. We would therefore predict a slight difference in the behavior of subject and object with respect to a following
process-external modifier; the slightly reduced prominence of the object
may make it somewhat easier to avoid construing it as a reference point.
The distinction should, however, be relatively subtle because of the
overall tendency for any prominent nominal to be construed as a reference point in relation to less-prominent material which follows it in the
linear string; the difference should be more obvious when the linear-
order effect is removed, as when the modifier is preposed (this is discussed in §4.3 below).

The data indicate that there is in fact a subtle distinction between
subject and object. Speakers' judgments vary, but sentences like the following are often judged acceptable; at the least, they are not as bad as
(8b) above (*She falls in love with Tom Cruise in *Kathleen Turner's* latest
movie), which bears out the point that there is a difference between
subject and object in these constructions. (15b–c) are from Reinhart
(1983).

(15)   a.   ?Kathleen Turner falls in love with *him* in *Tom Cruise's* latest movie.
       b.   ?Rosa is kissing *him* passionately in *Ben's* high school picture.
       c.   ?People still regard *him* highly in *Carter's* home town.

The less-than-full acceptability of these constructions reflects the fact
that backwards anaphora almost invariably involves a pronounced
asymmetry in prominence between the pronoun and the antecedent,
such that the antecedent stands out as a clear reference point in relation
to the pronoun (this is discussed in some detail in §4.2). In (15), the
conception designated by the full noun phrase (which is not profiled)
is in fact less prominent than the conception corresponding to the pro-

noun (which is profiled); the marginal acceptability of these constructions is explained, as noted, by the fact that the object does not stand out as figure within the processual profile, and can therefore be (more or less) disregarded as a reference point.

Constructions of this sort have been discussed previously in the literature. Bolinger (1979) credits Lakoff (1968) with the initial observation that pronominal objects are much more likely to corefer with a following full nominal than are pronominal subjects. Bolinger suggests that the reason is that a subject is much more likely than an object to be considered a topic, and that it is anomalous for a full nominal in the rheme or "focus" to corefer with a pronominal topic. This is essentially the analysis I am proposing here, using the model of reference points and dominions.

4.2.2 Process-Internal Modifiers

Process-internal modifiers are those which elaborate notions which are intrinsic to the conception invoked by the verbal head, but which are not profiled by the verb (elements which elaborate the profile are, by definition, complements rather than modifiers). Following Fillmore (1977), Langacker (1991:343), Croft (1991), and Talmy (1995), I assume that the conception of an event may presuppose some sort of setting within which various participants move about and/or interact. In describing an event, the speaker focuses on certain selected participants, imposing a limited scope or window of attention (Fillmore 1977; Langacker 1987a; Talmy 1995) within which one or two (at most, three) participants may be profiled as arguments of the verb. Other facets of the event conception, such as additional participants (e.g., instruments, sources, goals) or aspects of the temporal and spatial setting, may be expressed by modifiers. Such modifiers are process internal in that they elaborate portions of the conception prefigured by the verbal head.

Modifiers which elaborate notions connected to specific participants in the process are also considered to be internal to the process conception. For example, modifiers describing the state of mind of the subject would be construed as elaborating an internal part of the process in accordance with the notions of conceptual connectedness developed above. The conception of the subject, invoked as part of the process conception, implies the conception of the subject's state of awareness, his motives and goals, and so forth. That conception may be merely implicit, not part of the processual profile, and it may not be particularly salient unless it is explicitly coded by a modifier; such a modifier would nevertheless be an elaboration of a process-internal conception.

It was noted above that process-external modifiers which follow the clause are construed as belonging to the dominion of the subject, but may (to some extent) be construed as external to the dominion of the object. The process-internal modifiers pattern differently: Because they are conceptually more closely connected with the internal conceptual structure of the profiled process, they are construed as belonging to the dominions of any profiled participants within the process.[7] This explains data such as (16), which clearly pattern differently than data involving process-external modifiers, such as (17).[8]

(16) a. Mary gave *John* a hamster for *his* birthday.
      b. **He* gave *himself* a hamster for *John*'s birthday.
      c. *Mary gave *him* a hamster for *John*'s birthday.

(17) a. Mary gave *him* a million dollars in *John*'s fantasy.
      b. Mary gave *him* a million dollars—according to *John*, anyway.

The modifier in each sentence of (16) is construed as representing, in part, the subject's conception of the purpose of the event—the subject's intent that the gift be "for his birthday." Whereas the process-external modifiers, as in (17), provide a "conceptual address" within which the conceptualizer situates the entire clause (the world of John's fantasy or statements attributed to John), the process-internal modifier describes the conceptual context of the process as conceived by the *subject* of the clause. Although the modifier does not describe a participant in the action chain, it describes a sort of abstract goal, which is the subject's conception of the purpose of the action conceived as a whole. It is therefore construed as part of the subject's dominion, and correspondence between a pronominal subject and a full nominal in the modifier is unacceptable, as in (16b). It is also construed as being within the dominion of the object, as in (16c)—not because there is an intrinsic connection between the direct object and the modifier, but because the object is salient within the clause and the modifier is construed as an internal part of the process.

The pair in (18) involves correspondence between an indirect object (a secondary landmark) and a nominal in a modifier. My intuition is that (18b) is not quite as bad as (16c) above, where the correspondence was between a primary landmark and a nominal in the modifier. However, all four of the native speakers that I consulted judged (18b) to be unacceptable with coreference.

(18) a.   Mary gave a hamster to *John* for *his* birthday.
      b. *Mary gave a hamster to *him* for *John*'s birthday.

The conception of an instrument is an internal part of the process conception, as it is part of the action chain. When it is elaborated by a modifier, it is construed as belonging to the dominions of any profiled participants in the process. This explains the judgments on the following sentences.

(19) a.   Mary tickled *Joe* with *his* peacock feather.
      b. *She* tickled Joe with *Mary*'s peacock feather.
      c. *Mary tickled *him* with *Joe*'s peacock feather.

The phrase *with X's peacock feather* elaborates the instrument in the conceived process. It is not profiled by the verb, but it is nevertheless a participant within the event conception. The modifying phrase is therefore construed as internal to the verb, and hence is understood to be in the dominion of the subject (as in [19b]), and the object (as in [19c]). This is borne out by the fact that the four speakers I consulted all judged (19c) to be unacceptable with coreference. This modifier can be contrasted with the modifier in (20), which does not describe a direct participant in the process, but rather describes a part of the larger circumstances surrounding the process. (This example was pointed out to me by Farrell Ackerman.) The same speakers who unequivocally rejected (19c) either accepted this example completely (one speaker) or judged it marginally acceptable and clearly better than (19c) (three speakers).

(20) Mary tickled *him*, with *Joe*'s father looking on approvingly.

As with other process-external modifiers, however, correspondence between a pronominal *subject* and a full nominal is not acceptable. As in the other cases discussed above, a modifier which is attached to the clause and which follows the clause is construed as part of the dominion of the subject. This explains (21), where coreference is unacceptable (though perhaps a sharp intonation break would improve it).

(21)   *He* was tickled, with *Joe*'s father looking on approvingly.

This also explains data such as (22), in which the modifier in each example corresponds to and elaborates the temporal setting of the profiled process.

(22) a.   *John* took a nap when *he* got home.
      b. *He* took a nap when *John* got home.
      c. I paid *John* before *he* left.

    d. *I paid *him* before John left.
    e.   Mary spoke with *Ralph* when *he* got back.
    f. *Mary spoke with *him* when *Ralph* got back.

The notion that the process-internal modifier belongs in the object's dominion is somewhat tenuous, in just the same way that the assignment of a process-external modifier to the subject's dominion was argued to be somewhat tenuous in the examples in §4.2.1 above. There is no profiled relation directly linking the object and the modifier, as the object is not the figure of a relation elaborated by the modifier. Rather the object is a relatively prominent element within a larger conceptual structure which elaborates the trajector of the modifier. If there is some sort of conceptual discontinuity, the modifier may not be construed as closely connected with the object. The following example, from Brugman and Lakoff (1987), illustrates the effect of a subtle conceptual discontinuity:

(23)   a. *Mary hit *him* just before *John* got up.
       b.   Mary hit *him* before *John* had a chance to get up.

In (23b), the modifier is not construed as merely an elaboration of notions prefigured by the process—it does not function merely to spell out the temporal setting of the event. In a sense, it does describe the temporal setting of the main-clause process, but it locates that process relative to an event which did not occur, and it functions not so much to elaborate the temporal setting of the main-clause process as to make the point that John did not, in fact, have a chance to get up. The conceptual connection between the actual event (profiled in the main clause) and the preempted or irrealis event (described by the subordinate clause) is more attenuated than the connection between the clauses in (23a), where the two clauses together describe a single event which occurred in reality. The conceptual discontinuity between the realis and irrealis clauses in (23b) makes it easier to construe the second clause as (relatively) loosely connected with the profiled process, and hence outside the dominion of the object.

    (24a), from Bolinger (1979), is another example of the effect of a subtle conceptual discontinuity, involving a modifier which Bolinger would term an afterthought. It is construed as relatively external to the process in that it gives the speaker's judgment of the event, and thus functions more as a process-external evaluation than as a process-internal setting. In (24b), the modifier is much more likely to be construed as elaborating the temporal setting for the process, which is a process-internal notion; hence the modifier is construed as belonging to the dominion of the object. (Bolinger gives [24b] a question mark, but some speakers judge it to be fully unacceptable.)

(24)   a.   I don't believe *him* when *John* tells a story like that.
       b.   ?I don't believe *him* when *John* tells a story.

4.2.3 Complement and Quasi-Complement Locative Relations

On the continuum from more external to more internal elements, the last group we must consider involves locative phrases which are so closely connected with the process conception that some would be considered complements, and others would be considered to be in between modifier and complement status. The modifier / complement distinction in CG is a matter of degree, as it depends upon the extent to which the element in question elaborates a *salient* (i.e., profiled) subpart of the conception invoked by the head (Langacker 1987a), and profiling itself is a matter of degree. The particular locative relations to be discussed here describe a portion of the setting which is construed as the location of the landmark of the process.

In some instances, as with *put* (e.g., *He put a plate on the table*), the phrase which describes part of the setting is clearly a complement, as the location in which something is put is intuitively a central part of the meaning of *put* (the location is obligatorily coded as well, but CG generally avoids relying exclusively on distributional tests of that kind; see Langacker 1987a:306). In other cases, as with *see* (e.g., *He saw a snake near him*), the classification of the locative phrase is somewhat less obvious, but the locative still has some complement-like properties. In the case of *see*, we do not see things as isolated objects; rather we see things within the context encompassed by our field of vision. Assuming that this notion is an intrinsic and salient part of the meaning of the expression *see*, the locative phrase which locates the direct object also elaborates the conception of the area which the person sees (this analysis was suggested to me by Ronald Langacker). It is therefore akin to a complement of the verb, although it is not obligatorily elaborated by an overt locative phrase. Rather than sort out the precise complement / modifier status of each example, I will call all of these phrases quasi-complements for convenience. (25) gives two examples of complement or quasi-complement phrases.

(25) a.   John put a plate on the table.
      b.   Dan saw a snake near his foot.

An important characteristic of these constructions is that the primary landmark in each sentence corresponds to the trajector of the locative phrase. Whereas in the previous examples I have pointed out that there is generally no intrinsic or direct conceptual connection between the direct object and the modifying phrase, in these examples there is in fact a direct conceptual link between the two—the direct object corresponds to, and elaborates, a salient part of the conception profiled by the locative phrase. In (25a), *on the table* profiles a path leading from some unspecified point to the table. The path conception corresponds to part of the path profiled by the verb *put*. The trajector of the relation *to the table* corresponds to the direct object of *put*. In (25b) the profile of *a snake* corresponds to the trajector of the relation profiled by *near his foot*. This correspondence is significant in explaining the behavior of elements within the locative relation with respect to the direct object of the verb when the locative phrase is preposed (discussed in §4.3.6).

These process-internal elements are construed as being within the subject's dominion. Since the trajector of the locative corresponds to the direct object, the locative relation is also in the direct object's dominion. The behavior of the locative phrase with respect to pronominal anaphora follows from these points, and is illustrated by the examples in (26).

(26) a.   *John* saw a snake next to *him*.
      b.   **He* saw a snake next to *John*.
      c.   John saw *Sally* next to *her* car.
      d.   **John saw *her* next to *Sally*'s car.

4.3 PREPOSED MODIFIERS

Constructions involving preposed modifiers illustrate the significance of linear word order in this model. It should be emphasized that, since CG is not a transformational theory, there is no notion of preposing as an operation deriving surface structures from underlying structures. The term "preposed modifier" is useful in that it captures the intuition that these constructions are semantically similar to constructions with canonical word order. I therefore adopt the terms "preposed" and "preposing" as theory-neutral terms, without any accompanying notion of transformation or derivation.

The anaphora possibilities in preposed modifier constructions follow directly from the general principles of linear order developed
above. In a number of (nonpreposed) modifier constructions, a modifier
may be construed within the dominion of a reference point solely on
the basis of linear order, as the two are only weakly interconnected (see,
e.g., the analysis of process-external modifiers). For such configurations,
a change in word order changes the construal of reference point relations. Where the modifier is more strongly connected with the reference
point, differences in linear order do not have such a significant effect.[9]

4.3.1 Semantics of Preposing

A speaker's knowledge of the conventional structures of English must
include the inventory of schemas sanctioning specific types of preposing constructions. We may also assume that speakers have a schematic
representation of the general semantic import of preposing. Although
the anaphora facts involving preposed modifier constructions can be
captured simply in terms of the linear-order effects described in §4.1.1
above, it is worthwhile to consider briefly the semantic characteristics
of preposing constructions.

Reinhart (1983) points out several relevant facets of the semantics
of preposed modifiers. Essentially, the preposed modifier is construed
as "old information" in some sense. Some or all of the material in the
clause is interpreted as "new" information or the "focus" of the construction. Reinhart makes the observation that the material construed
as new is the material which *would* be c-commanded by the preposed
modifier, *if the preposed modifier were in canonical position*. So when an S-
modifier is preposed (adjoined to S'), the entire clause may be interpreted as in some sense new. When a VP-modifier is preposed (adjoined
to S), the VP (and only the VP) is expected to be new, and the subject
is typically old information. Figure 4.1, based on Reinhart's figures, illustrates the distinction; the old information nodes are circled.

Reinhart illustrates her claims about the distribution of new information by pointing out that indefinite subjects are acceptable when an
S-modifier is preposed, but relatively unacceptable when a VP-modifier
is preposed. VP-modifiers generally require that the subject be old information, as illustrated by the sentences in (27), involving S-modifiers,
and the sentences in (28), involving VP-modifiers (these examples are
from Reinhart [1983]).

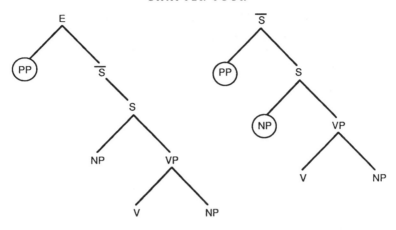

Figure 4.1   Preposed modifiers

(27)   a.   In Ben's picture, a fat woman is riding a horse.
       b.   In Ben's family, a cousin always did the dishes.
       c.   With such poor security arrangements, a thief managed to walk
            off with the office football pool.
       d.   In spite of the efforts of the police, a bomb exploded yesterday in
            the courthouse.

(28)   a.   #In Ben's picture, a fat woman found a scratch.
       b.   #In Ben's office, a stranger spent the night.
       c.   #With the boss, a client has been arguing bitterly.
       d.   #In a great huff, someone just left the boss's office.

Looking at these constructions from a CG perspective, we can make
the observation that the new information in each case corresponds to
the trajector of the preposed modifier. A sentential or process-external
modifier is one whose trajector is elaborated by the entire clausal conception. A verb phrase modifier (a process-internal modifier) takes part
or all of the event conception (the action chain) as the correspondent
to its trajector. The locative phrases which I called quasi-complements
generally take only the processual landmark as the correspondent to
the trajector. In each case, preposing the modifier backgrounds the less-
prominent parts of the modifying relation (i.e., the modifying relation
itself, including its landmark), and focuses attention on the correspondent to the most prominent part of the modifying relation, which is its
figure (trajector). The following sentences illustrate this point.

(29)   a.   In Ben's picture, a fat woman is riding a horse.
       b.   In Ben's picture, Sally found a scratch.
       c.   With a peacock feather, Rosa tickled Jim.

In (29a), the trajector of *in Ben's picture* corresponds to the entire clausal conception relative to which the modifier functions as a space builder. Preposing the modifier sets the scene for the entire clause. In (29b), the trajector of *in Ben's picture* corresponds to the search domain within which the agent found the scratch. Preposing the modifier focuses attention on just that part of the clausal conception. In (29c), the preposed instrument focuses attention on the action which is carried out through the instrument, specifically, tickling Jim.

The observation that only the material c-commanded by the modifier's original position in the sentence should be new, and the rest of the material is expected to be old, is explained if we can make the assumption that, because the construction functions to focus attention on the material which elaborates the trajector of the modifier—similar to a spotlight focused on one part of the clausal conception—it would be inconsistent to try to introduce new material outside that tightly focused area. As indicated by the examples Reinhart (1983) provides, it is not entirely unacceptable to do so, but it is less than completely conventional.

In discussing the behavior of preposed modifiers, it should be made clear that modifiers are not intrinsically categorized as external or internal independently of the specific details of the constructions and contexts in which they appear. The same modifier may be construed in different ways in different constructions and different contexts. Some modifiers which are typically construed as process-internal when they appear clause-finally may be construed as process-external when preposed. This is particularly true for the modifiers which describe temporal setting, as they seem to alternate between two general kinds of construal: They may be construed primarily as a description of the temporal setting of the main-clause process or as a description of a relatively independent event which is merely being coordinated in time with the main-clause process.[10]

4.3.2 Preposed Process-External Modifiers and the Subject

The process-external modifiers are those which do not elaborate any intrinsic part of the processual conception, such as *in her latest movie* in the sentence *Kathleen Turner falls in love with Tom Cruise in her latest movie.* Such modifiers, when they are in canonical position, are construed as being within the dominion of the subject simply because they are subordinate to the clause and they follow the clause. Preposing changes this situation, as illustrated by the examples in (30).

(30)   a.   In *Kathleen Turner*'s new movie, *she* falls in love with Tom Cruise.
       b.   In *her* new movie, *Kathleen Turner* falls in love with Tom Cruise.

The modifier in (30a) is not automatically assigned to the dominion of the subject. The preposed process-external modifier can be construed as outside the subject's dominion, and so one can introduce the referent there with a full noun phrase, as in (30a). One can also, optionally, construe the modifier as belonging to the subject's dominion, and use that reference point / dominion relationship to sanction backwards anaphora, as in (30b).

The same pattern of optional forward or backwards anaphora is found with all preposed process-external modifiers. The sentences in (31) give additional illustration of this pattern (31c–d are from Reinhart [1983]).

(31)   a.   In *Carter*'s home town, *he* is still considered a genius.
       b.   In *his* home town, *Carter* is still considered a genius.
       c.   In Dan's picture of *Rosa*, *she*'s riding a horse.
       d.   In Dan's picture of *her*, *Rosa* is riding a horse.

4.3.3   Preposed Process-External Modifiers and the Object

In §4.2.1 it was noted that a pronominal object, unlike a pronominal subject, can correspond with a full nominal in a sentential (i.e., process-external) modifier (Lakoff 1968). One example of this is repeated here as (32a). When the modifier is preposed, correspondence between the two is, of course, acceptable, as the pronoun and full noun phrase are more separate conceptually. In fact, here forward anaphora seems somewhat more likely than backwards anaphora. Backwards anaphora, as in (32c), is not impossible, but it seems less likely that the object would be taken as having sufficient prominence in the larger context to serve as an antecedent for a preceding pronoun. To the extent that constructions like (32c) occur, it seems most likely that they would be used in circumstances where the referent has already been established in the discourse (see §5.4).

(32) a. They still consider *him* a genius in *Carter*'s home town.
      b. In *Carter*'s home town, they still consider *him* a genius.
      c. In *his* home town, they still consider *Carter* a genius.

4.3.4 Preposed Process-Internal Modifiers and the Subject

Modifiers construed as internal to the process conception are those which elaborate some notion which is prefigured by the profiled process, albeit peripherally (as explained above, elements which elaborate central, profiled parts of the process conception are not modifiers, but complements). Such modifiers are therefore construed as belonging to the dominions of both subject and object, when they are in canonical position, following the clause. Preposing removes one of the cues encouraging the conceptualizer to construe the modifier as belonging to those dominions. However, the intrinsic conceptual connection between the process and the modifier should mean that the modifier cannot be removed from the dominion of the subject, as the subject is a reference point in relation to everything contained within (i.e., elaborating) the process conception.

   The basic prediction is that, to the extent that a modifier elaborates notions which are intrinsic to the process conception (albeit not profiled by the verb), preposing the modifier should be insufficient to remove the modifier from the subject's dominion. Given that conceptual connectivity is a matter of degree, we can expect some variability in the data. We can predict that the slightly less-internal modifiers (e.g., those describing the setting) are more easily removed from the subject's dominion than the more fully internal modifiers (e.g., those describing additional participants in the action chain), and that other factors, including contextual considerations, may affect the judgments. In this section I will first present a few examples of modifiers which are fully internal to the process conception, and then turn to examples of modifiers whose status is more marginal.

   Modifiers which elaborate nonprofiled participants in the process, such as instruments, are internal to the process conception, and cannot be removed from the subject's dominion by preposing. Correspondence between a pronominal subject and a full noun phrase in the modifier is therefore unacceptable. An illustration of this is the data in (33), taken from Reinhart (1983). (33a) bears out the point that this is a process-internal modifier, as it is construed as part of the object's dominion.

(33b) illustrates that preposing is insufficient to remove the modifier from the dominion of the subject.

(33) a. *Rosa tickled *him* with *Dan*'s feather.
      b. *With *Rosa*'s feather, *she* tickled Dan.

A modifier of an embedded clause is also internal to the main-clause process, just as any other modifier of a clausal complement. Preposing such a modifier therefore does not remove it from the dominion of the subject. The data in (34) are from Reinhart (1983), and the judgments given are those she reports.

(34) a. *In *Ben*'s picture, *he* promised Rosa that she would look attractive.
      b. *In *Ben*'s next picture for Vogue magazine, *he* promised Rosa that she would look attractive.

Modifiers describing the spatial and temporal setting for the process are internal to the process conception, though slightly less so than modifiers describing participants in the action chain. Modifiers describing the temporal setting are somewhat more external than those describing the spatial setting, as they do not describe the spatial locations of the participants themselves. This observation leads to the prediction that it should be slightly easier to construe a preposed temporal modifier as external to the dominion of the subject, as compared with a preposed spatial modifier. This prediction seems to be borne out. Of six speakers I consulted, four judged (35a) to be better than (35b) (one found both acceptable, one found neither acceptable).

(35) a. %Before *John*'s quals, *he* took a shower.
      b. %In *John*'s apartment, *he* smokes pot.

The difference between (35a) and (35b) is in the amount of conceptual overlap between the modifier and the process. In (35a), the qualifying exam itself is not a part of the conceived process of taking a shower; rather it describes a point in time external to the showering process. By contrast, the modifier in (35b) describes a more-internal part of the profiled process: The apartment is where John is located when he smokes pot.

There is a certain ambiguity to temporal modifiers, particularly temporal modifiers which incorporate a complete finite clause. They may be construed as merely defining the temporal setting, or they may be construed as describing a relatively separate process which 'sets the scene' for the main-clause process. When such modifiers follow the clause, they tend to be construed as internal to the process conception

(Bolinger [1979] describes this in terms of the verb's 'capturing' the temporal modifier), but when they are preposed, they are much more likely to be construed as describing a relatively independent event which functions as background to the main-clause process and hence to escape the subject's dominion (see n. 10). This explains data such as (36).

(36) a. When *Ralph* got back from the store, *he* took a nap.
   b. Before *Samantha* went out, *she* cleaned the cat box.

These examples contrast with (35a) above (*Before John's quals.* . . .) in that the incorporation of a full finite clause (i.e., an independently grounded clause) in the modifier seems strongly to encourage the construal of the modifier as relatively external to the main-clause process. Matthiesen and Thompson (1988) argue that it is misleading to think of the first clause as an adverb attached to the second, and propose that the first clause may more accurately be considered a satellite in relationship to the nucleus of the second clause. Their analysis would seem to support the analysis presented here, though they do not address the relevance of their claims to pronominal anaphora.

A modifier which elaborates the goal or motivating circumstances of an action (as in *John gave himself a hamster for his birthday*) describes a sort of abstract setting, the purpose or motivation for the action as conceived by the agent. It therefore tends to be construed as an internal part of the process conception, and hence as part of the subject's dominion. Phrases such as *for his birthday* may be somewhat ambiguous, however, as they may be taken to represent the agent's conception of the motivation (which would be process internal), or they may be the speaker's assessment of the circumstances (which would be process external). When such phrases are preposed, they can marginally be construed as external to the subject's dominion. (The percent symbol indicates variable judgments).

(37) a. For *his* birthday, *John* gave himself a hamster.
   b. %For *John's* birthday, *he* gave himself a hamster.

Some speakers who were consulted judged (37b) to be unacceptable, but several others volunteered that (37b) would be acceptable only in a context such as (38), which would promote construing the modifier as a topic, with the entire clause functioning as a comment on the topic.

(38) For Mary's birthday, we had a big bash, and then for Susie's birthday, we all went out to dinner, and then for John's birthday, he gave himself a hamster.

Preposed modifiers illustrate the effects of one other subtle distinction in degrees of connectivity. As explained in §2.1.3, an e-site within a relation is elaborated by the entire nominal whose head corresponds to the trajector or landmark of the relation. The various modifiers and complements of that nominal therefore behave as if they were directly interconnected with the other arguments of the relation, although only the profile of the nominal participates directly in the relation. In assembling a sentence such as *Dan saw a snake near his foot*, the profile of the nominal *his foot* corresponds to and elaborates the landmark of the relation *near*, and both the profile of *foot* and the possessor designated by the pronoun are construed within the dominions of the subject and landmark (i.e., *Dan* and *a snake*).

There is, however, a slight difference between the profiled nominal conception and the associated modifier, as noted in §2.1.3. The nominal profile (in this case the profile of *foot*) is incorporated as the landmark of *near* and participates directly in that relation, which in turn is part of the relational conception expressed by the entire clause. The conception expressed as a possessive pronoun is construed within the same dominion only because it is closely associated with the nominal profile; it does not directly participate in the larger profiled relations.

The difference is usually not significant for determining coreference possibilities involving full noun phrases (though it is significant in determining the distribution of reflexives; see §7.5 on the participant/nonparticipant distinction). Generally speaking, a nominal conception which functions as a reference point in relationship to another nominal is salient enough that it will also be construed as a reference point in relationship to nonprofiled elements attached to the nominal profile. This is especially so when the reference point precedes the nominal in the linear string because of the linear order effects explained in §4.1.2 above. However, where a nominal precedes the reference point in question, so that the construal of the nominal as internal to the reference point's dominion is based solely on semantic connectivity, subtle gradations in connectivity are more significant.

In these three pairs of examples, the critical issue is not the absolute judgments (both sentences are more or less unacceptable in two of the pairs) but the relative rankings. The (b) sentence in each pair is more acceptable than the (a) sentence, although a c-command-based account would predict equal unacceptability for both. In each case, the relevant nominal in the (b) sentence does not directly correspond to a participant in the profiled process. (41) (pointed out to me by Michael Hegarty) contrasts a process-internal modifier with a complement. (41a) may have an additional complication inasmuch as a reflexive might be more appropriately used in place of the full noun phrase.

(39) a. *In front of *Mary*, *she* saw a crack in the snow.
      b. ?In front of *Mary*'s skis, *she* saw a crack in the snow.

(40) a. *Near *Dan*, *he* saw a snake.
      b. Near the woman *Dan* was talking to, *he* saw a snake.

(41) a. **John*, *he* could never criticize.
      b. ?*John*'s best friend, *he* could never criticize.

Clearly this is an area which warrants further study, although the subtlety of judgments in some of these cases suggests that reaction time studies or surveys of large numbers of speakers might be necessary to pin down the effects of this subtle distinction in semantic connectivity.

In some cases lengthening a preposed modifier increases the likelihood that it will be accorded topic status (as noted by Reinhart [1983]), hence as external to the process conception. This may be a factor in (42) below, as suggested by Reinhart. Lakoff (1968) has also noted that, when preposed locative modifiers are lengthened, the anaphora possibilities become freer, as in (43).

(42) a. *In *Zelda*'s armchair, *she* spent *her* sweetest hours.
      b. In the armchair that *Zelda* stole from the Salvation Army, *she* spent *her* sweetest hours.

(43) a. *In *John*'s apartment, *he* smokes pot.
      b. In *John*'s incredibly elegant new pad on 5th Avenue, *he* smokes pot.

The effects of lengthening the preposed phrase are evident only when the phrase is one which describes a setting, not a participant in the clause. Added length promotes construing the phrase as a topic, hence as process external. The process-external construal is only possible with setting modifiers, which are less internal than participants, when the preposed locative phrase is more strongly connected with the subject's dominion—for example, when it is actually a complement of the verb—increased length does not make forward anaphora acceptable (see discussion of example [48] below).

4.3.5 Preposed Process-Internal Modifiers and the Object

When process-internal modifiers appear in canonical (postverbal) position, they are construed as belonging to the dominion of the object. As explained above, this is not because there is a profiled relation directly interconnecting the object and the modifier, but because the object is salient in the general conceptual structure to which the modifier is attached, and the modifier follows the object in the linear string. This involves weaker connectivity, analogous to the situation with process-external modifiers which follow the clause and tend to be construed as belonging to the dominion of the subject. The construal in both cases is based primarily on prominence and linear order, as connectivity is weak.

In §4.3.2 above, we saw that preposing a process-external modifier makes it possible to construe it as outside the dominion of the subject. Preposing a process-internal modifier does not remove it from the dominion of the subject, because of strong connectivity. But it does remove it from the dominion of the object in just the same way that preposing an external modifier removes it from the dominion of the subject. This explains contrasts such as (44).

(44) a. *Rosa tickled *him* with *Dan*'s feather.
      b. With *Dan*'s feather, Rosa tickled *him*.

A spatial setting is an internal part of the process conception (i.e., it is where the participants are actually located), and so even preposed, it is unlikely to be construed as sufficiently separate from the clause that it can be considered to be outside the subject's dominion. But it does become sufficiently separate from the object to be construed outside the object's dominion. The following examples (from Reinhart [1983]) illustrate the consequences for anaphora of this distinction.

(45) a. In *his* apartment, *John* smokes pot.
      b. *In *John*'s apartment, *he* smokes pot.
      c. In *his* apartment, Rosa showed *Dan* her new tricks.
      d. In *Dan*'s apartment, Rosa showed *him* her new tricks.

Purposive *for* clauses, which describe the agent's conception of the motivating circumstances of the profiled process, are also internal to the clause but not directly connected with the object. Preposing therefore makes it possible to construe the modifier outside the object's dominion. This explains the contrast in (46).

(46) a. *I gave *him* a hamster for *John*'s birthday.
      b. For *John*'s birthday, I gave *him* a hamster.

4.3.6 Preposed Quasi-Complements

The last set of items to discuss is the quasi-complements. These are strongly interconnected with both the subject and object of the verb. With respect to coreference involving the processual trajector (the subject), they behave in just the same way as any other preposed process-internal modifiers, such as those discussed in §4.3.4 above. A pronoun in the preposed quasi-complement can correspond with the subject, but a full noun phrase in the preposed phrase cannot correspond with a pronominal subject, as it is connected with the subject's dominion by virtue of elaborating an intrinsic part of the process conception. This explains the data in (47).

(47) a. *Near *Dan*, *he* saw a snake.
      b.   Near *him*, *Dan* saw a snake.

As Reinhart (1983) notes, lengthening the phrase in constructions such as these does not make coreference acceptable, as illustrated by the data in (48).

(48) a. *In *Ben*'s box, *he* placed some cigars.
      b. *In *Ben*'s most precious Chinese box, *he* placed some cigars.

The reason that lengthening does not make an appreciable difference is that increasing the length serves to enhance the topicality of the preposed phrase, and when the preposed phrase is so tightly interconnected with the processual conception (elaborating part of the profile), it is simply not possible to construe it as a clause-external topic.

One last point to be addressed is that neither forward nor backwards anaphora is acceptable with a preposed modifier and an object nominal. The sentences in (49) illustrate the data to be explained.

(49) a. *In *Sam*'s office, Mary saw *him*.
      b. *In *the kitten*'s box, I put *it*.
      c. *In *his* office, Mary saw *Sam*.
      d. *In *its* box, I put *the kitten*.

(49a–b) are unacceptable because the pronoun corresponds to the trajector of each prepositional phrase, and so merely preposing the phrase is not adequate to overcome the effects of strong connectivity. The unacceptability of (49c–d) pertains to the observation that the element corresponding to the trajector of the modifier is brought into focus by the preposing construction (§4.3.1). The element which elaborates the figure of the modifying relation is expected to be new or contrastive information. If the direct object actually corresponds with part of the modifying phrase which has been set up as background information, then it is not sufficiently new or contrastive to fit the specifications of the construction.

If a nominalized process is substituted for the noun, so that there is in fact something new elaborating the trajector of the modifier—hence something new in the context set up by the modifier—the construction is (more or less) acceptable:

(50)   ?In *his* office, I saw *Sam* working on a paper.

4.4 SUMMARY

In this chapter I have argued that prominence (as defined by figure/ground organization and profiling) and conceptual connectivity (as defined by elaboration of interconnecting relations such as process conceptions) determine the possibilities for coreference both within head/complement structure and within the more weakly interconnected structures involving modifiers. More specifically, I claim that modifiers vary in the extent to which they are construed as an internal part of the event conception invoked by the verb, and that they therefore vary in the extent to which they are conceptually interconnected with the profiled arguments of the verb. Linear word order contributes to determining the construal of modifiers as internal or external to the dominions of the profiled nominals within the clause, but its effects are more apparent where connectivity is weaker.

BEYOND THE ANAPHORA
CONSTRAINTS

The discussion of the reference point model in the preceding chapters focused on data of the type typically covered in the generative literature on structural anaphora constraints (e.g., Langacker 1969; Reinhart 1976, 1983). So long as we focus on those data, it may appear that the reference point model covers only the same ground as the c-command analysis. Its most visible advantage so far is that it provides a conceptual-semantic explanation for the constraints rather than a list of structural conditions. To the extent that the reference point model extends beyond the data which have been tacitly considered as the core anaphora data, there is additional support for the superiority of this analysis. In this chapter I address two such areas. The first half examines backwards anaphora constructions, focusing not on determining which configurations are made possible by the conventions of English but instead on examining the patterns of backwards anaphora found in actual usage and explaining the relative frequency and rarity of the various constructions.

The second half of the chapter situates the reference point model developed here in the context of published studies of discourse topicality and coreference. The claim that the constructs of the reference point analysis are fundamentally semantic rather than structural (in the sense of autonomous syntactic tree structures) is supported by the discourse analysis literature, in which identical or equivalent constructs are utilized with equivalent functions. The reference point model of sentence-internal anaphora patterns is thus shown to be unifiable with discourse analysis in a way in which autonomous syntactic constraints are not. I focus on interpreting an array of studies illustrating the effects of discourse unit boundaries on coreference patterns, illustrating the far end of the continuum of conceptual connectivity, which extends from the strong connectivity of head / complement structures to the weaker connectivity of head / modifier configurations, and then to the weakest connectivity, discourse unit boundaries.

5.1 BACKWARDS ANAPHORA

Backwards anaphora is of interest for several reasons. Structural accounts of the anaphora constraints have typically assumed that the syntax is insensitive to linear order, and that forward and backwards anaphora is therefore equivalent in status from the point of view of syntax (Reinhart [1983] notes that there is no doubt a discourse-level preference for forward anaphora). From a CG perspective, there is no sharp division between syntax and discourse. The reference point model considers linear order as one factor contributing to the determination of reference point organization at all levels of complexity, both within and across clauses. Backwards anaphora is significantly different from forward anaphora in that it requires that other factors outweigh the effects of linear order.

The approach taken here is unlike the approach to backwards anaphora taken within generative literature on the anaphora constraints. The literature on constraints has largely confined analysis of backwards anaphora to a few isolated examples, almost always invented, many of which are atypical of actual usage and produce mixed judgments from speakers. Here I report on a corpus of 500 examples of backwards anaphora drawn from texts, focusing on the properties which characterize typical backwards anaphora in actual usage. I argue that the most typical backwards anaphora constructions are those in which factors other than linear order combine to establish most clearly the reference point status of the antecedent. In particular, backwards anaphora typically involves a significant asymmetry in prominence between the nominal conceptions corresponding to the pronoun and the antecedent.[1] I demonstrate that the relative typicality of various backwards anaphora constructions is explained by the same factors which explain the constraints on pronominal coreference discussed in the previous chapters.

5.1.1 Backwards Anaphora versus Repeat Identification

Some researchers have questioned whether backwards anaphora even exists. Bolinger (1977), Karttunen (1968), Kuno (1972, 1975), and Delisle

(1973), among others, have put forth what Carden (1982) calls the "Forward Only" hypothesis, which is that pronouns in English always follow their antecedents. According to the Forward Only hypothesis, apparent cases of backwards anaphora are just examples of "repeat identification" of a referent taken out of context (see esp. Bolinger 1977). Carden (1982) provides a strong rebuttal of this hypothesis based on a corpus of approximately 800 examples of backwards anaphora drawn from texts (Carden does not, however, attempt to characterize the semantics of backwards anaphora constructions).

I have collected a corpus of 500 examples of backwards anaphora found in written texts (most were collected as they were encountered in everyday reading, but a large number were collected by deliberately searching through texts, mostly popular magazines). Examples were collected from almost every imaginable source: magazines, novels, newspapers, placards at museums, signs on buses, and the inscriptions on the walls of the Lincoln Memorial. My goal in collecting those data was to obtain as accurate a sample as possible of the backwards anaphora patterns in use in written (American) English, and to that end, I made a concerted effort to record every example encountered.

All of the sentences in the corpus are genuine backwards anaphora; none of the sentences are examples of repeat identification of a referent. The criterion for inclusion in the corpus was that there must be no plausible antecedent for the pronoun other than the noun which appeared to its right. If there were another potential antecedent to the pronoun, it would be impossible to be certain whether the construction was genuine backwards anaphora or whether the full noun phrase which followed the pronoun was merely a renaming of the referent, serving no antecedent function. Some examples of genuine backwards anaphora were no doubt excluded, along with examples of repeat identification, because they could not be identified as backwards anaphora with certainty.[2]

This corpus of 500 examples of indisputable backwards anaphora constructions seems to be conclusive evidence against the claim that there is no genuine backwards anaphora in English. Backwards anaphora is used to introduce referents into the written discourse, including referents whom the reader has never heard of before (contra Bolinger's [1977] claim that apparent backwards anaphora might occur only when the referent is famous, and so can be presupposed).

The corpus also provides evidence against a somewhat more-complex version of the "no backwards anaphora" hypothesis. Apparent backwards anaphora could be analyzed as a kind of stylistic trick in which the text is written as if the referent were already established in the discourse, and the pronoun corefers with this (unspecified) discourse referent. Eventually the reader is informed of the identity of the referent. This kind of stylistic device is used in posters advertising movies and in teasers for television news programs, and in other places where the writer may wish to create suspense, to involve the reader or viewer emotionally. Carden (1982) calls this the "Withheld Antecedent" style and points out that it differs from backwards anaphora in that the suspenseful use of pronouns may continue for several sentences before the referent is finally identified, whereas ordinary backwards anaphora includes both pronoun and antecedent within a single sentence.

Evidence against what we may call the "underspecified discourse referent" analysis of backwards anaphora is provided by constructions drawn from contexts in which another referent is already established as the topic of discussion, so that without the nominal which follows the pronoun, the pronoun would unquestionably be taken to corefer with the other, previously established referent. This is exemplified by (1), in which the preceding context is included along with the backwards anaphora example itself.

(1) a. And Najibullah never misses a chance to manifest his piety in public. In his letter to Gorbachev, Khomeini referred to the failure of the atheist state in the Soviet Union to destroy Islam. (*The Nation* 10/16/89)

   b. The 1976 case (Runyon vs. McCrary) involved a private school which had refused to admit blacks. When it upheld legal sanctions against the school, the Court was interpreting an 1866 law that bans discrimination in private contracts. (Letter from the NAACP Legal Defense Fund)

   c. Colie is a seeker. Robin is a discoverer. With a major college scholarship awaiting her signature, Colie has grabbed the brass ring. (San Diego *University City Light* 2/89; Robin is also female)

In each of these sentences, the pronoun would corefer with a referent previously established in the discourse were it not for the nominal antecedent which follows it. This illustrates that backwards anaphora may be used even where an attempt to recover the referent from the larger context would give the wrong interpretation, seriously undermining the claim that apparent backwards anaphora implies the referent's availability in the larger context (as suggested by Bolinger [1977]).

5.2. THE PROTOTYPICAL CONFIGURATION

As explained in §2.1 and §2.4, CG captures specific grammatical patterns in terms of constructional schemas, templates which speakers extract from exposure to actually occurring expressions, and which are then used to create new expressions. Constructional schemas are part of a speaker's inventory of conventionally established units, along with words, morphemes, and fixed phrases. (This view of the place of constructions is also a fundamental tenet of Construction Grammar; see Taylor 1989; Fillmore and Kay 1993; Goldberg 1995.) Given these assumptions about the architecture of a grammar, it would not be sufficient merely to say that the rules of English don't rule out backwards anaphora. Backwards anaphora must rather be specifically sanctioned by a constructional schema or a network of interrelated schemas, which are acquired by speakers through exposure to actually occurring expressions. In this chapter I argue that the specific constructional schemas which are most frequently used (as indicated by analysis of the corpus) exhibit recurrent characteristics which can be explained in terms of the larger model of anaphora constraints presented here.

As explained in the preceding chapters, prominence and linear order both contribute to the construal of reference point organization. Backwards anaphora is, in a sense, backwards: One of the cues signaling potential reference point relationships is misleading, and could potentially lead a conceptualizer to construe the pronoun as a reference point with the full nominal in its dominion. We may reasonably predict that backwards anaphora constructions will tend to involve marked prominence asymmetries between pronoun and antecedent (i.e., at the semantic pole) to facilitate the correct construal of their relationship.

It should be noted that this is not simply a matter of communicative clarity or the writer's wish to avoid confusing the reader, though this may conceivably play a role. The fundamental question for any anaphora construction is whether it is conceptually coherent or, in other words, whether the conceptualizer (a reader, writer, speaker, hearer, etc.), guided by the established conventions of the language, can arrive at a construal in which the putative antecedent functions as a reference point in relationship to the pronoun. If we assumed that this question were fundamentally or solely one of clear communication, we could make the bizarre prediction that speakers will freely use, in the privacy of their own thoughts, constructions such as *He loves John's mother* (with coreference), and that they will avoid them in interpersonal usage just so as to avoid confusing their audience.

The prediction concerning prominence asymmetries is borne out by the backwards anaphora corpus, in which the vast majority of examples were found to exhibit the following characteristics.

(2)   i.   The antecedent is the most prominent nominal conception in the sentence.

  ii. The pronoun is semantically backgrounded relative to the antecedent.

  iii. The larger phrase containing the pronoun is also subordinated to a more prominent linguistic unit (which indicates further backgrounding of the pronoun).

The specific prominence notions involved here are figure / ground organization and profiling, just as in the rest of the reference point model. Backwards anaphora constructions which failed to exhibit marked prominence asymmetries of this kind were found to be relatively rare in the corpus, and seemed to be motivated by more subtle prominence considerations such as discourse focus and/or backgrounding of clauses, as discussed below.

One construction type, exemplified in (3), stood out as a candidate for the status of prototype (for discussion of the notion of constructional prototypes, see Lakoff 1987; Taylor 1989; Deane 1992). The antecedent is the subject, the most prominent nominal in the clause. The pronoun is contained within a preposed (i.e., clause-initial) modifier, which is, like all modifiers, unprofiled in the composite conception, therefore significantly less prominent than the arguments of the verb.[3] This preposed phrase is additionally set off from the main portion of the clause by an intonation break (represented in writing by punctuation), which may also serve to signal backgrounding relative to the main clause. Within the preposed phrase, the pronoun itself expresses another modifying relation: It is a possessor attached to another noun. Its own status as part of a modifying phrase within a modifier renders it one step further removed from prominence, and that much less likely to be misconstrued as a reference point in relation to the full noun phrase.

(3)   a.   In his *Prairie Home Companion* radio series, Garrison Keillor brought a remote part of Minnesota to life. (San Diego *Reader* 3/16/89)

  b.   Much to his profound amazement, Grandfather Sol woke up alive shortly after midnight on the eleventh day of Adar. (K. Lasky, *The Night Journey*, p. 76)

Constructions like those in (3) account for 307 of the 500 examples collected, or 61% of the corpus. (This accords with Carden's [1982] observation that a large portion of the examples he collected consisted of a possessive pronoun anteceded by a full noun phrase in subject position.) On the basis of overwhelming frequency of occurrence, we can assume that this is the most strongly entrenched schema for backwards anaphora. Another construction type, exemplified in (4), accounts for an additional 19% of the corpus. In this construction, a subject pronoun in a preposed modifier takes as its antecedent the subject of the main clause.[4]

(4) a. Less than a week before he was to face trial on felony charges relating to his activities in the Iran-Contra scandal, Richard Secord copped a plea. (*Time* 11/20/89)

  b. Before he was shot dead by police on a field near the international border, Roger Varela was out of work and "bored." (*Los Angeles Times* 2/2/91)

As in (4), 80% of the backwards anaphora constructions in the corpus which involved a clause within a preposed modifier had the subject of the main clause as antecedent for the pronoun. At first sight this appears to be evidence that the main-clause subject, as most prominent nominal in the clause, is particularly qualified to function as antecedent for cross-clausal anaphora as well (this claim was made in van Hoek [1992]). The general claim about the significance of subjecthood is borne out by the corpus overall, in which 88% of all the examples collected had the subject of the (main) clause functioning as antecedent. But this specific construction type, involving a preposed clausal modifier, does not provide strong evidence for the claim, as it may also reflect some other factor, such as a preference for parallelism of function in cross-clausal anaphora (Grober, Beardsley, and Caramazza 1978).

To test whether the preference for subjects-as-antecedents was special to backwards anaphora, I collected a corpus of 100 examples of forward anaphora involving the same basic grammatical configuration—a clause in a preposed modifier, as in (5). (The examples were all collected from popular magazines, mostly various issues of *Reader's Digest*.)

(5) a. As T. J. returned to his seat, he moved his chair close to the last row of students. (*Reader's Digest* 4/91)

  b. When a Cockney lad named Maurice Joseph Micklewhite, Jr. was 19, he was sent to the Korean war. (*Reader's Digest* 11/91)

In 78 of 100 examples, the antecedent for the pronoun was the subject of the clause in the preposed modifier. The preference for the subject as antecedent in this kind of construction is therefore not necessarily a special property of backwards anaphora, but may reflect a more general tendency for the same referent to have the same grammatical role in both clauses in this kind of construction. (These need not be mutually exclusive analyses; my point here is simply that the backwards anaphora data from these constructions are not conclusive evidence for the analysis put forth in van Hoek [1992].)

The fact that subjects are preferred overall as antecedents in backwards anaphora is nevertheless significant. The general (though not absolute) tendency for subjects to be old or given information is well known (Hopper 1979; Givón 1983b, 1984, 1989, 1994; Chafe 1991, 1994). In a study of written narrative, Chafe (1991) observes that there are restrictions (albeit not incontrovertible ones) on the introduction of new referents in subject position. The majority of examples in the backwards anaphora corpus described here involve newly introduced referents, and yet there is an overwhelming preference for them to be subjects. In §5.3.1 below I suggest an analysis in terms of Chafe's (1991, 1994) observation that subjects which are not given tend at least to be accessible, meaning that they are in some way prefigured by the preceding discourse. I suggest that one of the functions of backwards anaphora may be the concise introduction of new information into a discourse (here meaning written text), and that typical backwards anaphora constructions serve to make a referent somewhat more accessible (in Chafe's sense) before it is fully introduced with a full noun phrase.

5.2.1 Other Prominence Asymmetries

The predicted prominence asymmetry between pronoun and antecedent (i.e., between the conceptions encoded by each) manifested itself in a number of different ways. In the backwards anaphora corpus, there was a clear tendency for the antecedent conception to be profiled (i.e., to be an argument of the verb), and an equally strong tendency for the conception corresponding to the pronoun to be unprofiled (i.e., contained in a modifier). This tendency can be separated from the preference for subjects as antecedents (which automatically fit the pattern). 423 of the 500 examples involved the subject of the main clause as antecedent for the pronoun, but even in the 77 examples in which the antecedent was not the main-clause subject, it was three times more likely that the antecedent would be profiled at the highest level of organization than that it would not be. Only 19 examples were found in which the antecedent would be considered to be unprofiled (i.e., it was part of a modifier), as opposed to 58 examples in which the antecedent was not the subject of the clause, but was nevertheless a complement of the verb (e.g., a direct object) or a complement of a verb which was itself embedded as a complement of the main-clause verb (and therefore profiled in the composite conception).

There were no examples of constructions in which the pronoun coded a profiled entity and the antecedent did not. This pattern would be exemplified by sentences such as the invented (6), a type which is often cited in the anaphora literature (Reinhart [1983] gives several invented examples of this kind, listing them as grammatical). The pronoun corresponds to an argument of the verb, while the full noun phrase is in a modifier, hence unprofiled.

(6)   They still consider *him* a genius in *Carter*'s home town.

We can predict that these examples will be very rare, at least as examples of genuine backwards anaphora (repeated identification of a referent has different requirements from those of backwards anaphora; see §5.4 below), since the entity corresponding to the pronoun is more prominent than that of the full noun phrase. As noted, no examples in the corpus had this kind of profiling pattern. Not only were none found that precisely fit the constructional pattern exemplified by (6), but no examples were found of other constructional patterns involving a profiled pronominal argument and an unprofiled antecedent. (7) gives additional invented examples of the kinds of constructions which were not found.

(7)   a.   *It* may not be much, but *the trailer park*'s residents say it's all
              they've got.
       b.   Penelope hit *him*, and then *John*'s roommate threw *him* out.
       c.   They talked to *him* briefly, just before *John* left for Indonesia.

These constructions do not seem impossible with coreference, but they are not typical of the backwards anaphora constructions which were found. If they were used at all, they would presumably be most likely as examples of repeat identification of a referent, where it is not required that the conception coded by the full noun phrase be prominent (since it does not function as an antecedent for the pronoun). If genuine backwards anaphora examples of this kind occur, they are sufficiently rare that they did not turn up in the sample of 500 sentences collected for the corpus.

The sentences in (8) exemplify the three profiling patterns which were found in the corpus. In (8a), the full nominal corresponds to a profiled participant, as it is a complement of one of the main verbs (both conjoined clauses are considered in CG to be profiled [Langacker 1991: 429]), and the pronoun, as a modifier, does not. In (8b), neither one corresponds to a profiled conception. In (8c), both the full nominal and the pronoun correspond to profiled entities.

(8)   a.   His office has a commanding view of the Potomac, and Michael
             Deaver combed the world to select the best furniture. . . . (News-
             week 1/18/88)
       b.   To their supporters, the case for the Justice Department's orga-
             nized crime strike forces is open and shut. (Los Angeles Times
             4/24/89)
       c.   It may not be great, but "Footsteps" is not that bad. (Title of arti-
             cle in San Diego University City Light)

The intuitive idea that the antecedent must be prominent is thus specifically definable in terms of trajector/landmark alignment, in the preference for subjects as antecedents, and in terms of the profile/base distinction. Only nineteen examples were found (in the entire corpus of 500 sentences) in which the conception coded by the full noun phrase was not profiled. As noted, no examples were found in which the pronominal conception was profiled and the conception encoded by the full noun phrase was not.

Even in the nineteen cases in which the antecedent was not part of the composite profile, there is still an apparent tendency for it to be conceptually "central" in some sense. Although the analysis of such a small number of examples is necessarily rather subjective, these examples provide interesting clues to the underlying dynamics of backwards anaphora. One sense in which antecedents may be considered relatively central is that they may be conceptually closely connected to the main-clause profile via semantic connection with one of the arguments of the verb. The antecedent nominals in (9) are landmarks of the preposition of, therefore functioning as quasi-complements of arguments of the verb (for analysis of of-phrases, see Jackendoff 1977; Langacker 1992; Taylor 1994).

(9)   a.   Despite its long reach, the testing activities of ETS are not over-
             seen by any public agency. (Readers Digest 3/80)

b. Never mind their guilt or innocence, the executions of atomic spies Julius and Ethel Rosenberg 36 years ago were illegal and represent a breakdown in the criminal justice system. (*San Diego Union* 8 / 89)

As noted, only nineteen examples were found in which the antecedent was not profiled. In seven of those, the antecedent was the object of an *of*-phrase attached to one of the arguments of the verb. *Of*-phrases correspond to some conception which is intrinsic to the meaning of the head noun, and are in that sense conceptually bound up with the head noun and are almost included in its profile (Langacker 1992). Though they are not part of the composite profile, they can be considered almost as central as actual arguments of the verb.

In five other examples (out of the nineteen involving nonprofiled antecedents), the antecedent was a possessor attached to the subject nominal, therefore closely connected with the most prominent nominal in the clause. (10) illustrates this pattern.

(10) a. Without his own dramatic presence, Andy Warhol's work remains great art. (*Los Angeles Herald Examiner* 2 / 6 / 89)

b. As he walked past City Hall on Wednesday, attorney David Miller's eyes were drawn to a banner proclaiming "DRUG FREE— THE WAY TO BE." (*San Diego Union* 11 / 12 / 89)

Though there were few examples of this construction type, it was slightly rarer for the pronouns in backwards anaphora constructions (which are conceptually backgrounded) to appear as possessors attached directly to the main-clause subject (as discussed below).

A different kind of conceptual prominence can be provided by visual cues. Several examples like those in (11–12) were included in the corpus. These examples are obviously not exact visual reproductions of the originals, but I have attempted to reproduce the proportional sizing of the letters and the font styles.

(11) *This, the last of my books to have the benefit of his help and advice during its making, is dedicated to the memory of my husband,*
GEOFFREY LOFTS 1905–1948

(Norah Lofts, *Women in the Old Testament*, dedication page)

(12) *With some in his own party skeptical and the whole GOP gleeful, is California ready for....* **The Rebirth of Jerry Brown?** (*Los Angeles Herald Examiner* 2 / 6 / 89, title of article)

The Jerry Brown sentence is a particularly clear example of visual prominence in backwards anaphora. The contrast between the large boldface font and the small italicized font makes it clear that the full nominal is central and prominent, part of the focus, while the pronoun is part of the periphery.

5.2.2 Backwards Anaphora as a Focusing Device

Given the informal observation that backwards anaphora is "backwards," in the sense described above, we may reasonably ask what motivation a writer would have for using it. The prominence asymmetry characteristic of backwards anaphora may provide one of the motivations. Backwards anaphora may serve a foregrounding function, signaling that the conception most immediately containing the antecedent is to be construed as more prominent than the backgrounded conception containing the pronoun. Mittwoch (1983) makes this point for one specific type of backwards anaphora construction (see §5.3 below), but it seems to hold more generally.

We can observe, first of all, that backwards anaphora is frequently used where a referent is to be described by a particularly "heavy" noun phrase. As illustrated by the examples in (13), the noun phrase may incorporate a great deal of background information about the referent's identity and role in the situation.

(13) a. As his team walked off the Kearny High soccer field Friday, University City High boys' soccer team coach Donaldo Viana was not happy at what he had just witnessed. (San Diego *University City Light* 2/2/89)
      b. If you missed his face in the curriculum guide to the Soviet arts festival, Mikhail Gorbachev look-alike Ronald Knapp will be on the "Tonight Show" with Johnny Carson on Oct. 26. (*San Diego Union* 10/6/89)
      c. Although he'd prefer to be a "towel boy in a Turkish prison," a financially embarrassed Dan agrees to tutor Bull in the "subtleties of seduction." (*TV Guide*, date unavailable)

These could be rephrased using forward anaphora simply by reversing the positions of pronoun and full noun phrase, but the results would be rather awkward as compared with the constructions used in the actual texts. Introducing so much information in a semantically backgrounded position (possessive noun phrase in a modifier) feels somewhat less natural than packaging it as part of the subject nominal in the main clause. This observation raises questions about the oft-noted tendency for the subject to correspond to information which is already "given" or "active" (e.g., Hopper 1979; Givón 1976, 1989; Chafe 1991, 1994), an issue which I address below.

If typical backwards anaphora (i.e., with main-clause subject as antecedent) involves placing the antecedent in a prominent position, in somewhat less-typical backwards anaphora the positioning of the antecedent may serve to underscore the prominence of the position it is placed in. The examples in (14) could be rephrased using forward anaphora, but as in (13) above, the results would be somewhat awkward and would also lose the focusing effect of the original constructions.

(14)   a.   Though it was completed in 1989, you'd like to nominate erstwhile journalist Michael Moore's *Roger and Me* as the first film of the nineties. (*Tikkun* 11/89)

   b.   It's the time honored way their yarns are dyed that give our authentic Madras Plaids their timeless beauty. (Lands' End catalog 1/90)

   c.   By matching his parents' characters and backgrounds with the findings of scholarly studies, they decided that Michael Lee Hall faced a precise 40% chance of being abused within the next five years. (*Los Angeles Times* 2/1/89)

Two other examples from the corpus illustrate this point particularly clearly and merit individual discussion. (15) is the title of a newspaper article (the source information was unfortunately not preserved with the clipping). There is a clear intuitive sense in which the embedded clause is the focus or point of the construction. It is the central assertion of the sentence, and is therefore "dominant" in the sense of Erteschik (1973) and Erteschik and Lappin (1979), while the main clause functions only as background. The foreground/background relations here can be assumed to facilitate construing the embedded nominal *Mandela* as a reference point in relation to the pronoun. Note that this sentence is most naturally read with a pause setting off the embedded clause (i.e., "Even his admirers admit—Mandela is no miracle worker"). This reflects the independent status of the embedded clause vis-à-vis the discourse context, as it stands out as the central assertion of the overall construction.

(15)   Even his admirers admit Mandela is no miracle worker (newspaper article title)

It would not be impossible to reverse the order of pronoun and antecedent, but the result (*Even Mandela's admirers admit he's no miracle worker*) seems intuitively to reduce the sense of the embedded clause as an independent conception, standing out as the focus of the sentence. The revised sentence would tend to be pronounced differently from the original, reflecting the increased semantic dependence of the embedded clause on the main clause, as it would be much less natural (though not impossible) to have a pause between *admit* and *he.*

A similar example is (16), the complete text of the inscription on the wall behind the statue of Abraham Lincoln at the Lincoln Memorial in Washington, D.C.

(16)   In this temple, as in the hearts of the people for whom he saved the Union, the memory of Abraham Lincoln is enshrined forever.

It seems intuitively clear that the focus of the construction is the profiled main clause, "the memory of Abraham Lincoln is enshrined forever." The antecedent is not the subject of the sentence, but it is closely associated with it (in the sense explained above, in the discussion of *of*-phrases), and is therefore part of the focus of the overall construction. Here again, the arrangement of the full noun phrase and pronoun underscores the focus on the clause containing the full noun phrase.

While it would not be impossible to reverse the positions of pronoun and antecedent, the result would not be nearly as appropriate for the formal and rather dramatic context of the inscription: *In this temple, as in the hearts of those for whom Abraham Lincoln saved the Union, his memory is enshrined forever.* Here the referent is identified almost casually, as part of the background information, while the main clause contains a pronoun which is referentially dependent on information introduced as part of the periphery. From examples like these we can see that the positioning of pronoun and antecedent is not simply a matter of the relationship between those two elements, but that it conveys a great deal of information about the conceived prominence of the subparts of the construction.

5.3 THE PRONOUN AS PERIPHERAL ELEMENT

While the antecedent for backwards anaphora tends strongly to be prominent or central within the construction, there is a corresponding tendency for the pronominal conception to be backgrounded or peripheral. We can assume that this facilitates construing the pronoun within the dominion of the antecedent and avoiding the construal of the pronoun as a reference point. (As noted above, this is not simply a matter of the speaker/writer being clear for the benefit of the audience; rather it is a question of the conceptualizer's ability to construe the antecedent as a reference point in relationship to the pronoun.)

In the vast majority of backwards anaphora constructions I have collected, the pronoun was contained in a preposed modifying phrase that formed an intonation unit (in the sense of Chafe [1987, 1994]) separate from the main clause. As noted above, 80% of the examples in the corpus involved a pronoun in a preposed phrase, with the antecedent the subject of the profiled clause. Even in constructions in which the antecedent was not the clausal subject, there was still a tendency for the pronoun to be in a preposed phrase. Constructions like (17) were somewhat more common than constructions like (18)—67% of the examples involving a nonsubject antecedent had the pronoun in a preposed phrase.

(17) a. Mistaking him for a burglar, Barbara shoots Carol's boyfriend. (*Chicago Tribune* 1/5/91, blurb for a TV program)
   b. Once it's built in Simi Valley, California, scholars will flock to the Ronald Reagan Presidential Library to sift through state papers. (*Time* 1/16/89)
   c. Aside from his schoolboy experiences, one cannot present George Orwell as a victim of child abuse. (Leonard Shengold, *Soul Murder*, p. 69)

(18) An unsolved murder and his twin brother put Father D. in double jeopardy. (*TV Guide* 2/7/90, text of advertisement)

The pronoun in a backwards anaphora construction tends to be in a structure that is clearly backgrounded relative to the main clause. Constructions exactly parallel to the oft-cited (19a) seem to be extremely rare, as indicated by their lack of representation in the corpus (note however that [18] and [20c] are partially similar). The sentences in (19b–c) were taken from contexts in which the referent was already the discourse topic, so that the full noun phrase was not necessarily the antecedent for the pronoun (see §5.4). These examples were not included in the backwards anaphora corpus, as it is not clear whether they are genuine backwards anaphora.

(19) a. *His* mother loves *John*.
   b. Her mother motioned Sashie to the other side of the room (Laskie, *The Night Journey*, p. 81)
   c. His research led Finder into the sewers of Paris (*San Diego Union* 3/11/91)

There are several differences between these examples and the protoypi-
cal construction. The full nominal is not the subject of its clause, and
the pronoun is not in a phrase that is obviously backgrounded relative
to the main clause. Although the nominal is profiled (i.e., it is a main-
clause argument) and the pronoun is unprofiled (a modifier), the difference in prominence between the two is not as pronounced as in the
more typical examples. We can predict that this construction type will
be rare as an example of genuine backwards anaphora, though it might
appear as repeat identification (as in 19b–c, and see below).[5] This prediction is borne out by the data in the corpus.

    While nothing exactly parallel to (19a) was found, several examples
of roughly similar constructions turned up, of which a few are given
in (20) (an additional example is discussed as [28b], below). These examples differ from (19a) in a few key respects.

(20) a.   An old flame's appearance at his high school reunion prompts
           Jack (Morgan Stevens) to dwell on precious moments of the past.
           (*TV Guide* 3/12/88)
      b.   His son's freakish death brings new pain to guitarist Eric Clapton.
           (*People* 4/1/91, title of article)
      c.   Their dome-shaped heads and smaller ears set Asiatic apart from
           African elephants. (first line on the sign for the Asiatic elephant
           pen at the San Diego Zoo)

In (20a–b), the pronoun is several relational links removed from the
profile of the clause, therefore further backgrounded than the pronoun
in *His mother loves John*. (20c) most closely resembles (19a), with the
possessor directly connected to the subject nominal, but even it involves
a more elaborate noun phrase than simply "his mother." We can specu-
late that this has the effect of making the pronoun more clearly part of
the background. Even so, these examples constitute only a very small
fraction (approximately 2%) of the corpus of 500 examples. The relative
rarity of these examples is explained by the general principle that the
pronoun in backwards anaphora tends to be contained within a phrase
which is clearly backgrounded and peripheral to the main clause.

    It is of interest that most of these examples came from very special-
ized contexts, such as picture captions, single-line blurbs from TV listings, or subtitles at the heads of articles. This does not reflect the compo-
sition of the overall backwards anaphora corpus, in which the majority
of examples were taken from longer texts. The fact that these sentences
were almost all found as single sentences in specialized contexts is

therefore not due to a general property of backwards anaphora constructions, but must be explained by some peculiarity of this construction type. It is reasonable to suppose that these constructions would be more likely in special contexts in which the writer is striving for a maximally compact statement—contexts such as subtitles and captions, placards in museums, and television program listings. In longer texts, where the writer presumably does not need to employ such a compact (and awkward) style, these constructions are almost never found.[6] Nevertheless, I will suggest below that this observation about the distribution of the rarer examples offers a clue to one of the discourse functions of the more typical backwards anaphora as well.

Several backwards anaphora examples were parenthetical constructions, as in (21). Parentheticals involve incidental or background information which interrupts the main clause, with a strong intonation break differentiating it from the main-clause material. The parenthetical material is clearly less prominent or central than the profile of the main clause, again facilitating backgrounding of the pronoun.

(21) a. It was 6:10 p.m.—almost time for her break—when Claudia
          Hawkins pulled her airport shuttle into Lot C. (*Los Angeles Times*
          2/2/91)
      b. Today in Monte Carlo—the same princely locale where eight
          years ago he retired—tennis legend Bjorn Borg attempted a come-
          back of his own. (*San Diego Tribune* 4/23/91)
      c. At the end of that time—and none knew who had started it—a ru-
          mour went through the jungle that there was better food and wa-
          ter to be found in such and such a valley. (Rudyard Kipling, *The
          Jungle Books*)

Another kind of semantic backgrounding involves the use of conjoined clauses, in which the first clause functions as background for the second conjunct, which is the focus or point of the construction in an intuitive sense. These constructions seem always to use the conjunction *but* (Mittwoch 1983) (though compare example [8a] above). Mittwoch (1983) describes these constructions in some detail, though she uses only invented examples, and argues that a crucial characteristic is that "the second conjunct represents the speaker's main point. . . . It is therefore the appropriate point for the introduction of the new information represented by the antecedent" (1983:133). She suggests also that the second conjunct may be considered to be dominant (Erteschik 1973; Erteschik and Lapin 1979), that is, that the second conjunct may be considered the part of the construction which the speaker particularly intends to draw attention to (though she proposes this only as a speculation, noting that the specific tests for dominance proposed by Erteschik and Lappin [1979] do not seem to be fine-grained enough to provide supporting evidence). The sentences in (22) are examples of unequal conjoined structures in actual usage, drawn from the corpus.

(22)   a.   It may not be great, but 'Footsteps' isn't that bad. (San Diego *University City Light*, 2/2/89, title of article)

       b.   It's tabloid TV however you look at it, but at least NBC's "Unsolved Mysteries" is striving to be different from "America's Most Wanted." (*San Diego Tribune* 10/5/89)

       c.   His beloved old white convertible was in terrible shape, but my stepfather refused to get rid of it. (*Reader's Digest* 2/89)

In these constructions, both the pronoun and the full noun phrase are profiled within their respective clauses (conjoined structures are typically analyzed as involving two profiles; see Langacker 1991:429), and would therefore be considered equally prominent if profiling were the only kind of prominence considered. The backgrounding of the first clause relative to the second, as described by Mittwoch (1983), preserves the pattern of backgrounding the pronoun relative to the antecedent.

     Mittwoch (1983:134) writes, "Whereas normally BA [backwards anaphora] is associated with syntactic subordination, my claim is that in such conjoint sentences it functions on its own as a marker of pragmatic subordination." In other words, given that a prominence asymmetry is required for backwards anaphora, the use of backwards anaphora can itself serve as a signal that the conjuncts are construed as unequal in prominence. As noted in §5.2.2 above, the equivalent observation can be made for backwards anaphora generally, not only for the unequal-conjuncts constructions.

5.3.1 Backwards Anaphora and the Given/Accessible/ New Distinction

Backwards anaphora constructions frequently involve introduction of a "new" entity (by which I mean one not previously mentioned in the text) in subject position. The fact that subjects are the preferred antecedents for backwards anaphora is exactly as predicted by the reference point model given the claim that subjects are the most prominent nominals in their clauses, but it is, at least on first sight, surprising in light of the frequent observation that subjects tend to be "given" information, for example, entities already under discussion (e.g., Hopper 1979; Chafe 1991, 1994).

An additional potential oddity is that the majority of examples in the corpus involved a prepositional phrase preceding the clause, as in (23). Reinhart (1983:75–80) notes that these constructions, in which a so-called VP-modifier appears at the beginning of the clause, do not seem to allow for the introduction of entirely new material in subject position, as illustrated by Reinhart's examples quoted in (24a–b), contrasted with (24c–d) (the # sign is used to indicate awkwardness).

(23) a. In his Aug. 21 letter, Jared Taylor seeks to refute comments made by Gloria Allred (*San Jose Mercury News* 8/30/89)
      b. In her recent Warhol memoir, "Famous for Fifteen Minutes," former superstar Ultra Violet observed that most of the Factory faithful were, like herself and Andy, fallen-away Catholics. (*Los Angeles Times* 2/6/89)

(24) a. #In Ben's picture, a fat woman found a scratch.
      b. #In a great huff, someone left the boss's office.
      c. In Ben's picture, Sally found a scratch.
      d. In a great huff, Bill left the Boss's office.

The preposed prepositional phrase seems to focus attention on the predicate in the clause (intuitively speaking, the construction "shines a spotlight" on the predicate), to the exclusion of the subject, making the subject position an unlikely place to introduce new material (see §4.3.1). Yet this is the preferred configuration for backwards anaphora constructions, including those which introduce an entirely new referent into the discourse. The new entities introduced differ from those in Reinhart's examples above in that they are not usually indefinite noun phrases (on the contrary, the vast majority are personal names), but they are at least not given information.

These facts become much less puzzling if viewed in light of Chafe's (1991, 1994) observation that subjects which are not given tend strongly to be accessible, where the term is used to mean that they are not fully active in the addressee's consciousness, but are rather semi-active or within the peripheral awareness of the addressee. Chafe (1994) notes that entities may become accessible through inference and/or physical presence in the immediate environment, both of which are situations in which an entity is in peripheral awareness but has not been specifically focused upon or individually designated by a nominal.

Backwards anaphora constructions can be analyzed in terms of Chafe's notion of accessibility. The clause-initial modifier may serve to set up the context for the following clause, providing a transition between the preceding context (which may be, so to speak, a lack of context, in the case of discourse-initial clauses) and the main clause. This is not a fundamentally new claim; Chafe (1984), Ramsay (1987), and Longacre and Thompson (1985), among others, have done studies of sentence-initial modifiers containing full clauses (e.g., "if" and "when" clauses) suggesting that they serve this kind of contextualizing function.

What is new here is the claim that this contextualizing function of sentence-initial modifiers provides part of the rationale for (typical) backwards anaphora in that the sentence-initial modifier provides a sort of pre-activation of the referent prior to its identification with a full noun phrase. The full noun phrase, for its part, functions as a reference point in relationship to the pronoun. The result is that the backwards anaphora configuration becomes a particularly economical, concise way to introduce new referents into the discourse, by allowing a preposed modifier to supply the needed context for the subject nominal, while the subject nominal functions as antecedent for the pronoun in the modifier.

The studies of clause-initial modifiers cited above do not address backwards anaphora, nor do they analyze preposed prepositional phrases of the type found most commonly in backwards anaphora (as exemplified by [23]). To resolve the seeming paradox brought up by Reinhart's observations on sentences like (24) above, I suggest that, although the clause-initial prepositional phrase may focus attention only on the predicate, it can nevertheless serve a contextualizing function for the clause as a whole, sufficient to permit construing the subject as accessible (in Chafe's [1991, 1994] sense).

Consider (23a) above, the first line of a letter to a newspaper editor. The phrase "In his Aug. 21 letter . . ." makes clear the relevance of Jared Taylor's name: He wrote a letter to the editor, to which this letter is a response. If the author had begun simply, "Jared Taylor seeks to refute comments by Gloria Allred . . . ," the implication would be that the reader should already know who Jared Taylor is (e.g., he might be a famous politician). The prepositional phrase in (23a) narrows the domain which the reader has to consider.

Similar remarks apply to (23b), which is the first mention of Ultra Violet in the text. The reader might have heard of Ultra Violet (this is clearly not assumed, since the author provides additional identification, i.e., "former superstar"), but the prepositional phrase clarifies her connection with Andy Warhol, the topic of the article. If the sentence began, "Former superstar Ultra Violet observed . . . ," the reader might wonder what relevance or expertise Ultra Violet has in connection with Warhol.

The same contextualizing function is of course found with clause-initial modifiers containing clauses, such as *if* or *when* clauses (Chafe 1984; Ramsay 1987; Matthiesen and Thompson 1988). (25a) involves something like a forward anaphoric relationship; the phrase "former coach" is to be construed as "former coach *of the Chargers.*" Without the preposed phrase, the subject nominal would be interpreted differently.

(25) a. On the day the Chargers named Dan Henning as his successor, former coach Al Saunders was closing in on a position as receivers coach of the Kansas City Chiefs. (*Los Angeles Times* 2/10/89, first line of article)

      b. When her son was sentenced to life imprisonment, Mrs. Coe hired a hit man to kill the judge and the Spokane prosecutor. (*Parade* 2/26/89)

(25b) demonstrates that this contextualizing function is not limited to setting the stage for the subject, but applies to the predicate as well. In the context in which this sentence was found, where Mrs. Coe's son's situation had not been explained, it would definitely be anomalous to begin a sentence with "Mrs. Coe hired a hit man to kill the judge and the Spokane prosecutor. . . ." The preposed modifier makes possible the use of the definite nominal forms, by setting up a frame in which *the judge* and *the prosecutor* can be construed as unique (see Langacker 1991:97–98; Hawkins 1978).

As indicated by (25b), it is not necessarily the case that an instance of backwards anaphora is motivated solely by the need to contextualize the subject of the main clause. In some cases the preposing of the modifier may be motivated by the need to set the scene for some other portion of the clause, and no doubt other considerations enter into the use of backwards anaphora as well. Nevertheless, it seems that at least some of the time, backwards anaphora serves as a device for introducing new information in a concise fashion. In a sense, we have interlocked contextualizing relationships within the same construction: The modifier sets up the context for the subject, while the subject functions as a reference point and antecedent in relationship to the pronoun.[7]

Bolinger (1977) gives a possible counterargument to this analysis.

To illustrate his claim that famous entities can be accessed by (apparent) backwards anaphora—since their fame facilitates speaking about them as if they were presupposed—he contrasts backwards anaphora referring to a famous person and a "nonentity." His examples are given in (26).

(26)   a.   In his *Memoirs,* Winston Churchill tells us. . . .
       b.   *In his term paper, Jerry Jones tells us. . . .

These examples do not prove Bolinger's claim (that there is no genuine backwards anaphora; there is only repeat identification of referents and reference to presupposable entities, e.g., famous people). Rather they provide further illustration of the function of the preposed modifier in setting the scene for the conception, which includes the subject nominal. In (26a), the modifier *in his "Memoirs"* tells us a great deal about the subject of the clause. Even without the name or any supporting context, we know that this person is an author of a specific book entitled *Memoirs* and that he is almost certain to be famous (unknown people rarely write memoirs). The modifier in (26b) does not provide enough information to set the scene for the clause effectively. We do not know the topic of the term paper nor how the speaker knows about it. The construction is greatly improved if the paper is described in a more informative way, even if the reader has never heard of the author before:

(27)   In his paper "David Koresh and the Hermeneutics of Biblical Criticism," Jerry Jones writes. . . .

This kind of construction is used frequently as a device for introducing new sources of information into a newspaper or magazine article. It seems that the difficulty with Bolinger's example is not in the choice of antecedent but in the modifier's inability to set the scene for the following clause.

5.4 REPEAT IDENTIFICATION

One of the claims being made here is that backwards anaphora is characterized by a clear prominence asymmetry between the pronoun and antecedent motivated by the linear order's giving a misleading cue to reference point organization. If this is the correct functional explanation for the patterns found, then "repeat identification" of a referent that is already prominent in the discourse should not reflect such restrictions, since the pronoun can find its antecedent in the larger discourse context.

If the characteristics of backwards anaphora described here are attributed to other factors, and functional considerations of backgrounding and prominence do not play a role in facilitating construal of the antecedence relationship, then we will predict (other things being equal) that repeat identification constructions will display all the same characteristics as backwards anaphora.

A corpus of 100 repeat-identification examples was collected by specifically searching through texts (rather than by simply noting down any examples that were encountered in everyday reading, as was done with backwards anaphora).[8] The criterion for inclusion in the corpus was that the reference of the pronoun must be clear and easily identifiable from the preceding context, so that the following noun phrase was not needed as an antecedent. Without the capability of reading the authors' minds, however, it was not possible to be sure of filtering out every example of genuine backwards anaphora. No doubt some of these examples were intended to be read as backwards anaphora, with the full noun phrase as antecedent, even though the pronoun could also have picked up its reference from the preceding discourse. Despite the impossibility of obtaining an absolutely pure sample, we can see clearly from the data that repeat identification does not pattern exactly as backwards anaphora does.

A simple count of repeat identification patterns shows striking differences from the backwards anaphora patterns. Only 31 out of 100 repeat identification examples fit the pattern which I have identified as the predominant backwards anaphora pattern, and which accounted for 61% of the backwards anaphora corpus: possessive pronoun in a preposed modifier phrase, full nominal as subject of the main clause. Moreover, whereas 88% of the backwards anaphora constructions had the subject of the main clause as antecedent, only 61% of the repeat identification sentences fit this description.

More significant, a large number of the examples seem unlike anything found in genuine backwards anaphora. Several construction types which are unattested in the backwards anaphora corpus occur more than once in the repeat identification corpus. In (28a), the first pronoun elaborates the primary object of the verb *tell*, so it is profiled in the composite conception, while the full noun phrase *Sara* appears in an unprofiled modifying phrase—a configuration which is unattested in the backwards anaphora corpus, as discussed above. Five examples of this kind were found in a corpus one-fifth the size of the backwards anaphora corpus.

(28) a.   Margaret and Dewi told her about her legs as soon as Sara re-
           gained consciousness. (*Reader's Digest* 6/94)
      b.   Furthermore, his studio gave Les a place to perfect his multiple-
           recording techniques. (*Reader's Digest* 7/93)
      c.   Her mother and sister so despaired of Kerri's recovering that they
           actually discussed the service they would have when she died.
           (*Reader's Digest* 4/91)

(28b) is a construction parallel to the oft-cited *His mother loves John*, at
least insofar as it involves a possessive pronominal attached to the subject and a coreferential nominal in object position. This is another construction type which is unattested in the backwards anaphora corpus
(though as explained above, variants of this configuration are found
which more closely conform to the backgrounding-of-pronoun pattern
found in typical backwards anaphora). (28c) would be even more atypical as an example of backwards anaphora than (28b): The pronominal
possessor is directly attached to the subject and the full noun phrase is
itself a possessor, and is therefore not included in the clausal profile.
(No examples of type [28c] were found in the backwards anaphora corpus.) Four examples of the construction type exemplified by (28b–c)
were found in the repeat identification corpus (I have also encountered
other examples outside the collection which went into the corpus). Despite the small sizes of the corpora, the findings suggest strongly that
there is a difference between repeat identification and backwards
anaphora.

Additional isolated examples were found which are unlike anything in the backwards anaphora corpus. In (29a), the full noun phrase
is a direct object in a coordinate structure; in the backwards anaphora
corpus, all the coordinate structure examples had the antecedent in subject position within its clause. (29b) is almost a mirror image of the backwards anaphora construction type involving parenthetical expressions;
the pronoun codes an argument in the main clause, while the name,
which is not needed as an antecedent, occurs in a backgrounded, parenthetical expression. Such a configuration was not found in any genuine
backwards anaphora construction. (Italic has been added for clarity.)

(29) a.   Facts were familiar tools for *him*, and yet something attached to
           this fact had caused *Data* to state what Lore already knew. (Diane
           Carey, *Descent*, p. 176)
      b.   Police arrested *him* and returned the car—which *Johnson* had
           stripped of the couple's belongings—to Lucero. (*Reader's Digest*
           6/94)

There is also a subtle, qualitative difference between the backwards anaphora corpus and the repeat identification corpus. The backwards anaphora examples can be categorized, almost without exception, in terms of one constructional pattern or another. In contrast, many of the repeat identification examples seem to be one of a kind. Some repeat identification constructional patterns seem to be more or less conventionally established, such as the pattern exemplified by (19b–c) above and repeated here as (30), which were collected separately from the repeat identification corpus (though they meet the contextual requirement for repeat identification, not backwards anaphora).

(30) a. Her mother motioned Sashie to the other side of the room.
          (Laskie, *The Night Journey*, p. 81)
      b. His research led Finder into the sewers of Paris. (*San Diego Union* 3/11/91)

While some repeat identification examples seem to fit familiar constructional patterns, it seems in other cases that repeat identification requires only that a writer use a pronoun and then, somewhat later in the sentence, use a full noun phrase which happens to refer to the same person. No special repeat identification schema is required. Sentences which illustrate this point are in (31), with italics added for clarity.

(31) a. When *she* and Toby then made love, the drug seemed to heighten the event beyond anything else *Kerri* had ever experienced. (*Reader's Digest* 4/91)
      b. *Her* mother returned at 3 P.M., opened *Diane's* door and found her lying face down on her bed. (*Reader's Digest* 4/91)
      c. If the air pressure around *his* arm could be made to equal the pressure on the rest of *his* submerged body, the force holding *Decker* would be neutralized, and divers could pull him free. (*Reader's Digest* 9/93)

The overall difference between backwards anaphora and repeat identification seems fairly clear, although, as noted, it is not possible to find a perfectly clear dividing line between the two.

5.5 SUMMARY

In this study I have argued that backwards anaphora constructions exhibit distinct patterning which can be explained only if we focus attention on backwards anaphora as a constructional category in its own

right rather than consider it merely as something which is not ruled
out by general anaphora constraints. At the same time, the reference
point model of anaphora constraints offers an explanation for many
of the patterns observed. The assumption that backwards anaphora is
subject to special requirements owing to the "backwards" (in terms of
linear order) relationship between pronoun and antecedent is given
support by the finding that repeat identification exhibits much freer
patterning than genuine backwards anaphora.

The uses of backwards anaphora and repeat identification reflect
principles governing the introduction of referents into a discourse and
their accessibility for subsequent reference back. The details of the construction types attested, however, are fully explicable by the terms of
the reference point model, which also accounts for the sentence-internal
anaphora constraints. In the second half of this chapter I further exam-
ine the relationship between the sentence-internal application of the reference point model and the principles of accessibility and coreference
in cross-sentential discourse.

5.6 ANAPHORA IN DISCOURSE

In contrast to structural models of the anaphora constraints, which have
viewed intra- and interclausal coreference patterns as separate domains
of study, the reference point model posits that the same factors determine the organization of reference points (and hence the possibilities
for reference and coreference) at all levels of organization. This is essentially the view taken by Ariel (1988, 1990), Givón (1979a, 1983a, 1983b,
1984, 1989), Chafe (1987, 1991, 1994), and others working within Accessibility theory and/or Information Flow theory, though none of those
researchers has done a detailed study of the intrasentential and in-
traclausal anaphora constraints of the type done here. In this section I
cite a number of studies from the literature on accessibility, reference
tracking, and discourse-level coreference with the goal of setting the
reference point model of intrasentential anaphora constraints in the
larger context of cross-sentential studies of coreference.

5.6.1 Discourse Topics as Reference Points

A vast body of literature has focused on the factors influencing topic
continuity or accessibility in discourse (Givón 1979a, 1983a, 1983b, 1984,

1989; Tomlin 1987b; Fox 1987a, 1987b; Ariel 1988, 1990 et al.). It is by now well established that accessibility cannot be predicted solely (or even primarily) in terms of linear distance notions, such as the number of clauses intervening between mentions of a referent. Rather, reference patterns in both spoken and written discourse reflect notions of salience and conceptual connectivity which contribute to a complex, hierarchical conceptual organization at the discourse level.

A number of researchers have argued that the choice of referring forms reflects the salience of referents in the discourse context (as opposed to merely the linear distance since last mention) (e.g., Karmiloff-Smith 1981; Morrow 1985; Tomlin 1987b; Fox 1987a, 1987b). As Tomlin (1987b:457) states, "Pronouns are used to make reference when a particular referent is in a state of high focus or 'foregrounded,' in a given linguistic context." A variety of studies (see references below) have found that a referent which is highly topical tends to be referenced with a pronoun, while a referent that is less prominent, even if more recently mentioned, will frequently be described by a full noun phrase.

In studies of spoken narrative, Karmiloff-Smith (1981, 1985) has suggested that there is a "thematic constraint" operative in narrative by which speakers tend to reserve pronominal reference for the character construed as the main character, while secondary characters tend to be invoked by full noun phrases. Speakers do make pronominal reference to secondary characters, but there is a strong tendency for pronouns to be reserved for reference to the main character. (Karmiloff-Smith [1985] notes that this principle holds even for narratives involving characters differing in gender, where pronouns could in principle be used for reference to both characters without danger of confusion.)

Karmiloff-Smith (1981) claims that speakers use full noun phrases in positions in which a pronoun would be completely unambiguous, and that they use pronouns in positions in which the number of intervening clauses since the last mention of the referent might lead one to expect a full noun phrase. She explains these observations with the hypothesis that pronominal reference reflects not merely distance since last mention but also the thematic status of the referent within the larger narrative structure. Her hypothesis is that "anaphoric pronominalization functions as an implicit instruction to the addressee *not* to recompute for retrieval of an antecedent referent but rather to treat the pronoun (or, par excellence, zero anaphora) as the default case for the thematic subject of a span of utterances, and to take it that deviations therefrom will be marked clearly linguistically by use of full noun phrases" (p. 77). She supports this hypothesis with a developmental study of children's elicited narratives, which shows that children's referential patterns come to reflect the thematic constraint. For example, one older child (Karmiloff-Smith [p. 140] does not give the exact age) told a story (elicited by picture book) as follows.

(32)   A little boy is walking along on a sunny day. He sees a balloon man. The balloon man gives him a balloon. He [the boy] walks off home. . . .

Karmiloff-Smith points out that the repetition of the descriptive noun phrase 'the balloon man' is not required to avoid ambiguity, but rather reflects the thematic constraint which reserves pronominal reference for the main character, the boy.

A number of other researchers have found that, in nonnarrative discourse as well, speakers distinguish between topics and nontopics, and reserve pronouns for reference to the topic (as listeners, they also tend to interpret pronouns as referring to the topic in cases of potential ambiguity) (e.g., Broadbent 1973; Levy 1982; Redeker 1985; Ariel 1990). Again, it is not that pronouns are never used for reference to less-central referents in the discourse, but that there is a tendency for pronominal reference to be associated with topichood.

The central notion of prominence thus plays a critical role in determining referential possibilities both within and across sentences. There are some differences in the specific manifestations of this notion at these levels, however. The distinction between primary and secondary topics at the discourse/narrative level in some ways resembles the figure/ground (subject/nonsubject) distinction within clauses (see §5.6.2 below). The topical referent is also typically the character from whose point of view the narrative is construed (Bamberg 1987; Morrow 1985; McGann and Schwartz 1988; Hewitt 1995; Bruder and Wiebe 1995), an observation reminiscent of the familiar association between subjecthood and point of view (DeLancey 1981; Kuno 1987; and see §8.1).

The studies cited here suggest that the discourse topic (or main character) in some ways functions as a discourse-level parallel to the clause-internal notion of subject as figure within the conception. There are more specific associations between discourse topic status and subjecthood; the following section summarizes some of the relevant findings from the literature.

5.6.2 Subject as Reference Point Inside and Outside the Clause

One of the key points of the reference-point model of anaphora patterns is that the figure within a relational conception is the reference point for accessing the rest of that conception. One instantiation of this general notion is the claim that the subject of a clause is a reference point, with the rest of the clause in its dominion. With respect to the role of subjects, this claim essentially amounts to a restatement, from a CG point of view, of Chafe's (1987:36) observation that a typical strategy for presentation of information is "employing a subject to express the starting point and proceeding with a predicate which adds information about that starting point." At the discourse level, this facet of reference point organization is reflected in the familiar observation that clausal subjects tend to be entities which are already established in the discourse and have more or less topical status (e.g., Givón 1976, 1978, 1979a, 1983b, 1984, 1994; Chafe 1976, 1987, 1991, 1994; Tomlin 1983).

One manifestation of this is that subjects tend to be definite (Givón 1979:26–28). Givón notes that languages provide various means for avoiding the use of indefinite subjects, such as presentational-*there* constructions. A sentence such as (33a) is somewhat awkward, while the paraphrase in (33b) is perfectly natural.

(33)   a.   ?A tree is in the front yard.
       b.   There is a tree in the front yard.

Chafe (1976, 1987, 1991, 1994) has made similar observations within the context of his Information Flow theory. As explained in §5.3.1 above, Chafe (1991) analyzed transcripts of spontaneous conversation and found that subjects in spoken conversation are very rarely new (i.e., not at all in the addressee's awareness). Even subjects coded as full noun phrases tended to be either given (currently active in the addressee's awareness) or accessible (not fully active, but semi-active as part of the background context).

Chafe explains the fact that subjects tend overwhelmingly to be given or accessible in terms of their function as starting points, given the reasonable assumption that the entities suited to function as starting points are those which are already in the speaker's and addressee's awarenesses. The reference point model makes the same claim, though it arrives at it through principles of clause-internal semantic organization (a "bottom-up" approach which converges with Chafe's "top-down" approach). More generally, the first reference point through which one accesses any grounded unit (i.e., any conception expressed by a finite clause or full nominal) tends to be an entity which is already accessible in the larger context (see §3.3.3). The subject is the primary reference point within the clause, with the rest of the clause in its dominion. Within nominals, the possessor (if there is one) is the primary reference point, as one makes mental contact with the rest of the nominal through the possessor. Both subjects and possessors tend to be "high continuity," that is, already accessible within the discourse context (Givón 1983b; Brown 1983; for analysis of possessors only, see also Deane 1992; Taylor 1994).

Although there is a strong correlation between clause-internal or phrase-internal reference point status and the notion of discourse-level given information, it should be emphasized that these are distinct notions, and reference points are not defined as given information. The subject's role as a clause-internal reference point or starting point does not depend on its being given information within the larger discourse, although there is a natural tendency for it to be such (Chafe [1991, 1994] makes this distinction explicit as well).[9]

5.6.3 Conceptual Connectivity in Discourse

It is by now well-established that discourse is not composed merely of sequences of sentences, but is hierarchically organized into units of varying kinds (e.g., Givón 1983b, 1984; Hinds 1979; Longacre 1979; Fox 1987a, 1987b; Chafe 1987, 1991, 1994; Tomlin 1984, 1987b). Depending on the medium (spoken or written) and the genre, discourse units of various kinds are construed as connected units, that is, dominions, for purposes of anaphora. Chapters 3 and 4 discussed the role of conceptual connectivity in determining when a conception is likely to be construed as a part of a previously established dominion or when it may more readily be construed as external to a dominion. Conceptual connectivity plays a role at the cross-sentential level as well. In particular, conceptual breaks or junctures can bring about 'closure' of a dominion. Here I will review findings by a number of researchers in studies of conversation, expository prose, and written narrative, interpreting the various claims reported in terms of the reference point model.

A number of researchers have argued that a model based solely (or even primarily) on linear distance between mentions of a referent cannot explain the selection of specific forms to access that referent. This point has been made in response to research by Givón (1983b) and

Clancy (1980), among others, who note that pronouns tend to occur when the referent has been mentioned very recently (typically in the previous sentence), while full noun phrases are more likely to occur when there has been relatively more material intervening since the last mention of the referent. Tomlin (1987b) calls the analysis put forth by these studies the "recency / distance" hypothesis.

Fox (1987a), Tomlin (1987b), and Ariel (1990) have pointed out that, while the recency / distance model captures some of the relevant facts, it is not ultimately an adequate model. Although it is true that, statistically speaking, the use of pronouns and full noun phrases tends to correlate with the distance between the current and previous mentions of the referent, the statement of this general tendency does not accurately describe the range of variability across specific cases. A full noun phrase may be used even when its referent was mentioned via a pronoun in the immediately preceding sentence. A pronoun may be used even when a few sentences have intervened since the last mention of the referent. The alternative which a number of researchers have proposed to the recency / distance model is based on taking into account the hierarchical structure of discourse and of spoken and written texts. They seek to explain the distribution of pronouns and full noun phrases in terms of structural units and unit boundaries.

In this section I review studies done by several different researchers concerning discourse unit boundaries. These represent the extreme end of the continuum of connectivity described in §4.1, which ranges from strongest connectivity (within head / complement structures) to weaker connectivity (nominals more loosely associated within a single sentence or discourse unit), and which now can be seen to culminate in situations where a reference point is separated from another conception by a discourse unit boundary, with the result that the second conception is construed as external to the dominion of the reference point.

5.6.3.1 Ariel's Notion of Unity

Ariel's (1990) Accessibility theory is in many respects parallel to my reference point model in defining the domains in which different referring forms tend to appear, although the scope of the phenomena addressed by her model is different from that addressed here. Ariel does not address the clause-internal anaphora constraints in English, but focuses on developing a fine-grained "accessibility hierarchy" which differentiates among more than a dozen kinds of nominal forms and accounts for findings across a large number of languages.[10]

Ariel proposes a notion of "unity" which functions in some ways equivalent to my notion of semantic connectivity. She defines unity as "being in the same frame or world or paragraph or segment" (1990: 29), and argues that this notion plays a crucial role in determining the selection of nominal forms. Citing Sanford and Garrod (1981), she lists notions such as change of scene, passage of time in the narrative world, and so on as influencing unity at the discourse level, and hence the accessibility of referents. Unity is not precisely equivalent to my notion of connectivity (which includes the strong connectivity provided by explicit relational interconnections within head/complement structure), but corresponds more to my notion of weaker connectivity: co-containment within a single unit of some kind without direct relational interconnections.

Ariel illustrates the significance of unity by pointing out that in many languages it is common to find renaming of referents following paragraph boundaries. In her own study of Hebrew texts, she found that continuing discourse topics were commonly referenced via full nominals in the first sentence of paragraphs (full nominals appeared 75% of the time). Although she does not directly address any English data concerning renaming of referents at discourse unit boundaries, her comments on the general patterns found cross-linguistically are congruent with the studies of English I cite below, and she finds that various textual unit boundaries promote the use of full noun phrases for reference to entities previously established as discourse topics.

5.6.3.2 Reference and Episode Boundaries

One kind of textual unit is the narrative episode. In his study of reference in elicited English narrative, Tomlin (1987b:455) argues that "the syntax of reference is directly a function of episodic or thematic boundaries." Tomlin hypothesizes that discourse-level reference patterns are directly tied to attention and shifts in attention. Specifically, "During the on-line process of discourse production, the speaker uses a pronoun to maintain reference as long as attention is sustained on that referent. Whenever attention focus is disrupted, the speaker reinstates reference with a full noun, no matter how few clauses intervene between subsequent references" (1987b:458).

Tomlin defines **episode** as "a semantic unit in discourse organization consisting of a set of related propositions governed by a macroproposition or paragraph level theme" (1987b:460). "Episode boundaries" are "major breaks, or attention shifts, in the flow of information in discourse." Drawing on work by van Dijk and Kintsch (1983), he notes that episode boundaries in narration generally correlate with major changes in time, place, or characters. Noting that such text-based definitions of episode boundary tend to lead to circularity of argumentation, Tomlin devised two studies using perceptual cues to trigger episode boundaries in speakers' elicited narratives artificially. In one study, an elicitation of narrative using a videotaped cartoon, episode boundaries were triggered by video cuts accompanied by major scenery changes. In the other study, an elicitation of narrative using a series of slides, episode boundaries were expected to be triggered by the transition between slides. In both studies, the expectation was that a major disruption in the flow of visual information (a change in the scenery, or the gap between slides) would motivate the marking of an episode boundary, for example, by reintroduction of the characters after the boundary.

The finding from both studies was that subjects were much more likely to use full noun phrases after episode boundaries and to use pronouns to maintain reference within episodes. The elicitation of narrative using slides had three different conditions, varying the presentation of the slides in order to induce the episode boundaries at different points in the narrative. In one condition, the subjects saw the slides one at a time, and were asked to produce the story as the slides appeared. In the other two conditions, subjects saw the slides in pairs (one group saw the first slide alone, then saw slides 2–3, 4–5, and so on in pairs; the other group saw slides 1–2, 3–4, and so on). The hypothesis was that the interval between slides would be treated as an episode boundary. Tomlin's finding was that, no matter how the slides were grouped for presentation, subjects were significantly more likely to use full noun phrases to reestablish reference after an (artificially induced) episode boundary than within episodes.

In both the videotape elicitation and the slide elicitation, Tomlin found that there were some instances of the use of full noun phrases to make reference within episodes to characters previously mentioned within the same episode, but the majority of those examples support his hypothesis that shifts in attention motivate reidentifying the referents with full noun phrases. One context in which speakers tended to use full noun phrases was during or just after an evaluative comment, when the speaker "shifts his rhetorical activity from narrating events to evaluating them" (1987b:469). Tomlin analyzes this as an instance of attention shift. He gives the example in (34), among others.

(34)   That crab just tipped the top of its shell. I don't believe that, do you?
       And that crab's just going away.

In the terms of the reference point model, it appears that shifts in attention correlate with closure of a dominion. If a reference point is a conception which is an active or central part of the background into which new material is contextualized, a shift in attention can be thought of as disrupting the maintenance of previously established background information and thereby shutting down previously established dominions. Whether reference point/dominion organization should be equated directly with "attention flow" is still an open question, but Tomlin's study (and Chafe's [1987, 1991, 1994] Information Flow theory) suggests that this may be a reasonable interpretation.

5.6.3.3 Open and Closed Sequences in Spoken Discourse

The patterns of anaphoric reference in spontaneous conversation are also sensitive to notions of conceptual connectedness and discontinuity. Fox (1987a) makes this point in her analysis of spontaneous conversation. She claims that the basic pattern in environments of different-gender referents (i.e., where the pronouns are disambiguated by gender marking) is for a referent to be introduced by a full noun phrase, and to be referred to by a pronoun thereafter, so long as the speaker understands that the sequence containing the referent is not yet "closed." She finds further that full noun phrases may be used, even when the referent has been recently mentioned, provided that there has been closure of the previous sequence in which the referent was active. In other words, the mere linear distance between the current reference and the last previous reference is not sufficient to explain the choice of a pronoun or a full noun phrase in a particular context. Rather, some more abstract notion of conceptual continuity or discontinuity must be invoked.

One of the ways in which a discourse sequence can come to be construed as closed, under Fox's analysis, is when there has been a **re-turn pop**—a return to a topic that was previously under discussion. The material that is "popped over" is closed off. Subsequent reference to someone who was last referenced in the closed-off segment tends to use a full noun phrase even if the linear distance between the current mention and the previous mention is only one or two sentences. Fox gives as an example the discourse sequence in (35). As in §2.3.2, I have chosen to represent Fox's examples in more or less standard orthography rather than reproduce her semiphonetic transcription system. The beginning of the return pop is underlined here.

(35) M: Well, anyway, listen, I gotta go, I gotta do a lot of studying. Oh, and Hillary said she'd call me if she was going to go to the library with me. But I don't think she will. *So anyway.* Tch. I'm gonna go have these xeroxed and I'll come back in a little bit.

     R: Okay. Say hi to Hillary for me.

The marker *so anyway* signals a return to the previous topic, M's intention to go. Under Fox's analysis, this closes off the sequence involving Hillary, with the consequence that R uses a full noun phrase for subsequent reference to Hillary even though the linear distance between the preceding pronoun and the current mention is quite small. In the terms of my model, closure of the discourse sequence represents a conceptual disjuncture which motivates construing subsequent material as being outside the dominion of the previously established reference point. This makes the use of a full noun phrase much more likely. (This phenomenon is also compatible with Tomlin's (1987b) notion of attention shift as a crucial factor, as a return pop seems quite clearly to represent a shift of attention to a previously discussed topic.)

5.6.3.4 Rhetorical Structure in Expository Prose

Different written genres show different kinds of structural organization, with differing effects on the use of pronouns and full noun phrases. A number of these superficially different patterns can be described as instantiations of the same schematic notion: Conceptual unit boundaries tend to correlate with dominion boundaries. The exact nature of these conceptual units, and the factors which tend to be construed as unit boundaries, vary from one genre to another, but the basic pattern is the same.

For (1987a) reports on her studies of anaphora in written expository prose. As in her study of anaphora in spoken conversation, she finds that the distribution of full noun phrases does not depend merely on the linear distance between the current and previous mention of the referent, but crucially involves notions of textual units and unit boundaries. She draws on a theory of rhetorical structure analysis drawn largely from Mann, Matthiessen, and Thompson 1988; Grimes (1975), and McKeown (1982). In this theory, the smallest unit of text is the proposition. Propositions are organized into larger units consisting (usually) of a nucleus, which "realizes the main goals of the writer," and an adjunct, which provides supplementary information pertaining to the material presented in the nucleus (Fox 1987a:79). Nuclei and adjuncts are organized into **rhetorical structures** of various types. The most central type of rhetorical structure within the model is the **Issue** structure, which consists of a nucleus which presents a claim, plus one or more adjuncts of the following types: an **elaboration** adjunct, which provides details about the central claim; an **evidence** adjunct, which provides evidence in support of the claim; and/or a **background** adjunct, which provides background information pertaining to the claim.

Fox discusses almost a dozen additional kinds of rhetorical structures, but the Issue structure is identified as particularly crucial for describing expository prose, and it is sufficient here for illustrating the point that conceptual organization at the discourse level affects pronominal anaphora patterns. Fox argues that full noun phrases are used not only to identify referents, but also to demarcate textual boundaries. She shows that even when just one referent is the topic of discussion throughout a text, full nominals may be used for reference at the beginnings of new rhetorical units. For example, the Issue structure involves a nucleus and a number of satellite structures which provide supporting information pertaining to the nucleus. Each of the satellite structures functions as a rhetorical unit, and the onset of each such rhetorical unit is marked by the use of a full noun phrase for reference.

Fox gives a number of examples, of which I will cite just one here. This example involves a single Issue structure, introduced by the first sentence, with four background structures and one elaboration structure. According to Fox's analysis, the background structures begin with lines 3, 4, 6, and 9. Of those, the last three contain references to James Albertson, the topic of the text. Albertson is renamed in each of these lines, although in lines 6 and 9 a pronoun would have been unambiguous.

(36) 1. James S. Albertson has been appointed acting academic vice president by the Regents following President Saxon's recommendation.
2. The appointment is effective from March 1 until a permanent academic vice president is named.
3. Academic Vice President Donald C. Swain earlier was named president of the University of Louisville.
4. Albertson will be responsible for academic planning and program review, student affairs, financial aid, admissions, student loan collections, student affirmative action, basic skills, the Education Abroad Program, library plans and policies and UC Press.
5. He also is responsible for UC Extension, summer sessions, instructional media, Continuing Education of the Bar, and liaison with

the Academic Senate, the Student Body Presidents' Council and the California Postsecondary Education Commission.

6. Albertson has been special assistant to Swain since 1978.
7. For four years prior to that he was assistant academic vice president.
8. He joined UC in 1973 as director of analytical studies.
9. Albertson is a graduate in classics at St. Louis University.
10. He earned his M.A. in philosophy there in 1953 and received the Ph.D. in physics in 1958 at Harvard.
11. He joined the faculty at Loyola University of Los Angeles in 1962 and became chairman of the department before he left in 1968 to join the faculty of the University of Santa Clara as professor of physics.
12. He was also academic vice president at Santa Clara. (*University Bulletin* 3/23/81; cited in Fox 1987a:111–12)

Albertson is referenced with a full noun phrase in sentences 6 and 9 even though reference was made via a pronoun in the immediately preceding sentence. Fox's analysis is that the use of a full noun phrase in a context in which a pronoun would have been unambiguous signals the beginning of a new rhetorical unit. With respect to the overall model of anaphora I am developing, the crucial observation is that the onset of a new conceptual unit (and hence the closure of a preceding unit) is associated with the use of a full noun phrase for a referent previously referenced via a pronoun.

The use of full nominals at the onset of new rhetorical units seems to be quite common (Fox provides figures for her data indicating that it is a common device), but it is not mandatory. Speakers do not judge a construction deviant simply because a pronoun is used at the beginning of a new rhetorical unit. What we are dealing with here is a distinct tendency rather than a hard and fast rule. Nevertheless, it is a tendency which reflects the same notions drawn on to predict the anaphora possibilities within the sentence. While pronouns represent continuation of a nominal conception that is already part of the immediate conceptual context, full nominals are associated with the onset of a new conceptual unit, and tend to appear when the speaker or writer feels that a previously established conceptual unit has reached closure.

5.6.3.5 Development Structures in Popular Narrative

The schematic notion of full nominals demarcating textual unit boundaries is instantiated in popular fiction as well. Fox (1987b) has carried out studies of pronominal anaphora in popular written narrative, using sources such as science fiction novels. Her finding is that full noun phrases are used at the onset of a particular kind of narrative unit termed a **development structure**. A development structure begins when a character takes action, typically in response to a previous event. The actor is commonly (though not invariably) referenced with a full nominal even when reference to the same character was made in the previous development structure, and even when pronominal reference would have been unambiguous. Fox gives the following examples, among others (the relevant nominal is italicized).

(37)   She [Ripley] did not see the massive hand reaching out for her from the concealment of deep shadow. But Jones did. He yowled.
       Ripley spun, found herself facing the creature. It had been in the shuttle all the time. (Alan Dean Foster, *Alien*, p. 267; cited by Fox 1987b:169)

(38)   But the man drew his knees up and pulled himself into a kneeling position. He looked at Susan and managed a smile despite the intense pain of his broken rib. "I like 'em . . . when they fight back," he grunted between clenched teeth.
       Susan picked up the fire extinguisher and threw it as hard as she could at the kneeling figure. (Robin Cook, *Coma*, p. 241; cited by Fox 1987b:169)

In each of these examples, the scene involves only one female character. The pronoun *she* could have been substituted for the italicized names, with no possibility for ambiguity. The appearance of the full noun phrase is motivated by the development unit boundary. This analysis seems also to be congruent with Tomlin's (1987b) notion that shifts in attention are the critical factor. A development unit boundary represents a shift of attention onto the actions of a character who is taking up the agentive role.

5.7 SUMMARY

To summarize, the model of reference point organization developed in the previous chapters is essentially a clause-internal application of discourse-level conceptual notions of accessibility or "topic continuity." The claim that the subject functions as the primary reference point for the clause, a claim motivated by the CG-internal claim that the subject is the conceptual figure within the clause, is congruent with observations by Givón (1976, 1979a, 1983b, 1994), Chafe (1976, 1987, 1991, 1994), and other researchers concerning the role of the subject in discourse and the relationship between subjecthood and discourse topic status.

The critical role of conceptual connectivity in defining the anaphora constraints is also mirrored in the discourse-level anaphora patterns. The comparative flexibility of judgments at the cross-sentential level is also explained in these terms. In §4.1 it was noted that strong connectivity (when elements are interconnected by virtue of elaborating a single explicitly coded relation) gives rise to the most unequivocal judgments concerning coreference possibilities. Where connections are weaker, as at discourse unit boundaries, there is greater flexibility in construal. The seeming disparity between the unequivocal judgments within clauses and the flexibility of judgments at the discourse level is not an indication that we are dealing with fundamentally different sets of principles, but rather illustrates the import of different degrees of connectivity.

BOUND ANAPHORA

In this chapter I apply the reference point model to the analysis of bound anaphora, constructions in which a pronoun takes a quantifier expression as an antecedent. Bound anaphora is subject to narrow constraints which are usually stated structurally in terms of c-command. The data in (1) illustrate the point that bound readings are not freely available. (The judgments given apply only to the bound readings.)

(1)   a.   *Everyone* loves *his* mother.
      b.   I interviewed *each senator* in *his* office.
      c.   **His* mother loves *everyone*.
      d.   **The neighbors of *each of the politicians* hate *him*.

One well-known analysis of these facts asserts that the antecedent must c-command the pronoun at some level of representation (Reinhart 1983). This approach accounts for many of the data, but has difficulty with the so-called donkey constructions (Geach 1962), exemplified by (2a), and inverse linking constructions in which the antecedent for the pronoun is a possessor rather than an argument of the verb, as in (2b). In each of these sentences the antecedent fails to c-command the pronoun.

(2)   a.   Every man who owns *a donkey* beats *it*.
      b.   *Each man's* mother gave *him* a tie for Christmas.

To resolve this problem, various researchers have proposed modifications of c-command or of the indexing procedures which determine which elements have scope over other elements (see, e.g., Haïk 1984; May 1985; Roberts 1987; Reinhart 1987).

Within the reference point model, bound anaphora is accounted for in terms of the same principles as ordinary coreference, with the addition of an appropriate conception of quantifier semantics. I draw on Langacker's (1991) analysis of quantifiers as mental space builders, and propose that bound anaphora is simply a correspondence between the semantic poles of a pronoun and an antecedent within the special mental space set up by a quantifier construction. The constraints on bound anaphora follow naturally from certain basic assumptions about the structures which can be construed to be included within the mental space set up by the quantifier, and from the requirement that the intended antecedent be sufficiently salient to function as a reference point within that mental space.

This analysis is based on many of the same intuitions as the analyses proposed by Kamp (1984), Heim (1982, 1990), and Roberts (1987). My analysis is similar to Kamp's in that I claim that bound anaphora is governed by the same basic principles which govern other forms of coreference and deictic use of pronouns. Like Kamp and Heim, I analyze bound anaphora as a configuration in which a quantifier expression sets up a particular kind of discourse context within which the pronoun-antecedent relationship must hold; constraints on bound anaphora are explained in terms of the principles which determine the setting up of these contexts. This is very similar to Kamp's Discourse Representations analysis; he claims that a pronoun must be linked with a referent in an appropriate Discourse Representation (DR), and that bound anaphora involves the additional requirement that the pronoun-antecedent relationship hold within the DR set up by the quantifying expression. Kamp and Heim do not, however, utilize the notion of degrees of conceptual salience in any significant way in their models (Heim mentions that it has some relevance [see below], but does not develop it in detail), nor do they deal with some of the restrictions on bound anaphora which are traditionally handled by c-command, and which will be a focus of discussion here.

The analysis closest to mine is Roberts's (1987). Working within the DR theory developed by Kamp, she proposes a set of principles according to which nominals within syntactic tree structures are mapped onto DRs. The constraints on bound anaphora fall out as a result of the mapping principles. In essence, she states that nominals are mapped onto a DR in order of their scope, so that an NP with wide scope is mapped first onto a DR—or in the terms of the model developed here, it sets up the context within which subsequent NPs are construed. This is obviously parallel to the notion of nominals functioning as reference points and setting up the dominions within which subsequent nominals are construed.

My analysis differs from Roberts's in the formulation of the principles determining which nominals set up the contexts within which other nominals are construed, that is, which nominals take scope over others. Roberts's scope principles are based in part on syntactic tree configurations. Unless a particular NP is flagged as taking wide scope, NPs are integrated into DRs in top-down and left-to-right order. In other words, nominals which asymmetrically c-command other nominals will take scope over them, and nominals which precede sister nominals in the linear string will take scope over their sisters. The exception to this is a configuration where one NP is marked to take wide scope over a constituent, which may be a VP, an NP, or an entire S. The wide-scope NP will be mapped onto a DR first, and mapping then proceeds in the usual order. In response to an observation by Edwin Williams, Roberts notes that her inventory of constituents over which a nominal may take scope is not motivated by general principles; as she puts it, she is "descriptively conservative" in limiting scope possibilities to this small set of constituent types (1987:286). She has to make two special exceptions to accommodate a particular scope phenomenon termed "inverse linking," to be discussed below in §6.3, involving possessive nominals and complements within NP.

The scope problem is framed here as the question of when a quantifier phrase can set up the specialized conceptual context described in Langacker (1991). In §6.3 I propose an explanation for the seemingly special behavior of possessive nominals and complements within nominals. The central notion I will be working with is closely related to Roberts's notion of distributivity, but I will not be attempting to propose a replacement for Roberts's extensive analysis of distributivity facts. Rather I will propose basic distributivity principles (in this model, principles which determine the availability of a 'replicate construal') sufficient to explain the bound anaphora facts.

6.1 QUANTIFIER SEMANTICS

I will focus here on bound anaphora involving the quantifiers *each*, *every* or *no*. Although *each* and *every* are universal quantifiers, the noun phrases they ground are singular. Under Langacker's (1991) analysis, *each* and *every* profile a single nominal instance against the background conception of a group. The profiled instance is construed as representa-

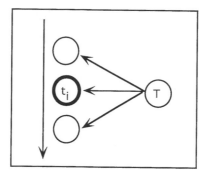

Figure 6.1   *Each*

tive, so that whatever properties are attributed to it are understood to apply to each element in the group. *Each* differs from *every* in that the instances in the group are subjectively ordered, as if being individually examined in turn. Vendler (1967:78) described this distinction as well, noting, "*Every* stresses completeness, or rather exhaustiveness. . . ; *each*, on the other hand, directs one's attentions to the individuals as they appear, in some succession or other, one by one." In Figure 6.1 the various nominal instances invoked by *each* are represented as small circles. They are construed as instances of a single nominal type, labeled T. The representative instance profiled by *each* is labeled t_i. The notion of sequential access of instances is indicated by the arrow.

When a nominal grounded by *each* or *every* combines with a verb (or other relational expression), the composite conception profiles a single representative instance of the relation type designated by the verb. This representative instance is construed against the background conception of multiple instances of the same relation type, which is termed a replicate construal of the relation. As only one instance is profiled, the verb will take singular morphology, as in *Every cat chases mice*, which describes the participation of a group of cats in multiple instances of mouse chasing, but does so through focus on just one representative instance. In Figure 6.2, the relation is represented by a squiggly arrow. The atomic relation instances making up the composite conception are all construed as instantiations of a single relation type, labeled T.

The quantifier *no* is characterized as a complex conception in which an entity is specified as being absent from some context, such as conceived reality. Langacker assumes that negation requires a comparison

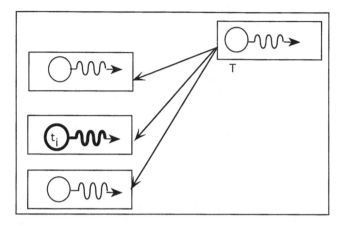

Figure 6.2   A replicate process

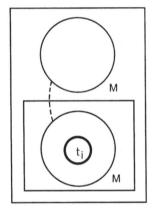

Figure 6.3   *No*

between backgrounded and foregrounded conceptions: It sets up a
mental space in which the entity is present (labeled M in Fig. 6.3), and
construes that mental space in relation to another mental space (also
labeled M), which is conceived as equivalent except in that the entity
is absent from it. The mental space which lacks the entity is conceived
as portraying the actual state of affairs, but it is meaningful only in
relation to the background conception of an equivalent state of affairs,
in which the negated entity is present.

When a quantified nominal combines with a verb, each instance of the nominal type in question participates in an instance of the process type. A sentence such as *Every dog chases cats* involves the conception that each instance of the nominal type *dog* participates in an instance of the process type *chase cats*. The clause profiles just one representative instance of this process type, but it is profiled against the background of a process conception construed as replicate (i.e., having multiple internal instances). The conceived process type is a kind of mental space whose properties are determined by the elements which make up the clausal profile. Bound anaphora is a configuration in which a pronoun-antecedent correspondence is included in the replicate relation.

6.2 BOUND ANAPHORA

Bound anaphora (in the sense of quantifier-bound pronouns) can be described as a pronoun-antecedent configuration contained entirely within the mental space set up by a quantifier expression (the meaning of "contained entirely" is discussed below). The expression *Every boy loves his mother* will serve as an illustration. The nominal *every boy* profiles one instance within a conceived group of instances of the type *boy*. The process *loves his mother* includes a correspondence between the possessor and the trajector of *loves*. When that trajector is put in correspondence with the nominal *every boy*, the result is the conception of a group of boys each of whom participates in an instance of the process type *loves his mother*. The correspondence between the possessor and the trajector is an internal part of the characterization of that process.

Note that the profile of the pronoun cannot correspond to anything outside that process conception, such as the conception of a specific person mentioned in the discourse. If it did correspond to anything external, it would be coreferential rather than bound (on the co-referential/bound distinction, see Evans 1982).

Since the correspondence between the pronoun and antecedent must be part of the representative process instance profiled by the clause, the profiles of both the pronoun and the antecedent must be included within the elements which make up that process conception. If the pronoun is outside that structure, perhaps in a separate sentence, it cannot be construed as bound. For example, in the sentences *Every boy loves his mother; he calls her every Mother's Day*, the pronouns in the second clause cannot be given a bound reading, as they are outside the replicate process conception set up by *Every boy loves his mother*.

Essentially the same remarks apply to constructions with *no*. Recall that the nominal instance grounded by *no* is an arbitrary instance which exists in a backgrounded relational conception, and which is invoked only for purposes of comparison with a foregrounded conception in which that instance is not present. If that nominal instance is to serve as the antecedent for a pronoun, the pronoun must be semantically included within the relation in which the instance is present. If the pronoun is semantically external to the overall construction (which portrays the nominal instance as absent), then of course that nominal conception is not accessible, as in (3a). There are exceptions to this generalization, in which a subordinating conjunction specifically indicates that subsequent clauses in the discourse are to be construed within the mental space set up by the quantifier, as in (3b).

(3)   a.   *No one* showed up; I guess *he* was busy.
       b.   *No one* should come unless *he* wants to.

Cross-sentential bound anaphora is generally impossible because of the requirement that the pronoun-antecedent correspondence be included in the clause which profiles the representative process instance. There is a distinct, but closely related, reading of quantifier constructions, in which the representative process instance becomes the **focus space** which subsequent discourse serves to elaborate (Fauconnier 1988; Dinsmore 1989). This usage seems to involve the description of generic situation types rather than specific scenes, as in (4). (4a is an invented example; 4b is from actual usage.)

(4)   a.   In chess, each player tries to capture the opponent's king. If he
             moves a piece into a position that attacks the king, then he must
             say "check." If his own king is attacked by a piece of the oppo-
             nent's, then he must either make a move to avoid the attack, or re-
             sign. (Dinsmore 1989)
       b.   Any large pieces of aluminum lying around are a hazard. Each
             piece has a definite potential for decapitation. Hurled on the tide
             of a 140-mile-an-hour wind, it can slice its way to, and through,
             bone. (Dave Barry, *Dave Barry's Greatest Hits*, p. 55)

It seems, intuitively, that these constructions are very similar to other quantifier constructions, but the representative instance profiled by the clause becomes the focus of attention to the extent that the notion of replication and of a backgrounded group fades still further into the background, and may disappear entirely. Subsequent discourse may then be contextualized within the mental space set up by the representative process instance (now the sole instance), and pronominal anaphora is possible across sentences. The difference between the replicate construal of the quantifier construction and the generic construal, as in (4), is essentially a shift in focus, and is no doubt a matter of degree.[1] Although I will restrict attention in this chapter to sentence-internal bound anaphora, it should be noted that the distinction between the fully replicate construal found in bound anaphora and the focus on just the representative instance, as in (4), is not clear-cut.

Karttunen (1976:377) has discussed similar examples, pointing out that the felicity of these examples is greatly improved if each sentence following the first includes another quantifier-like expression (*always*, *never*, etc.) which implies that it is a continuation of the situation description begun in the first sentence. Like those in (4), Karttunen's examples (given in [5], slightly modified) describe recurrent situations rather than individual events, although they differ from (4) in that each describes the actions of one person.

(5) a. Harvey courts *a girl* at every convention. *She* always comes to the banquet with him. *She* is usually also very pretty.
   b. Every time Bill comes here, he picks up *a book* and wants to borrow *it*. I never let him take *it*.

The conditions for obtaining a bound reading of a pronoun are summarized in (6). These are automatic consequences of the semantic characterization of bound anaphora and the general principles of the reference point model; they are not independent stipulations.

(6) i. The quantifier phrase must combine with a head (typically a verb) to profile a conception construed as a mental space.
   ii. The semantic poles of both the pronoun and the antecedent must be included within the mental space set up by the combination of the quantifier with the head (the profiled representative instance). They also must not correspond to any conception outside that mental space (as the reading would then be coreferential rather than bound).
   iii. The profile of the antecedent must be sufficiently salient to function as a reference point in relation to the pronoun, within the mental space set up by the quantifier and the head.

Each of these requirements is discussed separately below. §6.3 addresses the factors which determine when it is possible to obtain a replicate construal of a process (similar to the distributivity issues addressed by Roberts [1987], though as noted, I will not be pursuing the issue in anywhere near as great detail). §6.4 focuses on the requirement that the semantic poles of both the antecedent and the pronoun be included within the mental space set up by the quantifier construction. §6.5 addresses the requirement that the antecedent's profile be sufficiently salient within that mental space to function as a reference point.

6.3 THE REPLICATE PROCESS CONCEPTION

Determining when bound anaphora is possible requires first ascertaining the conditions under which a quantifier can motivate a replicate construal of a process or other relation (or, in the case of *no*, when *no* can set up a mental space within which the larger conception of which it is a part is construed). I will focus here on the combination of replicate quantifier constructions with verbs, producing replicate process construals. Essentially the same remarks apply to other kinds of expressions (e.g., complex nominals such as *everyone's belief in his own superiority*).

The quantifier phrase sets up a special kind of context within which the rest of the clause is construed. It thus functions as a reference point (van Hoek 1996b). The familiar factors determining reference point construal in general, prominence and connectivity, also determine when a quantifier phrase (by which I mean a quantified nominal such as *everyone* or *each boy*) can invoke a replicate construal of a conception.[2] A quantifier phrase (QP) tends to invoke a replicate construal of a head to the extent that that QP is salient and conceptually connected with the head.

Complements of a head elaborate portions of its profile, and so are prominent within the composite conception. Modifiers do not elaborate a subpart of the profile of the head, but are rather elaborated by the head. A complement therefore motivates a replicate construal of a head more readily than does a modifier. The canonical examples of bound anaphora (the examples commonly cited in the literature, and the constructions which native speakers accept without hesitation) involve QPs as complements of the profiled process. The QP is most typically the subject of the clause (the trajector, hence most prominent nominal in the clause). The sentences in (7) illustrate the typical bound anaphora configurations.

(7)   a.   *Each of the team leaders* did *her* best to get *her* team across safely.
      b.   *Each boy* asked *his* parents for a turtle.

The extent to which a modifier may invoke a replicate construal of the head is a matter of degree. Modifiers which serve to set up a context for the conception profiled by the head may induce a replicate construal of the head. One obvious example is possessors. A possessor functions as a reference point which conceptually locates the nominal instance profiled by the head noun (Langacker 1991), as in *Ralph's cat*, where the intended instance of the nominal type *cat* is located via its relationship to Ralph. A possessor construed as replicate induces a corresponding replicate construal of the possessum; the resulting replicate nominal conception invokes a replicate construal of the process conception, as in (8a).[3] Modifiers which function as mental space builders in relation to the clause, as in (8b–c), may also induce a replicate construal of the profiled process. The examples in (8) do not involve bound anaphora, but illustrate replicate construal only.

(8)   a.   Each candidate's speech has at least five pages devoted to economic issues.
      b.   In each of these movies, the hero is a cute but whiny little boy.
      c.   In every one of the past three presidential elections, the Republican candidate's platform was based on traditional values.

While some modifiers function specifically to set up conceptual contexts for their heads, it is perhaps more typical for modifiers to contribute to the type specification of the head noun (see Langacker 1991). Modifiers which contribute to the nominal type specification are included as part of the internal conceptual structure of the head, and so are generally not suited to function as starting points for accessing the nominal conception. Unlike complements, which are prominent within the composite conception (and so tend to function as reference points), modifiers are unprofiled within the composite conception. Modifiers which contribute to the type specification for the head noun are therefore much less likely to motivate a replicate construal of the head noun. If the head noun is not construed as replicate, the larger process conception which the nominal elaborates will also not be construed as replicate.

Failure of a replicate construal to spread from a type-conception modifier to a head noun is illustrated by (9). The examples in (9) are from Reinhart (1983), who gives them as evidence for the requirement that the antecedent in a bound anaphora construction must c-command the pronoun. Under the analysis presented here, the unacceptability of bound anaphora here is due to the failure to obtain a replicate construal of the subject nominal. To obtain a bound anaphoric reading, the subject nominal must invoke a replicate construal of the process conception profiled by the main clause, so that for each instance of *book in the library* there is an instance of *guy*, and so forth. In (9a), the replicate construal invoked by the quantifier phrase *every book in the library* does not include the head noun *guy*.[4] A parallel analysis applies to (9b).

(9)   a. *The guy who read *every book in the library* said *it* was boring.
       b. *The secretary who worked with *each of the managers* despises *him*.

To summarize, complements of a head are suited by virtue of their prominence to function as reference points in relation to the head, and a QP complement may therefore invoke a replicate construal of its head. Modifiers are significantly less prominent than complements within the composite conception and accordingly less able to motivate replicate construals of their associated heads. One notable exception to this is the class of modifiers whose function is specifically to "set up a context" for the head (possessors, mental space builders, etc., as illustrated above). Although further investigation is required, it appears that modifiers which elaborate a nominal type conception (as in [9]) tend not to be construed as invoking a replicate construal of the head noun. This is a matter of degree, however; the acceptability of a replicate construal of the nominal is highly variable and appears to depend upon a number of factors, including the specific lexical items selected as head noun and modifier.

There is an important class of exceptions, discussed by Jackendoff (1977) and Roberts (1987), who terms it "inverse linking." These are constructions in which a nominal contained within a larger nominal induces a replicate construal of that nominal (or, in Roberts's terms, takes wide scope over the nominal). The examples in (10) illustrate the kind of construction I have in mind. Because judgments seem highly variable for these constructions, I have selected a relatively large number of examples and collected judgments from nine different speakers. Before each example, I indicate the number of speakers who accepted the construction fully (indicated with a checkmark), found it marginal, or rejected it.[5]

(10) a. ✓3 ?3 *3 The president of *each country* spoke about *its* economic problems.
      b. ✓7 ?2   The bottom of *each statue* is engraved with *its* serial number.
      c. ✓5 ?2 *2 The cover of *each volume* is attached to *it* with a special glue.

d.　✓7　?2　The phone number for *each faculty member* is written just
below *his* name.[6]

e.　✓6　*3　*The chair of each committee* presented *his* concerns.

(10e) differs from (10a–d) in that the antecedent for the pronoun is the
entire nominal *the chair of each committee* rather than just the nominal
embedded in the modifier; this difference does not have a discernible
effect on the grammaticality judgments. The question for data such as
(10) is whether the quantifier in the modifier can motivate a replicate
construal of the head noun and of the process profiled by the entire
clause. The mixture of judgments indicates that it is indeed possible,
but also that this kind of construction deviates to some extent from the
typical patterns for bound anaphora.

That the nonhead nominal induces a replicate construal of the process conception is illustrated by the examples below ([11a] was pointed
out by a reviewer).

(11)　a.　The president of each country spoke about a crisis.
　　　b.　The cover on each book is a different color.

In (11a) there may be a different crisis for each president; (11b) is similarly construed as replicate. This indicates that the replicate construal
is able to spread from the quantifier phrase to the rest of the process
conception.

A critical factor, first pointed out by Jackendoff (1977), is that the
element containing the quantifier phrase is a complement or quasi-
complement rather than a typical modifier. In my terms, the import of
this distinction is that a complement is conceptually connected more
closely with the profile of the head than is a modifier, promoting spread
of the replicate construal. While other analysts (e.g., Larson 1985; Roberts 1987) have acknowledged the significance of the complement/
modifier distinction for producing a quantified (i.e., replicate or bound
anaphoric) reading in these constructions, they interpret the distinction
as a condition on the applicability of NP-adjunction or NP-indexing.
Roberts (1987:290–303) proposes a modification of NP-indexing to account for the ability of the quantifier phrase to get scope over the entire
clause. She stipulates that this is restricted to possessive NPs (e.g., *every
boy's mother*) and complements of NPs, such as in (10), though she spec-
ulates that the import of the complement/modifier distinction may
have to do with head-government of arguments (1987:297).[7]

To summarize, the elements which may invoke a replicate construal
of a conception fall into two categories, as described in (12).

(12)   i.   Replicate nominals functioning as complements, either of the pro-
            cess itself or of a nominal (which may in turn be a complement of
            the process, as in [10–11]).
      ii.   Replicate nominals within a modifier which functions to set up a
            conceptual context for its head; such modifiers are of two kinds,
            possessive relations and mental space builders.

These principles cover the typical bound anaphora configurations in
which the quantifier phrase c-commands the pronoun, as well as Roberts's (1987) special cases involving possessive nominals and complements of nominals, the configurations she terms "inverse linking"
(though as noted above, I am not attempting to provide a replacement
for Roberts's extensive analysis of quantifier scope and distributivity
facts; the discussion here is limited to providing a foundation for bound
anaphora).

6.4 REFERENCE POINT ORGANIZATION WITHIN THE
     COMPLEMENT CHAIN

Bound anaphora requires that the semantic pole of the pronoun be included within the special mental space set up by the quantifier construction, and within the dominion of the intended antecedent. The factors
determining the reference point status of putative antecedents are discussed in §6.6 below. Here I focus on the question of which elements
are construed as internal to the mental space set up by the quantifier
construction. The answer is to some extent a matter of degree, and depends upon the notions of connectivity discussed in the previous chapters. Complements of the verb and process-internal modifiers are conceptually included in the representative process instance profiled by the
clause, while process-external modifiers tend to be construed as external to that conception.

   Typical bound anaphora constructions involve pronouns which are
clearly downstream on the complement chain from their antecedents,
as exemplified by (13).

(13)   a.   *Everyone* loves *his* mother.
      b.   I gave *each student* a copy of *his* report.
      c.   *Each one* believes *he*'s the best.

When the pronoun is in a modifier of the clause or verb, its construal depends upon the precise semantic relationship between the
modifier and the rest of the process conception. Process-internal mod-

ifiers, as discussed in Chapter 4, are closely akin to complements in that they elaborate notions which are intrinsic to the process conception. They are conceptually included within the representative relation instance regardless of the linear ordering of the modifier and the rest of the clause. Bound anaphora is therefore possible, as exemplified in (14).

(14)   a.   *Each of the students* keeps a frog in *his* pocket.
        b.   *Each man* has a barbecue pit in *his* backyard.
        c.   In *his* pocket, *each of the students* keeps a frog.
        d.   In *his* backyard, *each man* has a barbecue pit.

Process-external modifiers which provide an assessment of the proposition put forth by the clause are typically separated from the clause by an intonation break. They are conceptually external to the process and therefore not construed as part of the representative process instance profiled by the clause. This is exemplified by the pair in (15). Linear order does not have an observable effect.

(15)   a.   **Each of the men* is a hero, according to *him*.
        b.   **According to *him*, *each of the men* is a hero.

The contrast between process-internal and process-external modifiers is exemplified by (16), which contrasts two different readings of *because*, root and epistemic (Sweetser 1984). The modifier in (16a) is process-internal as it describes the internal cause for the profiled process (see §4.2). Bound anaphora is therefore possible. The modifier in (16b) is process-external, as it provides information which the conceptualizer may use to judge the correctness of the assertion in the first clause. The modifier is external to the representative relation instance profiled by the clause, and so bound anaphora is not possible.

(16)   a.   *Each of those guys* gave *his* life because *he* loved her.
        b.   **Each of those guys* must've loved her, because *he* gave *his* life.

6.5 THE ANTECEDENT AS REFERENCE POINT

In addition to the requirement that the QP set up a mental space which includes the semantic poles of both antecedent and pronoun, there is also a requirement that the intended antecedent be conceptually salient within that mental space so that it can function as a reference point. In this section I discuss two classes of data involving failure to meet this condition: constructions in which backwards bound anaphora is unacceptable, and constructions involving an intended antecedent which is embedded within a modifying phrase.

6.5.1 Backwards Bound Anaphora

Backwards bound anaphora is subject to strict limitations. Sentences such as (17) indicate that backwards bound anaphora is at least sometimes possible. However, as illustrated by (17c–e), it is more constrained than ordinary backwards anaphora.

(17) a.   In *her* desk, *each of the secretaries* keeps a frog.
      b.   In *her* backyard, *each woman* has an apple tree.
      c.   *His mother loves *everyone*.
      d.   *His mother always says that *everyone* would grow up to be President.
      e.   *His* mother loves *John*.
      f.   *His* mother always said that *John* would grow up to be President.

In Chapter 5 I argued that backwards anaphora is distinct from forward anaphora in that linear word order could potentially lead the conceptualizer to misconstrue the pronoun as a reference point in relation to the intended antecedent. Backwards anaphora is nevertheless possible, at least in written English, provided that the antecedent's profile is sufficiently prominent to be correctly construed as a reference point in relation to the pronoun. The additional restrictions on backwards *bound* anaphora can be explained largely in terms of the observation that some of the factors which contribute to the prominence of the antecedent in typical backwards anaphora constructions are unavailable in a bound anaphora construction, with the result that the intended antecedent is insufficiently salient to function as a reference point within the mental space set up by the quantifier construction.[8]

Backwards anaphora involving a nonspecific antecedent is ruled out in constructions parallel to (17c–d), as illustrated by (18a–b) below. This fact has been pointed out as well by Heim (1982), who captures it in terms of her Extended Novelty-Familiarity Condition; essentially, indefinite NPs are ruled out in discourse contexts in which their referents have already been mentioned. Backwards anaphora with a nonspecific antecedent is much better in constructions parallel to (17a–b) above, as in (18c–d) below. (The less-than-complete acceptability of backwards anaphora here can be attributed to an independent factor, discussed in Reinhart [1983:77] and in §4.3.1, which is that sentence-initial modifiers of location indicate a tight focus on the verb and its object[s], to the exclusion of the subject; it is therefore somewhat odd to introduce new information in the subject position. The fact remains that these constructions are noticeably better than [18a–b].)

(18)   a.   *His mother loves a boy.
      b.   *His mother always says that a boy will grow up to be an axe murderer.
      c.   ?In his own home, a man should be safe from government intrusion.
      d.   ?In her purse, a woman usually keeps an assortment of odds and ends.

The role of (non)specificity can be explained in terms of salience. The salience of an entity is partly a matter of its being distinct from the surrounding context. One factor in determining the distinctness of a conception from its surroundings is the extent to which the conceptualizer has independent mental contact with that conception, separate from its role in the immediate context. A nonspecific nominal instance is one with which the conceptualizer has no independent mental contact or awareness. It therefore tends to be insufficiently salient to be construed as a reference point, at least where linear word order contributes to making such a construal less likely.

The profiled nominal instance which serves as the antecedent in a bound anaphora construction is necessarily construed as nonspecific in the sense that it is an arbitrary nominal instance selected as a representative instance within a group of equivalent instances. Backwards bound anaphora (similar to backwards anaphora involving other nonspecific antecedents) is therefore limited to configurations in which prominence asymmetries within the complement chain (i.e., within the grammatical relations hierarchy) motivate construing the intended antecedent as a reference point. When the antecedent corresponds to the trajector (subject) within the clause, its status as figure within the processual profile gives it sufficient prominence to be construed as a reference point in relation to the pronoun.

In Chapter 5 I reported on the study of a corpus of backwards anaphora examples, in which an overwhelming tendency for the antecedent to be the subject of its clause was observed. Backwards anaphora constructions in which the antecedent did not correspond to the subject of its clause made up only 15% of the corpus. In every one of those sentences, the antecedent was either definite or (rarely) indefinite but specific.

We can assume that, if backwards anaphora in a particular configuration is marginal even when a "heavy" nominal (such as a name or
definite descriptive noun phrase) is used as antecedent for the pronoun,
the additional reduction in salience brought about by using a nonspecific nominal (as in a bound anaphora construction) is sufficient to rule
out backwards anaphora altogether. Hence the restriction of backwards
bound anaphora to just those configurations in which the antecedent
is particularly prominent within the clause—configurations parallel
to the prototypical configuration for "plain coreference" backwards
anaphora.[9]

There are additional backwards bound anaphora facts which are
more difficult to account for. As Roberts (1987:96–97) notes, the facts
are complex. She cites the following example pointed out to her by Peter
Sells:

(19)   A plaque indicating the date of *its* incorporation may be found in *every
       American city*.

The analysis as it now stands predicts this sentence to be ungrammatical; I do not as yet have a solution for this problem, though I would
assume that the role of the quantifier phrase as a setting which encompasses the subject is a factor. Exploring this further will require a much
more detailed examination of the role of various elaborative relations
in determining quantifier scope and antecedence possibilities.

Overall, though, it seems that the majority of ungrammatical backwards bound anaphora examples can be explained in terms of insufficient salience of the intended antecedent. Other construction types provide additional evidence for the claim that bound anaphora may be
unacceptable in some configurations because the intended antecedent
is insufficiently salient to serve as a reference point. In §6.5.2 I discuss
several such cases.

6.5.2 Antecedents in Nominal Modifiers

The central observation to be explained in this section is that nominals
within the clause which are not complements of the profiled process
frequently cannot serve as antecedents for bound anaphora. It should
be emphasized that this is a matter of degree, and that there are clear
exceptions to this generalization; speaker judgments are also quite variable (see [10] above). The examples in (20) seem to be generally agreed
to be ungrammatical.

(20) a. ??/*Every lid to *a jar* should fit *it* perfectly.
      b. ??/*Each ad with *a former star athlete* made *him* look pathetic.

Under Reinhart's (1983) c-command analysis, the examples in (20) would be ruled out because the antecedent in each case, being embedded within the nominal modifier, does not c-command the pronoun. Without revisions, Reinhart's analysis offers no explanation for the acceptability of bound anaphora in constructions involving possessors and relative clauses, and predicts incorrectly that the examples in (21) should be ungrammatical.[10]

(21) a. *Each boy*'s mother packed *him* a lunch.
      b. Every woman who marries *a lawyer* divorces *him* soon after.

Some researchers have proposed revisions to the conditions on binding or indexing (e.g., Haïk 1984; May 1985; Roberts 1987; Reinhart 1987) to account for the grammaticality of sentences like those in (21). My analysis resembles the approach taken by Kamp (1984), Heim (1982), and particularly Roberts (1987) in assuming that the critical issue is the ability of the nominal within the modifying phrase to establish an accessible nominal conception within the local context (roughly equivalent to a Discourse Representation or File) set up by the quantifier phrase. The analysis also captures some of the same intuitions as that of Reinhart (1987). Following Heim (1982), Reinhart essentially claims that the critical issue in the donkey constructions is not the "scope" of the putative antecedent, the donkey-NP itself (e.g., *a lawyer* in [21b]), but the scope of the QP. Both the donkey-NP and the pronoun must appear within the scope of the QP, so that the donkey-NP may be interpreted as a variable (which functions similarly to the "arbitrary instance" in my model). Reinhart's analysis is stated ultimately in terms of c-command, however.

The analysis I present depends on the notions **nominal type** and **nominal instance** (Langacker 1991:55–58). The modifiers in the examples in (20) contribute to the type specifications of their head nouns. The analysis I propose for data such as (20) is that, under some circumstances, a nominal within a modifier is construed as merely part of the type description for the head noun, and that it is not construed as establishing an accessible nominal conception in the larger context. To put it another way, the nominal conception profiled by the noun within the modifier is insufficiently salient to function as a reference point.

This is by no means an entirely novel approach. A very similar analysis has been proposed in the literature for anaphora restrictions involving nominal compounds (Sproat and Ward 1987). In English, a nonhead noun in a compound cannot usually antecede a pronoun (Postal 1969), although this is to some extent a matter of degree (Lakoff and Ross 1972). Sproat and Ward (1987) argue that a pronominal antecedent must be salient, and that the nonhead noun in a compound describes a "kind" (equivalent to Langacker's notion of a type) and therefore fails to establish a salient instance conception which can antecede a pronoun.

Sproat and Ward demonstrate that under certain conditions, a nonhead noun in a compound can antecede a pronoun. In particular, anaphora is more likely to be acceptable when the antecedent is definite, for example, a proper name. The examples in (22) are from Sproat and Ward (1987).

(22)   a.   Bruce Springsteen fans would pay any amount of money to hear him in concert.
       b.   A: Are you a long-time "Jeopardy" fan?
            B: Yeah, I used to watch it with my grandfather.

Sproat and Ward's work demonstrates that there is variability in the extent to which a noun within a nominal type specification can be construed as establishing a distinct, salient instance which can then antecede a pronoun (a fact noted also by Lakoff and Ross [1972]). It is particularly significant that independent mental contact with the profiled entity—that is, specificity or definiteness—enhances its ability to be construed as an antecedent. Some possible reasons for this were discussed in the preceding section; I will assume that the critical factor is that independent mental contact contributes to making the nominal instance distinct.

To explain the bound anaphora data, I suggest that nominal constructions vary in the extent to which they portray nominals embedded within them as introducing distinct, salient nominal instances into the surrounding context. As the literature on compound nouns has shown, the nonhead noun in a compound tends to be construed as insufficiently distinct to function as an antecedent. I suggest that modifier phrases which consist of simply a prepositional phrase (e.g., *to a jar, with a stick*) also fail to promote a construal of the nominal profile as distinct, in much the same way that a compound construction promotes a construal of the nonhead nominal as indistinct.

We can assume that the effect is less dramatic in the case of modifying phrases than with compounds. The landmark of the modifying phrase (i.e., the nonhead noun) is a full nominal profiling a grounded instance of the nominal type (it often includes a grounding predication [typically *a*] which codes its relationship to the discourse context). Even a nonspecific nominal may therefore be construed as having its own relationship to the discourse context, independent from the head noun, and this will make it somewhat salient even if the surrounding construction overall does little or nothing to promote its salience. The nonhead noun in a compound is not a full grounded nominal, in fact it may not even profile an instance, but rather designates merely a type description. The nonsalience effects should therefore be more obvious with compounds than with nominals in modifiers; however, I will argue below that a nonsalience effect can be seen in bound anaphora constructions involving modifiers.

We also need to distinguish between kinds of modifying expressions. Relative clauses differ from prepositional phrases in that a relative clause includes a full finite (i.e., independently grounded) clause, which describes a situation or situation type which is independently located relative to the ground (i.e., it has its own tense). Most important, relative clauses seem to be most typically used to encode temporary interactions or situations involving the referent of the head noun, while prepositional phrases are more frequently used to describe relationships which are conceptually intrinsic to the meaning of the head noun. For example, the modifier in the nominal *lid to a jar* elaborates a conception that is intrinsic to the meaning of the noun *lid*—the conception that the lid belongs on some container. In the nominal *mother of the candidate*, the modifier *of the candidate* elaborates a notion which is intrinsic to the meaning of *mother*—the notion of offspring. Paraphrasing such intrinsic relations by means of a relative clause is generally infelicitous unless the relative clause contains additional information; merely adding a copula, as in *lid that is to a jar* or *mother who is of the candidate*, is generally insufficient to motivate the use of the relative clause construction.[11]

In contrast, a typical relative clause, as in *man who owns a donkey*, does not elaborate an intrinsic part of the conception described by the head noun. Rather it adds something entirely new, the notion of a separate relationship or situation in which this person participates. It seems intuitively likely that the nonhead noun inside such a construction would be construed as more separate, and hence more distinct, from the head noun than one which appears in a prepositional phrase construction. Note that I am not claiming that all relative clauses express temporary situations involving the head-noun referent, nor am I claiming that all prepositional phrase constructions which are used to refine the type specification for the head noun are quasi-complement phrases describing notions intrinsic to the head noun. What I am claiming is that there is a general tendency toward a division of labor between the two construction types, and that this reflects a semantic distinction in which prepositional phrase modifiers are conceptually more closely tied to the head noun than relative clauses.[12]

The import of this for bound anaphora is this: A bound anaphoric reading with a nonhead noun as antecedent requires that we have a one-to-one mapping between the replicate instances of the head-noun type invoked by the quantifier expression and the nominal instances described by the nonhead noun. In other words, we have to understand that *every lid to a jar* involves a one-to-one mapping of lids and jars, or that *every picture of a politician* involves a one-to-one mapping of pictures and politicians, so that the replicate construal invoked by the quantifier spreads to the modifier as well. Moreover, the representative nominal instance profiled by the nonhead noun (e.g., the representative jar or politician) must be sufficiently salient within the overall quantifier construction that it is accessible as an antecedent for the pronoun. I will claim that these requirements are mutually incompatible, and that the way in which the nonhead noun receives a replicate construal reduces its fitness to serve as an antecedent.

It appears that constructions which do not involve this kind of replicate construal allow for the nonhead noun to function as an antecedent, as in (23). In each of these examples, the nominal antecedent has an independent relationship to the context set up by the overall sentence, as indicated by its status as an independently grounded nominal (as explained above). The referents of these nominals are therefore accessible as antecedents relative to a following pronoun in just the same way that any ref ent mentioned in the discourse remains accessible relative to material which closely follows it in the linear string.[13]

(23) a.   The mother of *a child found abandoned in a hotel room* went to court this morning to seek custody of *him*.

   b.   The author of *a best-selling book on nutrition* will be autographing copies of *it* this afternoon at the university bookstore.

   c.   The mother of *a hyperactive child* has to keep *him* from eating sugar.

   d.   The lid to *a jar* should fit *it* perfectly.

Bound anaphora constructions differ in the nature of the connection of the nonhead noun to the surrounding context. To get a bound anaphoric reading involving an antecedent within a nominal modifier, we have to have a replicate construal mediated through the head noun. The nonhead noun (the antecedent) can have no independent relationship to the context whatsoever. Its construal as replicate is totally dependent on its relationship to the head noun and its role as part of the type description for the nominal concept profiled by the head noun. To attempt to access this nominal through the larger discourse context would require imposing a coreferent reading rather than a bound reading. Since this nominal conception's status within the replicate conception is mediated through its role as a type descriptor for the head noun, the only way in which it could be made salient would be if its role in that type description promoted construing it as salient. But I have argued above that plain prepositional phrase modifiers do little or nothing to establish the nonhead noun as salient.

In a sense, we arrive at an impasse. The intended antecedent must be conceptually contained entirely within the type conception for the head noun to which it is attached; otherwise, the necessary replicate construal will be unavailable. It is not possible to "bypass" the type conception and access this nominal conception as an independent entity, relying solely on its having been recently mentioned in the discourse (as in [23] above), as this would result in a coreferent, rather than bound, reading. And yet the nominal's role in the type description (the modifier construction) does little to promote its salience, making it unlikely that it will be judged sufficiently accessible to serve as antecedent for a pronoun. This explains data such as (24a–c). It should be emphasized that the difficulty in these constructions is the nonsalience of the intended antecedent, a factor which is very much a matter of degree; it is therefore to be expected that there will be variability in speaker judgments, as well as noticeable effects from small changes in word choice or discourse context. Both of these effects have been found in elicitation of judgments. Counterexamples do exist, such as (24d) (which was pointed out by a reviewer); here, although the construction involves a plain prepositional phrase modifier, the construction describes a relationship which is entirely extrinsic to the head noun—the conception of ownership. The bound anaphoric reading is acceptable, a fact which I would attribute to the nature of the relation being described rather than to the prepositional phrase construction itself.

(24)   a.   *Each picture of *a rock star* made *him* look diseased.
       b.   *Every lid to *a jar* should fit *it* perfectly.
       c.   ??Every novel about *a former president* portrays *him* as sleazy.
       d.   Every man with *a donkey* beats *it*.

The analysis predicts that bound anaphora should be more uniformly acceptable if the intended antecedent is embedded within a modifying relation which promotes its construal as distinct, such as a relative clause. This is of course the case, as attested by the well-known "donkey" constructions, exemplified in (25).[14] While speaker judgments for constructions like (24) are rather variable, it is clear that the sentences in (25) are far more universally accepted.

(25)   a.   Every man who owns *a donkey* feeds *it*.
       b.   Each of the women who married *a lawyer* divorced *him* within five
            years.
       c.   Everyone who brought *a stereo* had to insure *it*.

My analysis of "donkey" sentences bears a notable resemblance to that in Kamp (1984) and also that proposed in Heim (1990) in its claim that the relative clause makes salient a relationship between the head of the relative clause and the entity which functions as the antecedent for the pronoun. Heim (1990) describes the pronoun as being interpreted in terms of a function which has been made salient by the relative clause; for example, "it" in (25a) is interpreted as referring to "the donkey that he owns." My analysis, however, focuses on the role of conceptual salience, and degrees of salience, as a factor determining the availability of a bound-anaphoric reading; both Heim and Kamp acknowledge that some notion of salience may play a role, but they do not develop this in detail.

This analysis suggests a possible explanation for the relatively greater acceptability of the constructions which Roberts (1987) terms inverse linking constructions, such as in (10) above, repeated here. These tend to be at least marginally more acceptable than the constructions in which the quantifier is attached to the head noun, while the antecedent is contained in a modifying phrase. It seems intuitively clear that the quantifier has a quasi-emphatic effect, focusing attention on the nominal to which it is attached; the quantifier both picks out a representative instance of the nominal conception and makes that nominal the starting point from which the replicate construal spreads to the rest of the clause. Despite the difficulties in inducing the spread of a replicate construal from a noun that is not an argument of the verb (as discussed above), the increased salience of the nominal which is "put into focus" by the quantifier may contribute substantially to making a bound anaphoric reading available.

(10) a. ✓3 ?3 *3 The president of *each country* spoke about *its* economic problems.

b. ✓7 ?2 The bottom of *each statue* is engraved with *its* serial number.

c. ✓5 ?2 *2 The cover of *each volume* is attached to *it* with a special glue.

d. ✓7 ?2 The phone number for *each faculty member* is written just below *his* name.

e. ✓6 *3 *The chair* of each committee presented *his* concerns.

The analysis presented here also makes a clear prediction with respect to one additional construction type, which involves possessive relations. Under Langacker's (1991:168–69) analysis of possessive constructions, the possessor of a noun is not part of the type description for that noun; rather it profiles an independent and separate nominal instance through which the conceptualizer can make mental contact with the instance profiled by the head noun (as in an expression such as *the boy's knife*, in which the conceptualizer makes mental contact with or conceptually "picks out" the intended instance of *knife* through its association with the nominal instance profiled by *the boy*). The nominal instance profiled by a possessor should therefore be construed as sufficiently distinct from the head noun to function as an antecedent for a pronoun. This prediction is borne out by the examples in (26), which exemplify a construction type which is problematic for Reinhart's (1983) c-command analysis (though May [1985], Roberts [1987], and Reinhart [1987] capture these facts through modifications of the scope-indexing mechanisms and/or the definition of c-command).

(26) a. *Everyone's* mother loves *him*.
b. *Each woman's* fiancé left *her* at the altar.

6.6 SUMMARY

The restrictions on bound anaphora are explained here in terms of the requirement that the pronoun and antecedent (i.e., their respective semantic poles) be contained within the mental space set up by a quantifier construction, and the further requirement that the antecedent be sufficiently salient within that mental space to function as a reference point. These requirements arise automatically from the general anaphora principles developed in this work, combined with Langacker's (1991) analysis of quantifier semantics. Bound anaphora is therefore not fundamentally distinct from ordinary coreference, but is rather just another manifestation of the more general principles of pronominal anaphora.

REFLEXIVES

7.1 REFLEXIVES AND PRONOUNS

Traditional analyses of anaphora constraints have focused on explaining the more-or-less complementary distribution of reflexive and nonreflexive pronouns (which I will term, respectively, "reflexives" and "pronouns"). A significant complicating factor in analyzing reflexives is that they are used in at least three seemingly distinct ways: as markers of coreference among arguments (as in [1a]), as emphatic markers (as in [1b]), and as logophoric or POV indicators (as in [1c]).

(1) a. John saw himself.
     b. John himself knows I'm right.
     c. He sat down at the desk and opened the drawers. In the top right-hand one was an envelope addressed to himself. (David Lodge, *Changing Places*, p. 62); cited by Zribi-Hertz [1989])

Beginning with Lees and Klima's (1963) analysis, most generative analyses until recently focused on defining the structural constraints governing the use of reflexives in examples like (1a). Though the logophoric use of reflexives had long been noted (Ross 1970; Cantrall 1974; Kuno 1987), the relationship between these different uses of the reflexive has only recently become a central focus. Most of the research in this area has focused on defining the appropriate domains of application for the syntactic constraints which presumably govern examples like (1a) and the discourse rules governing examples like (1c) (e.g., Zribi-Hertz 1989; Pollard and Sag 1992, 1993; Reinhart and Reuland 1991, 1993).

In this chapter I offer an analysis of reflexives in English in terms of a network of constructional schemas organized around two distinct, but closely related, meanings of the reflexive, which may be considered prototypes (see Lakoff 1987; Taylor 1989; Deane 1992 for discussion of grammatical prototypes). I argue that the range of variation found in the uses of the reflexive in English reflects the development of an inventory of constructional schemas which retain, to varying degrees, the central semantic properties of one or both of the prototypical values.

The analysis proposed here closely resembles that of Deane (1992). Though independently developed, both analyses posit that the various reflexive constructions in English have developed from a central, prototypical construction in which the reflexive marks coreference between co-arguments of a single verb. The analyses differ primarily in the details, such as the application of the analysis to specific construction types, and the proposal presented here for semantically differentiating reflexives from nonreflexive pronouns.

7.2 PROTOTYPICAL VALUES OF THE REFLEXIVE

Several distinct themes recur in the analysis of reflexives. Various researchers have pointed out the significance of POV (Cantrall 1974; Kuno 1987; Zribi-Hertz 1989, 1994; Pollard and Sag 1992, 1993; Deane 1992; van Hoek 1992, 1995), emphasis or contrast (Reinhart and Reuland 1993; Baker 1995), and coreference between verbal arguments (e.g., Faltz 1985; Williams 1987, 1994; Pollard and Sag 1992, 1993; Dalrymple 1993; Kemmer 1993; Reinhart and Reuland 1991, 1993; Williams 1994). I suggest that the ubiquity of these notions arises from their presence in one or both of the two central values for the reflexive marker.

The reflexive marker is frequently used as an emphatic marker, a usage which historically preceded its use as a marker of coreference among verbal co-arguments (Faltz 1985; Baker 1995). The emphatic use is exemplified in (2). Some of the characteristics of the construction type in (2) are listed in (3).

(2)   a.   Sally herself knows she needs a new job.
       b.   I myself have often eaten gefilte fish.

(3)   i.   Proximity: the reflexive marker occurs directly adjacent (at the phonological pole) to a nominal with which it corresponds (at the semantic pole).
       ii.   Prominence: the antecedent is the most prominent nominal in relationship to the reflexive (i.e., the most prominent reference point).
      iii.   Contrast: there is an implied contrast between the entity desig-

nated by the reflexive and some (typically unspecified) set of possible entities (Planck 1979; Baker 1995).

This construction may have the status of a prototype. It occurs frequently, so it is highly entrenched, and it has several characteristics in common with other reflexive constructions which may be viewed as extensions from it. Although the use of the reflexive to mark coreference among verbal arguments is more commonly considered prototypical, as discussed below, there is no reason that the network of schemas for the reflexive marker should be organized around only one prototype. I will therefore tentatively identify the emphatic as a secondary or lesser prototype.

The most typical use of the reflexive marker (as determined by informal counts of tokens from texts, and by examples of usage elicited from native speakers) is that exemplified in (4), in which the reflexive codes a landmark of the verb which corresponds with the trajector.

(4) a.   John cut himself.
     b.   Sally saw herself.

This construction codes the configuration which Faltz (1985:3) uses to identify the **primary reflexive strategy** in a language. The primary reflexive strategy is the marking used in a situation in which the agent or experiencer argument of a two-place predicate corefers with the patient argument of that predicate (the situation type which Faltz terms the **archetypal reflexive context**), and which differentiates that configuration from one in which the agent or experiencer and patient do not corefer. Kemmer (1993:43) considers this situation type to be the "**semantic prototype** that forms the basis of the grammatical category of reflexive in human languages" and notes that cross-linguistically, if a language has a means for specifically marking coreference of participants in any situation type, this particular situation type will also be marked for coreference. Deane (1992) also proposes a characterization of the prototypical reflexive construction for English, in which an agentive subject corresponds with a nominal argument which codes a patient within the same clause. A number of researchers who do not use the term 'prototype' also characterize the central or primary reflexive configuration as one in which two arguments of the same verb corefer (e.g., Dalrymple 1993; Pollard and Sag 1992; Reinhart and Reuland 1991, 1993; Williams 1994). We can therefore assume there is broad agreement on at least this one point. I will henceforth refer to the schema which describes this construction as the "prototypical reflexive," and call the usage exemplified in (2) "the emphatic."

One point of terminology should be clarified here. The prototypical reflexive *construction* profiles a process with an agent and patient, which correspond. The reflexive pronoun itself profiles just one nominal entity, but it includes as an unprofiled part of its base the conception of a processual relation in which the landmark corresponds with the trajector. The reflexive pronoun itself profiles the landmark in that relation.

The semantic pole of the prototypical reflexive construction has the characteristics in (5), of which the first two closely resemble the characteristics of the emphatic marker, while the third arises from the nature of the event conception and the two roles taken by the single participant in it.

(5)   i.   Proximity: The antecedent and reflexive code arguments of the same verb (Pollard and Sag 1992; Dalrymple 1993; Reinhart and Reuland 1991, 1993; Williams 1987, 1994); they are thus strongly interconnected by virtue of directly elaborating the same profiled relation.

        ii. Prominence: The antecedent is the most prominent nominal in relationship to the reflexive (i.e., the most prominent reference point).

        iii. Subjectified view of the referent: The participant coded by the reflexive is "viewed" semisubjectively by the agent; that is, the agent cannot perceive him / herself as objectively as another person, and therefore perceives the recipient of the action differently than in an ordinary event involving two distinct participants.

From the first two properties listed in (5), it seems reasonable to view the reflexive prototype construction as a natural extension from the emphatic construction (Faltz 1985; Baker 1995:96). In both, the antecedent is highly prominent. Both also involve a notion of proximity, though in the prototypical reflexive construction, semantic proximity as defined by co-argument status replaces the requirement of linear adjacency found with the emphatic reflexive. This particular instantiation of semantic proximity—interconnection by participation in a linking relation—is carried out throughout most of the schemas in the network, in which the antecedent and reflexive consistently correspond to the "head" and "tail" of an interconnecting relation (though not always one that is explicitly coded by a verb).

Particularly significant is the third characteristic, the sense of a semisubjective view of the participant coded by the reflexive. As noted, a person acting on himself does not perceive the object of his action in the same way that he could perceive another person. Rather, he perceives himself semisubjectively: he has some objective perception of himself (in the sense of Langacker [1985]; see §2.3.2), but the roles of viewer and viewed are not entirely distinct. The conception of a semisubjective view of the reflexive referent arises because an agent is typically conceived as animate and aware of his actions, that is, as a viewer. As noted by Deane (1992), the implicit POV intrinsic to the reflexive prototype motivates the use of the reflexive marker as a POV marker in other contexts and construction types, and accounts for the pervasive association of reflexive marking with the notion of POV—an association which remains mysterious if we assume that the prototypical reflexive construction is to be accounted for purely in terms of structural relations or principles of argument structure.

The description of the relevant viewing relation requires some refinement, however, in order to differentiate reflexives from (nonreflexive) pronouns. The participant coded as the reflexive is construed semisubjectively by the agent (by virtue of their being the same person), and this fact is the basis for the extension of the reflexive into the domain of logophoricity. But I have claimed earlier in this work (see §2.3.2) that the referent of a (nonreflexive) pronoun is also construed semisubjectively. First- and second-person pronouns code discourse participants, that is, abstract viewers of the conception placed onstage by the speaker. Third-person pronouns code entities which are established within the offstage region, the context shared by speaker and addressee. The referent of a pronoun is therefore construed semisubjectively inasmuch as the speaker and addressee understand the pronoun in terms of the offstage, subjective conception of the referent. It appears that the pronoun and the reflexive both incorporate the notion of semisubjective viewing, making them appear indistinguishable.

The critical distinction is in the notion of onstage versus offstage perspective. The referent of the pronoun is viewed semisubjectively *from the offstage region*. That is, the discourse participants view the referent semisubjectively, since it is part of their shared background knowledge. The referent of the reflexive, in contrast, is viewed semisubjectively *within the onstage region*. That is, some participant in the scene views him/herself semisubjectively. The semisubjective perception of the referent is part of the agent's experience, part of the event conception being put onstage rather than just part of the experience of the speaker and addressee. This viewing relation is maintained throughout most of the extensions from the reflexive prototype.

This distinction can be seen clearly in sentences such as (6) and (7), from Cantrall (1974).

(6)   I can understand a father wanting his daughter to be like himself but I can't understand that ugly brute wanting his daughter to be like him.

In (6), the reflexive *himself* invokes the conception of the father as viewed from his own point of view; the pronoun *him* at the end of the sentence invokes the conception "him as I see him."

Cantrall also points out the following contrast (slightly paraphrased to remove a distractor):[1]

(7)   a.   The adults in the picture are facing away from us, with the children behind them.
       b.   The adults in the picture are facing away from us, with the children behind themselves.

Cantrall points out that, given the appropriate context, these two sentences have very different meanings. If they are applied as descriptions of a photograph, in which the adults have their backs turned to the camera, then (7a) could mean that the children are located "behind the adults" from the viewpoint of the speaker—that is, they are farther away from the camera. (7b) can mean only that the children were "behind the adults" from the adults' POV—closer to the camera. The distinction is one of perspective from offstage or from onstage. (7a) can also be understood to mean the children are behind the women's backs (closer to the camera), but this ambiguity can be attributed to the fact that people have an inherent front/back orientation. The offstage viewer can use *behind* to mean either "more distant from the viewer" or "behind as calculated relative to the inherent back of the landmark."

Cantrall (1974:147) also points out that an equivalent construction involving an inanimate entity is anomalous, providing further evidence that the notion of POV is critical:

(8)   a.   The house in the picture is facing away from us, with an elm tree behind it.[2]
       b.   *The house in the picture is facing away from us, with an elm tree behind itself.

The sentences in (9) exemplify the same principle.

(9)   a.   I'm finally starting to think about me, and I've decided that I like me.
       b.   You need to quit taking care of everyone else and take care of you for a change.

By using a pronoun, the speaker portrays the referent as semi-subjectively viewed from the offstage perspective but, critically, portrays the referent as more objectively viewed, *from the point of view of the trajector.* If the landmark were semisubjectively viewed from within the onstage region, a reflexive would be used; the contrast between the expected reflexive and the actual pronoun highlights the speaker's intended portrayal of the referent. The implication of (9a) is that the trajector of *like* perceives "me" objectively, as if she could stand outside herself and assess herself in the same way as she could assess another person. In (9b) the implication is that the addressee should show himself the same consideration that he presumably shows other people.

Ward (1983) notes that these constructions are most commonly found in contexts involving multiple parallel statements, such as (10).

(10) BJ: If you cut into a healthy body, you're going to hate your-
                   self for the rest of your life.
      Hawkeye: I *already* hate myself. I hate *me*; I hate *you*; and most of all, I
                   hate *this war*. (From "MASH"; cited by Ward [1983])

Ward analyzes these as constructions in which an open proposition is set up in the discourse and serves as background for a series of parallel statements. The interesting point for our purposes is that these constructions (not all of which require parallelism) also invoke a sense that the speaker or addressee perceives himself as he would look at another person, that is, more objectively than would be indicated by a reflexive.[3]

The notion of semisubjective construal from an onstage vantage point is extended into the logophoric use of the reflexive, as in (11). The antecedent for such a reflexive is the conception of a character in the narrative who serves as a POV.

(11) Carmen understood. Between her first lover and herself, it was no
      longer tennis; it was war. (Rita Mae Brown, *Sudden Death*, p. 58)

This construction differs from the prototype in several ways, making it an extension from the prototype rather than an instantiation of it. Most obviously, the antecedent does not correspond to the subject of its clause, and the reflexive does not correspond to the object. In terms of perspective taking, it again differs somewhat from the prototype. In the reflexive prototype construction, the character who views himself from an onstage perspective is an agent within the profiled clause that is the focus of the speaker and addressee's attention (i.e., squarely onstage). In the logophoric extension exemplified by (11), the conceived

POV is a character who may not play a role within the profiled clause, but is instead understood to be the discourse topic, as well as the POV through whose eyes the conception is filtered. To put it another way, the clause does not profile the conceived actions of an agent/POV, as in the reflexive prototype, but instead is construed as a description of the topic/POV's thoughts or perceptions. The POV may be considered to be onstage only if we extend the onstage notion to mean "within the story world (as opposed to the real-world discourse context)" rather than just "within the immediate scope of attention delimited by the clausal profile" (see §7.6.2).

7.3 THE SCHEMATIC REFLEXIVE CONFIGURATIONS

The major patterns of usage for reflexive markers are analyzed in terms of an inventory of constructional schemas extended from the central construction types described in the preceding section. We can assume that there is also a single superschema which is schematic for all of the conventional reflexive constructions in English. Such a schema must be nonspecific enough to generalize over both the prototypical reflexive and the emphatic reflexive, among others. It must specify only that the profile of the reflexive marker corresponds with a reference point which is in some abstract sense the "closest" either by virtue of linear adjacency or prominence (i.e., the reference point stands out as the most-prominent nominal conception in the local context, and less-prominent conceptions are disregarded, leaving this one as the "adjacent" reference point). There is presumably also a sense that that reference point is onstage, that is, conceived as a participant in the conception to which speaker and addressee are attending rather than being merely part of the offstage background context (this aspect of the reflexive's meaning may become rather attenuated in constructions referring to the speaker or addressee, as in *people like yourself*; see discussion below).[4]

In accordance with general principles of CG, I assume that such a superschema does little if any work in sanctioning the use of a reflexive marker in a particular context (see Langacker 1987a:381, 1988b). I therefore turn to the specific inventory of constructional schemas, in which the various characteristics of the emphatic reflexive and the prototypical reflexive (prominence, conceptual adjacency, POV) recur to varying degrees. In the discussion below, I will not attempt to provide an exhaustive list of all the constructional schemas for the use of the reflexive in English (there are no doubt hundreds of highly specific schemas, some representing individual constructions, with a great deal of variation between speakers). Rather I will focus on only the more central nodes in the network. Constraints on distribution are explained in terms of the interaction of schemas, discussed in §7.7.

7.4 EXTENSION FROM THE EMPHATIC REFLEXIVE

As exemplified by (12), there is an extension from the emphatic reflexive in which the emphatic marker follows the predicate rather than directly following its antecedent.

(12) a. John wants to talk to her himself.
    b. You can do that yourself.

The emphatic reflexives invoke the notion of contrast between the antecedent of the reflexive and other entities (Planck 1979; Baker 1995). This implies that the emphatic invokes, as part of its base, the conception of a background which includes a number of other nominal conceptions against which the profile of the antecedent stands out. In actual usage, it has been observed that the emphatic tends to appear in contexts in which the antecedent contrasts with other nominal conceptions (Ariel 1990).

    This extension from the emphatic reflexive construction described above maintains all of the core characteristics of the emphatic, though the notion of adjacency is instantiated in a somewhat more abstract way than linear adjacency. In the agentive emphatic construction exemplified in (12) above, the reflexive is included in a modifier of the process and hence is conceptually juxtaposed against the most prominent nominal within the processual profile, the subject (see §4.2.1).

7.5 NEAR EXTENSIONS FROM THE REFLEXIVE PROTOTYPE

Two other constructions may be considered very close extensions from the prototype in the sense that the reflexive and its antecedent correspond to co-arguments of the same verb. They differ from the prototype in the roles of the nominals: The antecedent does not correspond to the trajector, and/or the reflexive does not correspond to the primary landmark (i.e., the direct object). The former is exemplified by (13).

(13) a. I talked to Bill about himself.
    b. John told Sally about herself.

The construction exemplified by (13a) may not be fully entrenched for all speakers, as there is disagreement on the acceptability of these sentences (Kuno 1987).[5] The acceptability of these constructions depends on the conception that the participant coded as primary landmark of the process is also a cognizer, with awareness of himself, and that there is therefore a viewing relation (or construal relation) connecting the antecedent and the profile of the reflexive. Evidence for this is that, when the reflexive codes the participant that would be conceived as a viewer, and the antecedent codes the object of viewing, the construction is either very questionable or entirely unacceptable (as first pointed out by Kuno [1987]). This is illustrated by the examples in (14).

(14)   a. ??I'm tired of people explaining me to myself.
       b. *Mary discussed John with himself.
       c. *Mary talked about John to himself.

(14a) is closer to acceptable than (14b–c); some speakers accept it. The partial acceptability of (14a) may be due to the correspondence between the profile of the reflexive and the speaker's viewpoint, as well as with the subject of the matrix clause.

Jackendoff (1972) addresses data similar to (14) in terms of the thematic hierarchy Agent > Location, Source, Goal > Theme, developed by Gruber (1965). He argues for the principle that a reflexive cannot thematically outrank its antecedent (Dalrymple [1993] and Williams [1987, 1994] make similar proposals). The primary landmark in the acceptable sentences above would be considered to be the Goal (i.e., the person addressed), and the reflexive—describing what is talked about—the Theme. In the unacceptable sentences, the primary landmark is the Theme, and the reflexive codes the Goal. In the terms of the analysis presented here, the difficulty with these constructions is specifically that the reflexive codes the POV and the antecedent, the object of viewing. The construction therefore fails to preserve a significant part of the prototypical reflexive configuration.

The other near extension from the prototype is the configuration in which the antecedent is the subject of the clause, but the reflexive corresponds to a secondary landmark rather than the primary landmark. The examples in (15) illustrate this.

(15)   a.   I talked to John about myself.
       b.   Mary bought a book for herself.
       c.   Sam wrote a letter to himself.

As the most prominent nominal in the relation, the subject can be construed as the most salient reference point within the processual relation that includes the reflexive, though it is not the closest in terms of linear order. (The distinction between primary reference point status and linear proximity is discussed in relation to discourse-level coreference in §5.6.1.)

Not all constructions in which the object of a preposition corresponds to the subject of the clause are acceptable with a reflexive marker. For some speakers, the object of a preposition will be coded as a reflexive (rather than a nonreflexive pronoun) only if it is construed as elaborating a participant in the energetic interaction profiled by the verb; if it describes part of the setting, so that there is no energetic connection linking the antecedent and the anaphor, a pronoun will be used instead. For some speakers, therefore, there is a subtle distinction between the sentences in (16).

(16) a. *John* put the books under *him*.
       b. John put the books under himself.

In some dialects, the sentence in (16a) implies merely that John stored the books somewhere underneath him—perhaps beneath his chair. The most likely interpretation for (16b), for some speakers, is that John sat on the books, using them to boost himself up, or else sat directly on them in order to conceal them. Kuno (1987) discusses this observation in some detail, listing several similar pairs of sentences.

(17) a. *John* pulled the blanket over *him*.
       b. John pulled the blanket over himself.
       c. *John* hid the book behind *him*.
       d. John hid the book behind himself.
       e. *John* pulled Mary toward *him*.
       f. John pulled Mary toward himself.

The sentences involving reflexives imply that the action has a greater effect on the referent corresponding to the object of the preposition than do the sentences with nonreflexive pronouns. For instance, in (17d) the implication is that the book is physically in contact with John, whereas (17c) does not have such an implication. (17f) implies that John is somehow more involved in the action (perhaps emotionally) than in (17e).

The reflexive constructions resemble the prototype in two significant ways. First, the referent of the reflexive is more fully included in the processual conception, as the reflexive referent is conceived as a participant in the action rather than merely part of the setting (as in the pronominal examples).[6] Second, the agent presumably has greater self-awareness, as suggested by Cantrall (1974) and Kuno (1987); that is, it is part of the agent's intention that the action have an effect on him. The reflexive constructions again describe a conception which includes an onstage referent's semisubjective view of himself.

7.5.1 Nonprocessual Relations

A somewhat more distant set of extensions from the prototype involves constructions in which the landmark of a nonprocessual relation corresponds with the trajector of that relation, and is coded by a reflexive marker. This extension does not preserve the notion of a viewing relationship, but it includes a profiled interconnecting relation and the correspondence between trajector and landmark. These constructions tend to have idiomatic meanings, and are no doubt represented by highly specific schemas (e.g., *X in itself, X by itself*). (18) gives two examples.

(18)   a.   This in itself is not a big deal.
       b.   That book by itself is worth millions.

7.6 POV REFLEXIVES

The prototypical reflexive configuration includes the conception that the referent of the reflexive views himself, a situation which I have characterized as semisubjective perception from within the onstage region. Most of the extensions from the prototype preserve this notion. In some cases, the conceived viewing relation is the only interconnecting relation between the antecedent—the POV—and the reflexive, as there is no verb profiling the interaction.

7.6.1 Picture Nouns

So-called picture-noun noun phrases, as in (19), may include a reflexive marker whose profile is not connected with its antecedent by any profiled relation, but is connected to it by an implicit viewing relation (Cantrall [1974], Kuno [1987], Deane [1992], and Reinhart and Reuland [1991] also identify these constructions as involving logophoric reflexives, though this is not the traditional analysis within generative syntax.)

(19) a.   John recently read a book about himself.
      b.   Mary found a picture of herself in the paper.

The use of the reflexive marker in constructions of this type is sanctioned when the referent can be construed as perceiving the object named by the picture-noun phrase and perceiving that it is an image or description of himself, the perceiver. While some verbs (such as *look*) may possibly make the perceptual relation more salient by explicitly invoking perception or a related notion, the verb need not be a verb of perception, as evidenced by (20). The viewer's cognizance is implied as part of the typical experience of painting a picture, receiving a book, and so on.

(20) a.   Mary painted a portrait of herself.
      b.   Ralph sent Sally a book about herself.

Cantrall (1974) demonstrates that when the referent of the reflexive cannot be construed as perceiving the picture (or story, etc.), the sentence is ungrammatical. The following examples are from Cantrall (1974:107):

(21) a.   Funny stories about himself won't restore Tom to good humor.
      b.   *Funny stories about himself won't restore Tom to life.
      c.   The picture of himself that hangs in Nixon's study is quite dignified looking.
      d.   *The picture of himself that hangs in Lincoln's study is quite dignified looking.

In (21a–b), there is a difference between the situation in which Tom would be able to hear the stories and the situation in which he would not. (21c) was acceptable in 1974, when Nixon was alive and could potentially see the picture. (21c) and (21d) would both be acceptable under readings in which the president in question had painted the portrait himself, and thus could be understood to have the role of agent in relation to the picture.

Kuno (1987:179) captures the same generalization in his Awareness Condition on Picture Noun Reflexives, which he supports with a vast range of data, including the contrasts in (22–23).[7]

(22) a.   John was asked about all that gossip about himself.
      b.   *John was oblivious to all that gossip about himself.
      c.   *John* was oblivious to all that gossip about *him*.

(23) a.   Ironically, Mary owed her success partly to that scandalous rumor about herself that was going around.

    b. *Ironically, the book owed its success partly to that scandalous rumor about itself that was going around.

Another construction instantiating the POV reflexive schema is the configuration in which the possessor of a nominal antecedes a reflexive within a picture-noun phrase, as in (24).

(24)   a. *Sally*'s story about *herself*
       b. *John*'s picture of *himself*

The possessor in (24a) is an agent (the one who told the story), therefore automatically construed as a cognizer of the story. The relationship in (24b) is more ambiguous—John may be merely the possessor of the picture. A possessor is typically animate, and part of the typical possessive relation is that the possessor is aware of the possessum, has access to it, and potentially can view it. We can assume therefore that possessive constructions imply a viewing relation between the possessor and the possessum, which would make these constructions instantiations of the schema for viewpoint reflexives. It is not required that the conceptualizer have a strong sense of "empathy" with the possessor (in Kuno's [1987] sense of "empathy"); all that would be required to instantiate the viewpoint reflexive schema is that the conceptualizer recognize that the configuration involves a potential viewing relationship between the possessor and the picture noun.[8]

Jackendoff (1992) analyzes an interesting set of data which, in the present model, would be analyzed in terms of mental spaces. He points out that although a statue or other representation of a person can be referred to via the person's name, as in (25), there are tight restrictions on this usage when reflexives are involved, as in (26).

(25)   Ringo is the one in the middle [pointing to a set of wax figures of the Beatles].

(26)   The three surviving Beatles were touring the wax museum when there was a sudden earthquake, and Ringo fell on himself.

(26) can only mean that the real Ringo fell on the statue of Ringo, not that the statue toppled over onto the real person. A similar contrast is found in (27), also Jackendoff's (27) (adapted from Fauconnier 1985). The situation described by (27a) could be that of Richard Nixon going to see the opera *Nixon in China*. (27a) would mean that the real Nixon listened to the actor singing. (27b), intended to mean that the actor sang a special cadenza to the real Nixon, is unacceptable.

(27) a.   Nixon listened to himself singing to Mao.
      b.   *Nixon sang a special cadenza to himself.

Jackendoff analyzes these examples with his model of conceptual structure, which in some ways resembles the model developed here, although he does not attempt to provide a complete account of the c-
command constraints on coreference in terms of conceptual structure.
Essentially, he claims that the use of *Ringo* to mean "statue of Ringo"
and *Nixon* to mean "actor playing Nixon" sets up a conceptual structure
in which the notion of the real person is embedded as a sort of modifier
attached to the conception of the statue or actor; it does not participate
directly in the larger conceptual structure (e.g., the real Ringo isn't
the one that fell over, the real Nixon isn't singing, etc.) and so cannot
bind the reflexive within conceptual structure. His analysis draws on
a conceptual version of c-command in which the intended conceptual
antecedent cannot bind the reflexive, because it is contained in a modifier.

In the terms of my model, Jackendoff's data point to the importance of direct conceptual interconnection in the use of reflexives. It is
interesting to note that all of the grammatical examples involve configurations in which a person views a representation of himself—a statue,
an actor playing himself, and so on. All therefore incorporate the kind of
viewing relationship described here as a key component in the reflexive
prototype, as well as direct conceptual connectivity between the nominal entity named by the antecedent and the conception coded as the
reflexive. (26) above, *Ringo fell on himself*, means something like "Ringo
fell on (what he perceived as a representation of) himself." (27a) means
roughly "Nixon listened to (what he recognized as a portrayal of)
himself." The referent's perception of the image or performance as a
representation of himself activates the schema for POV-anteceded reflexives.

No special theoretical machinery is needed to explain the unacceptability of examples such as (27b), or the reading of (26) in which the
statue fell on the real Ringo. Each lacks the essential component of a
viewing relationship in which the POV perceives itself semisubjectively.
The acceptable examples all involve a kind of semisubjective self-
perception. Each picture, statue, actor, and so on is perceived objectively, but the viewer's conception that this is, in some sense, a portrayal
of his own self is crucially dependent on self-conception, which is by
nature semisubjective.

A similar analysis accounts for (28), a sentence type pointed out by Postal (1971) and also discussed by Jackendoff (1992).

(28)   a. ?*John worries himself.
       b.   John deliberately frightened himself.

Grimshaw (1990) explains this distinction in terms of **type-shifting** with respect to the subject of (28a). She claims that the subject in (28a) has been type-shifted, meaning that it does not refer to John per se but to properties of John or things that John does. She then proposes a constraint to the effect that an anaphor cannot be bound by a type-shifted antecedent. Jackendoff (1992) re-states this analysis in terms of his conceptual structure account of "statue" nouns, noting that this construction type is conceptually parallel to the impossible binding in sentences like (27b).

In the terms of my model, (28a) is deviant in that the POV is coded as landmark, while the trajector, *John*, codes the object of perception. The construction is in this respect parallel to (14b–c), discussed above. To the extent that (28a) is at all acceptable, it is presumably because correspondence between trajector and landmark of a verb partially satisfies the specifications of the reflexive prototype schema despite the incompatibility with respect to POV. (28b) has no POV conflict, as the subject is conceived as an agent deliberately acting upon himself, hence viewing himself.

7.6.2 Logophoric Reflexives in Written Narrative

A more distant extension from the prototype, found in written English, is represented by reflexives whose antecedent is a conceived POV in a narrative. The reflexive is possible if the text is construed as representing the thoughts or perceptions of one of the characters in a narrative (as in the "free indirect" narrative style) (Kuno 1987; Zribi-Hertz 1989; Pollard and Sag 1983, 1992). These constructions do not require that the antecedent and the reflexive be contained within the same sentence (though they may be). Zribi-Hertz gives a large number of examples from texts, including (29a–b).

(29)   a.   But aside from this, she was keenly conscious of the way in which such an estrangement would react on herself. (Edith Wharton, *The House of Mirth*, 1905:129)

b. And that was exactly it, he thought. He really didn't care too
    much what happened to himself. (Patricia Highsmith, *The Glass
    Cell*, 1973:79)

Zribi-Hertz (1989) gives the following examples of constructions in
which the reflexive is not sanctioned because it is contained within an
objectively-construed clause.

(30) a. He sat staring ahead of him with bright blue eyes that seemed a
          little screwed up, as if the glare of the East were still in them; and
          puckered at the corners as if the dust were still in them. Some
          thought had struck him [*himself] that made what the others were
          saying of no interest to him [*himself]. (Woolf, *The Years*, p. 6)
      b. She was not pretty, no, her size was against her [*herself]. (Vir-
          ginia Woolf, *The Years* p. 46)

In both of these examples, the clause containing the reflexive is conceived as objectively viewed, not viewed from the perspective of the
putative antecedent for the reflexive. In (30a), this is particularly clear,
as the description of the protagonist's appearance ("bright blue eyes
that seemed a little screwed up . . . and puckered at the corners". . .)
makes it obvious that we are looking at the protagonist from an outside
(narrator's) perspective. (30b) also is most easily read as an outside,
narrator's description of the character's appearance.

The claim that discourse-anteceded reflexives depend on the notion
of POV is not entirely uncontroversial. Baker (1995:67) claims that in
British English, locally free reflexives (i.e., those which do not have an
antecedent in the immediate clause) are not primarily logophoric, but
are rather markers of contrast and emphasis. He gives the following
examples (Baker 1995:68) of reflexives which do not correspond with a
local subject of consciousness, but rather correspond to a referent who
is prominent in the discourse and who is being contrasted with other
characters or entities in the discourse:

(31) a. If Cassandra has filled my bed with fleas, I am sure they must bite
          herself.
      b. But at the same time, she could not help thinking that no one
          could so well perform it as himself.[9]

Baker proposes that the logophoric use of the reflexive is just a subset of
the larger case of using reflexives as discourse-prominence and contrast
markers. He notes that a local subject of consciousness or conceived
POV is no doubt highly prominent, and so there is no need for a sepa-

rate statement concerning logophoric reflexives; they fall out as part of the more general pattern.

Baker's analysis is unsatisfying for American English. American English does not seem to allow for non-logophoric discourse reflexives as freely as in the dialect of British English Baker describes, but it clearly does permit the use of logophoric reflexives. This makes it difficult to treat logophoric reflexives as just a subset of the prominence-based reflexives. Baker is aware of this difficulty, but states that there is no need to state a general rule for logophoric reflexives in American English, that American speakers have no such general rule but instead have "a collection of highly idiosyncratic peripheral rules, this set representing the fragmented remains of the general rule still operative to a degree in British English" (1995:74, n. 10).

In the terms of the analysis presented here, the difference between British and American English would be captured in terms of different networks of schemas. British English includes an extension from the emphatic reflexive schema, one in which there is no requirement of linear adjacency, but in which the requirements of prominence and contrast still hold. American English does not have such an extension (or if it does, it does not appear to be as developed and entrenched as in the British dialect Baker describes, as many of Baker's examples seem unacceptable in American usage). It does however have an extension from the reflexive prototype which sanctions the use of logophoric reflexives without local antecedents. In these terms, there is no basis for calling one system or the other "fragmented"; the two dialects merely have somewhat different inventories of constructional schemas.

7.6.3 Reflexives and Discourse Participants

Ross (1970) first noticed constructions similar to those in (32), in which a reflexive referring to speaker or addressee appears with no overt antecedent.

(32) a.   Someone like yourself might appreciate these things.
      b.   We have received many letters from doctors such as yourself.
      c.   This book was written by Mary and myself.

These kinds of reflexives—first- and second-person reflexives with no overt antecedent—are quite limited in their distribution. They tend to appear in modifying phrases and elliptical expressions, and rarely appear as arguments of verbs. The following examples, all taken from actual usage, are representative of the kinds of constructions in which these reflexives are found.

(33) a.   Everyone except yourself? (line from the movie *Biloxi Blues*)
      b.   How about yourself? (line from the movie *The Milagro Beanfield War*)
      c.   "It's yourself I was hoping to see." (C. McLeod, *The Corpse in Oozak's Pond*, p. 135)

In these examples, the conception of the addressee as a speech-event participant (a conceptualizer) is the antecedent for the reflexive expression *yourself*; the addressee is conceived as metaphorically viewing the content of the predication, including the reference to the addressee himself. The use of the reflexive marker is sanctioned by the referent's role as object of the construal relation.

This construction type represents yet another extension from the prototype, as well as from the other POV uses of the reflexive. The use of the reflexive heightens the salience of one of the offstage participants and its role as viewer (i.e., conceptualizer), bringing it partially onstage (i.e., partially into awareness). The effect is not merely to identify one of the onstage participants as corresponding to an offstage entity (as is the case with pronouns), but effectively to bring part of the "audience" closer to the onstage region, highlighting its role as conceptualizer.

This account explains why the use of *yourself* is, in many contexts, construed as polite. The following example illustrates this (I have placed the relevant noun phrases in italics).

(34)   To illustrate how you are connected to international finance, let's look at how the banking system works. First, *people like yourself* deposit money in banks. The banks put the money in their safes, where the amounts gradually increase thanks to the sound banking practice of never lending money to *people like yourself*. (Dave Barry, *Bad Habits*, p. 83)

Replacing the last phrase in the paragraph with the near-equivalent phrasing *never lending money to people like you* changes the tone of the paragraph. The nonreflexive version comes closer to being genuinely insulting than the original, while the use of the reflexive marker in (34) adds a certain note of politeness. This pragmatic effect of increased politeness is further illustrated by the inappropriateness of the reflexive marker when the speaker's intent is to insult the addressee:

(35) a. People like you disgust me!
      b. *People like yourself disgust me!
      c. *With friends like yourself, who needs enemies?

The politeness effect can be attributed to the fact that the addressee's role as conceptualizer, and the construal relation connecting the (conception of the) addressee with the profile of the reflexive, are made more salient, as these are invoked to sanction the use of the reflexive marker. This implication of a heightened awareness or consideration of the addressee's viewpoint is felt to be more polite.

Baker (1995) proposes an alternative account of these facts. He notes that second-person logophoric forms are very rare, cross-linguistically, and suggests that it seems more likely that the polite use of *yourself* reflects the sense that the referent of the reflexive is the most prominent (therefore most important) person in the context. This seems plausible, but it leaves some questions unanswered. Baker claims that the American English equivalent to the British intensive-plus-contrastive reflexive form is a stressed (nonreflexive) pronoun. Such pronouns do not, however, convey politeness, as borne out by the distinction between (34) above and the modified version in (36), where italics represent emphatic stress.

(36) The banks put the money in their safes, where the amounts gradually increase thanks to the sound banking practice of never lending money to people like *you*.

Again, adding emphasis to the pronoun in (37) does nothing to increase the politeness of the statement—quite the contrary.

(37) People like *you* disgust me!

It is difficult to judge intuitively whether the use of the polite *yourself* is in fact logophoric, but it appears that the analysis of this use of the reflexive as a pure prominence marker is not unproblematic.

A further complication for Baker's analysis is that, at least in American English, there is clearly a requirement that third-person discourse-anteceded reflexives correspond to a conceived POV, as pointed out by Ross (1970) and Kuno (1987) and discussed below. Baker's analysis would presumably have to maintain that American English allows for the use of first- and second-person reflexive forms motivated solely by considerations of prominence, but imposes a logophoric requirement on third-person reflexives only.

Out of context, constructions parallel to (32) cannot be used in the third person (Ross 1970; Kuno 1987). This is illustrated by the following examples, which are ungrammatical so long as one does not imagine a special sanctioning discourse context.

(38) a. *Someone like himself might appreciate these things.
      b. *We have received quite a few letters from doctors such as herself.
      c. *This book was written by Mary and himself.

Embedded clauses may contain third-person reflexives analogous to (38), under certain conditions (Ross 1970; Kuno 1987). The conception of a speech-act participant may be invoked as an antecedent for a reflexive in reported speech (indirect quotation) even though the referent of the reflexive is not a participant in the speech event in which the entire sentence is uttered. Examples (39a–b) are invented ones given by Kuno (1987); (39c–d) are examples of actual usage, taken from written texts.

(39) a. May said this book was written by Tom and herself.
      b. I told Albert that physicists like himself were a godsend.
      c. In 1985, says Hefner, Leigh stole a videotape of a sexual frolic involving himself and some friends, thinking she could use it against him. (*People* magazine, exact citation unavailable)
      d. He said that the faculty tend to be cowardly about these things, himself included. (personal correspondence)

In these cases, the configuration which motivates the appearance of the reflexive marker is identical to that given for the *myself* and *yourself* examples discussed above, with the exception that the ground in which the implied POV is located is a surrogate ground, the conception of the ground of the original speech event. The surrogate ground conceptually includes the participants in the reported speech event. As illustrated by the constructions in (39), those conceived participants may antecede a reflexive.

Kuno (1987) provides further evidence that the referent's status as conceptualizer (i.e., POV) is a crucial factor, given in (40–41).

(40) a. According to John, the article was written by Ann and himself.
      b. *Speaking of John, the article was written by Ann and himself.

(41) a. John said to Mary that physicists like himself were a godsend.
      b. Mary said to John that physicists like himself were a godsend.
      c. Mary heard from John that physicists like himself were a godsend.
      d. *Mary heard about John that physicists like himself were a godsend.
      e. *Mary said about John that physicists like himself were a godsend.

These examples bear out the claim that a referent must be construed as a conceptualizer in order to antecede a reflexive in these constructions. Kuno (1987) and Ross (1970) propose essentially the same analysis, phrased in terms of the claim that a reflexive may corefer with a logophoric NP in a higher clause, a nominal describing a participant in the conception of the speech event in which the clause containing the reflexive is embedded. In the analysis I propose, this usage represents another extension from the reflexive prototype, in which the POV is conceptually onstage as speaker of the reported speech event.

7.7 CONSTRAINTS ON DISTRIBUTION OF REFLEXIVES

The distribution of pronouns and reflexives is determined by the interaction of the specific constructional schemas sanctioning their usage. Accordingly, reflexives are disallowed in many positions because their appearance would represent too great an extension from any conventionally established schema (e.g., reflexives in subject position, for which no sanctioning constructional schema has developed; see Deane [1992] for detailed discussion).

The possibilities for reflexive usage in a specific case are further constrained by the mechanisms underlying the selection of schemas to produce acceptability judgments. The analysis here is parallel to that of Deane (1992). For completeness' sake I describe the mechanisms which explain the constraints, but do not cover all of the points already covered by Deane. Rather I focus on certain examples which Deane does not discuss.

As explained in §2.4, acceptability judgments are analyzed in CG as categorizing judgments (Langacker 1987a, 1988b). The construction in question is compared with a schema selected as the categorizing schema, and is judged to be either an instantiation of the schema (hence fully sanctioned) or an extension from the schema, meaning that the construction conflicts in some respects with the specifications of the schema. An extension involving only a small deviation from the categorizing schema may be felt to be slightly unusual or innovative; an extension involving a large amount of conflict with the categorizing schema is felt to be unacceptable. Unacceptability is therefore a matter of degree, and depends upon the extent to which the construction conflicts with specifications which are felt to be central to the categorizing schema.

The categorizing schema is selected through competition among the various schemas that are activated by the expression in question (here I am describing the process from the point of view of the listener; see Chap. 2 n. 16). In expressions involving a reflexive marker, the appearance of the reflexive morpheme itself strongly invokes a number of reflexive schemas. Which schemas are most strongly activated depends on the extent to which other details of the construction match established constructional schemas (and the extent to which those schemas are entrenched). The closest match becomes the categorizing schema, in relation to which the particular construction is categorized as either an instantiation or an extension. If the specific construction has a different nominal as antecedent for the reflexive than that specified by the categorizing schema, the construction is categorized as an extension with a significant conflict in specifications, and so is judged anomalous.

The sentences in (42) will serve for illustration. Each of these constructions closely resembles the reflexive prototype schema in that a reflexive pronoun elaborates the landmark of the embedded process. The reflexive prototype is also highly entrenched by virtue of its frequent activation, while there is no competing entrenched schema that would specifically sanction correspondence between the matrix clause subject and the reflexive. The reflexive prototype schema is therefore selected as the categorizing schema, and the constructions are judged unacceptable. (This is essentially the same analysis as that of Deane [1992].)

(42) a. *John* wants Tom to phone *himself.*
      b. *Cyndi thought Tom loved herself.

Constructions in which the use of a reflexive marker is obligatory are also explained in terms of categorizing schemas. When a schema which would sanction the appearance of a reflexive marker is selected as the categorizing schema, the appearance of a pronoun is judged anomalous by comparison with that schema. A reflexive schema will always be selected as the categorizing schema whenever the landmark of a relation corresponds with the trajector of that relation, as in (43).

(43) a. *John* hurt *himself/*him.*
      b. *Sarah* cut *herself/*her.*
      c. Explaining *himself/*him* will be difficult for *John.*
      d. *This* in *itself/*it* is nothing to worry about.

Each of the constructions in (43) fits a schema for reflexives very closely: There is correspondence between two nominal conceptions, one of which elaborates the trajector of a relation, the other of which elaborates the landmark of the same relation. There is no specific schema sanctioning the use of a pronoun in this particular configuration, and so the reflexive schemas will win the competition on the basis of elaborative distance; that is, it much more closely resembles the target construction in its specifications. If a pronoun is used instead of the reflexive marker, there will be a discrepancy between the construction and the reflexive schema, and the construction will be judged to be anomalous.

The well-known sentence type exemplified by (44) and discussed in §7.2 above is an apparent exception to this pattern.

(44)　a.　I like me.
　　　　b.　You have to think about *you* for once.

These are not in fact counterexamples to the analysis. Speakers do notice the discrepancy between these constructions and the expected forms. This indicates that the reflexive prototype schema is selected as the categorizing schema, but that the deviation from the expected construction underscores the speaker's intention of evoking a special construal of the referent.

All of the construction types which require the use of a reflexive involve overtly coded relations involving the nominal participants. POV effects in the discourse do not force the use of a reflexive, as the viewing relation is only implicit, leaving the speaker free to decide whether such a viewing relation is a significant part of the conception and whether to mark it with a reflexive (see §8.2). There are, however, some constructions in which a POV-anteceded reflexive is considered to be obligatory. These are all constructions in which the POV is profiled by a nominal contained in the same clause as the reflexive. The sentences in (45) are examples of this.

(45)　a.　*John* found a picture of himself / *him* in the newspaper.
　　　　b.　*Mary* got ahold of a book about *herself* / *her*.
　　　　c.　Somebody told *Bill* a story about *himself* / ??*him*.

The reflexive marker is obligatory whether or not one has a strong awareness of "empathy" (in Kuno's [1987] sense), unlike the situation with discourse-level viewpoints. The obligatoriness of the reflexive marker is explained by the more-or-less overt coding of the conceptual interconnections between the antecedent and the referent of the reflexive (see also Deane 1992). The specific verbs are not necessarily verbs of perception per se, but they profile an interaction between participants which typically includes perception or viewing. The conceptual inter-connections are therefore made salient enough that a reflexive schema is strongly invoked, causing it to be selected in preference to any (nonre-flexive) pronominal schema.

As observed in §7.2 above, proximity between the nominal concep-tions corresponding to the reflexive and its antecedent is a component in all the conventionally established uses of the reflexive. Where overt nominal antecedents and overtly coded relational interconnections are involved, proximity means that they must correspond to participants within the same processual relation (though they may not directly elab-orate the verb, but may instead elaborate a relation coded by a preposi-tion, as in [17] above). At the discourse level, proximity means that the POV conceived as antecedent for the reflexive must be the one from which the reflexive is "viewed" rather than any more distant or external POV. This observation has been made by Kuno (1987), Zribi-Hertz (1989), and Pollard and Sag (1992) among others.

The antecedent for a third-person viewpoint reflexive must be the viewer the conceptualizer empathizes with as the reflexive is con-strued—in other words, the one from whose POV the reflexive is viewed. Switching to empathy with another viewpoint automatically makes the new viewpoint the closest, since it is the one directly con-nected with the predication. Pollard and Sag give the examples in (46).

(46) a. John was going to get even with Mary. That picture of himself in the paper would really annoy her, as would the other stunts he had planned.
      b. ?/*Mary was quite taken aback by the publicity John was receiving. That picture of himself in the paper had really annoyed her, and there was not much she could do about it.

The second sentence in (46a) is most likely viewed from John's perspec-tive, so John's viewpoint can antecede the reflexive. The second sen-tence in (46b) is most likely viewed from Mary's perspective; since Mary's is the active viewpoint, the viewpoint reflexive schema would sanction a reflexive anteceded by Mary, but not one anteceded by John. For some speakers, there is another reading in which the reflexive *him-self* is fully acceptable; that would be if John had arranged to get the picture printed in the newspaper, and Mary knew that this was so. Mary would be reacting to the idea that John had had the audacity to do such a thing. John's viewpoint as an indirect agent for the picture could then antecede the reflexive. The fact that only that specific context makes the reflexive acceptable simply underscores the point that a picture noun reflexive must be understood as corresponding to the immediately adjacent viewpoint.

Zribi-Hertz (1989) gives (47) as another example in which a reflexive is ruled out by a Domain of Point-of-View (DPV) boundary. Zribi-Hertz notes that the pronoun *they* explicitly names a subject-of-consciousness, which under her principles makes the clause a DPV boundary.

(47)   They stood now by the door waiting without visible impatience to see
        the last of me [*myself]. (Iris Murdoch, 1978, *A Severed Head*)

In the model presented here, the subject of the sentence is, by virtue of its being explicitly mentioned within the profiled interconnecting relation *see*, construed as more accessible in relation to the reflexive (i.e., more salient and more closely connected) than the conception of the speaker, which is not profiled and not part of any overtly mentioned relation which includes the reflexive. It is therefore the closest POV and blocks selection of the speaker's POV as antecedent.

As noted above, the profile of the reflexive must correspond with an antecedent which can be considered to be the most accessible in relation to the reflexive as determined by salience and conceptual connectedness (the relative entrenchment of schemas plays a role as well, as explained above). For complements within the complement chain (such as objects of verbs), the other complements are the nominals most closely connected and most salient in relation to them. Where the reflexive is contained in a modifying phrase, rather than a complement, it is more weakly connected with the process and may therefore be construed as connected with a POV other than the clausal subject. Sentences such as (48), which Zribi-Hertz terms comparative contexts, are therefore acceptable.

(48)   a.   They might appreciate somebody such as myself.
        b.   They would probably like to see somebody like yourself.

The observation made above, that "construal reflexives" are largely limited to modifiers and to elliptical phrases (*How about yourself?*, *Everyone except yourself?* and so forth), is explained by this model. Wherever the reflexive is strongly connected, semantically, with a close POV, that reference point will be selected as the obligatory antecedent. The construal reflexive schema, based on a correspondence between the profile of the reflexive and an unprofiled antecedent participating in an unprofiled relation, can compete for the status of categorizing schema only when there is no genuine competition.

Zribi-Hertz (1989) points out that comparative contexts are particularly likely to sanction the use of a logophoric reflexive, as in her examples cited in (49).

(49)   a.   The music made her think of her life as it seldom did; it exalted her (*herself).
       b.   The music made her think of her life as it seldom did; it exalted no one as it did herself.

Zribi-Hertz notes that in (49b), there is an implication that the referent is thinking to herself that the music exalts no one as it does herself. (49a) is more likely to be taken as an objective statement. The difference between these two is that the notion of comparison brings in the idea that the referent is an object of perception. As part of comparing her own reaction to music with other people's, she must observe her own reaction, as if viewing herself from the outside. That implicit viewing relation provides the interconnecting relationship between the antecedent and the reflexive which sanctions the reflexive. This is particularly so when the modifier involves a notion of comparison, which, as Deane (1992) points out, invokes the conception of a viewer who makes the comparison.

The picture is not as simple as it seems, however. Zribi-Hertz (1989) reports a number of exceptions to the generalization that POV reflexives are permitted only in modifier phrases. She notes that a more distant viewer may be selected (at least in some dialects) where there is sufficient contextual support. She gives the example in (50), among others, in which the selection of the viewer as antecedent seems to be supported by the conception that it is the dominant viewpoint which the speaker empathizes with throughout, a construal which is supported by the occurrence of certain modifiers.

(50)   Whom he [Philip] was supposed to be fooling, he couldn't imagine.
       Not the twins, surely, because Désirée, in the terrifying way of progressive American parents, believed in treating children like adults and had undoubtedly explained to them the precise nature of her relationship with himself. (David Lodge, *Changing Places*, p. 170)

Note that modifiers such as *surely* and *undoubtedly* represent the character's comment on the conception, and reinforce the awareness that we are looking at the conception "through his eyes". These kinds of clear contextual cues may be needed to support a construal in which the more distant POV is especially central to the construal of the construction, and hence the most accessible antecedent. Speakers I have consulted nevertheless find this sentence and similar examples cited by Zribi-Hertz unacceptable, indicating that there is significant dialectal variation.

POINT OF VIEW

The notion **point of view** has long been recognized as significant for pronominal anaphora (cf. Kuno 1987; Zribi-Hertz 1989; Pollard and Sag 1993), though it has generally been regarded as distinct from the core anaphora principles, perhaps in part because judgments of POV are relatively difficult to pin down. In contrast to most other models of the anaphora constraints, the reference point model takes POV effects to be central to the understanding of the general principles governing anaphora. As discussed in §3.2.2, the relationship between a conceived viewer and the material which is construed from its POV is taken as a model for the relationship between a reference point and the material in its dominion. In §3.4 I argued that there is also empirical evidence of greater interaction than is often acknowledged between the anaphora constraints and POV considerations.

My goal here is to shed more light on POV phenomena in anaphora, and to provide a principled explanation of why POV effects so often involve variable and slippery judgments while also demonstrating that the judgments are not always as variable and slippery as they sometimes appear. I will argue that the same basic notions which underlie the rest of the reference point model, namely prominence and conceptual-semantic connectivity, explain POV phenomena as well. I will also offer some speculations on the role of conceived viewing within the complement chain and the possibility that POV considerations are involved even within the data which are often taken to reflect purely syntactic anaphora constraints.

8.1 THE RELATIONSHIP BETWEEN REFERENCE POINT AND POV

I understand the term "point of view" to refer to the conception of an animate entity, typically a person, from whose perspective a conception is construed. The material 'viewed' from that POV is construed within a mental space representing the viewer's perceptions or thoughts. A POV configuration is an instantiation of the familiar reference point/ dominion configuration (cf. §3.2.2), with the added nuance that the material in its dominion is not merely associated with the POV but is also conceived as a representation of the POV's perceptions or thoughts.

It is not possible to draw a sharp distinction between POV effects and ordinary reference point phenomena, and in fact the role of POV effects in anaphora may be much more widespread than is generally recognized. Typically the role of empathy in anaphora is illustrated with examples such as the following (from Kuno 1987):

(1)   a.   *He* would be late, *John* said.
        b.   **John* would be late, *he* said.

(2)   *That *John* would be elected was anticipated by *him*.

In (1a–b), the preposed clause represents a statement from John's POV, and so the appearance of the full noun phrase in (1b) is anomalous. In (2), the sentential subject tends to be construed as a representation of John's thoughts (as this is part of the meaning of *anticipate*), and again the use of the full noun phrase is anomalous.[1]

Most discussion of the role of POV effects in anaphora focuses on examples like (1–2), in which other explanations for obligatory non-coreference (such as a c-command condition violation) would fail to explain the facts (e.g., Kuno 1987). But it is possible that even the central anaphora facts frequently involve POV considerations, which are difficult to tease out from other factors. It seems intuitively likely that examples in which a full nominal cannot corefer with a clausal subject typically include a POV conflict. We can consider (3) as an example. Some speakers report that the sentences in (3) sound as if Dan somehow saw himself at some distance away.

(3)   a.   **He* saw a snake near *Dan*.
        b.   **Near *Dan*, *he* saw a snake.

The extent to which there is felt to be a conflict involving the "view" taken of the referent may be variable, depending on the lexical items

involved—particularly, whether the verb explicitly invokes the conception of a viewing relation (or cognizing relation). But it is also possible
that the subject of a clause is typically, or at least frequently, construed
as the "viewer" of the material in the clause (DeLancey 1981; Kuno
1987). Crucial evidence for this observation will be difficult to find; here
I merely offer the suggestion that we may be dealing with POV factors
even in the central examples of the kind that is typically discussed in
the anaphora literature, and that it may very well be incorrect to think
of POV as a peripheral factor which comes into play only in the data
that cannot be explained in any other way. In this chapter I will focus,
however, on establishing that there is a principled explanation for the
oft-noted variability of POV effects, and that the factors which determine the anaphora constraints more generally also come into play here.

8.1.1 The Variability of POV Effects

The data in (4–5) illustrate POV effects which are not explained by
other factors in the reference point model (nor by analyses based on c-
command). (4a) is unacceptable to some speakers (the % symbol indicates variable judgments). In (5), the entities coded as pronouns are not
profiled in the composite structure, suggesting that they should not be
construed as reference points on the basis of prominence, though they
would presumably tend to be so construed on the basis of precedence
in the linear string. In each of the unacceptable sentences, the full noun
phrase corefers with a pronoun whose referent is understood to be a
conceptual viewer of the material which includes the full noun phrase
itself. (5) is from Reinhart (1983:175).

(4)   a. %The possibility that *Jim* might have AIDS frightened *him*.
       b.   The possibility that *Jim* might have AIDS was hidden from *him*.

(5)   a. *It should have bothered *her* that *Rosa*'s driving is dangerous.
       b. *It should have occurred to *her* that *Rosa*'s driving is dangerous.
       c.   Someone was shouting behind *her* that *Rosa*'s driving was insane.

The judgments involving conceived viewers in these constructions are
highly variable (see §3.1.3), but I argue below that this does not indicate
that the phenomena involved are fundamentally different from the
"core" anaphora data for which judgments are typically much clearer.
Before presenting the analysis, I will briefly review the relevant properties of mental spaces (Fauconnier 1985).
     One of the central points of Fauconnier's theory of mental spaces

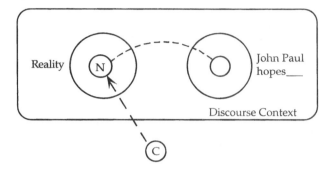

Figure 8.1   Accessing a conception within a speaker's reality

is that a conceived referent may be represented in multiple mental spaces, and that the nominal description used to access the referent may "point to" or access a conception in one mental space or another. This is exemplified by (6), from Fauconnier (1985).

(6)   Pope John Paul hopes *a former quarterback* will adopt needy children.

The relevant reading of (6) is that in which Pope John Paul is unaware that the referent is a former quarterback (he may only know the man from some other context). The nominal description *a former quarterback* applies to the speaker's conception of reality, in which the referent is a quarterback; that conception corresponds to the conception in the space set up by *Pope John Paul hopes*. . . . (This is illustrated in Fig. 8.1, in which the dotted line indicates the correspondence between the entities in the two mental spaces.) The crucial point is that a nominal description may be construed as a representation of the speaker's view of the referent (such as the speaker's conception of the referent "in reality") rather than as a representation of some other viewer's conception of the referent. Even when a nominal referent is construed as being represented in multiple mental spaces, the nominal description used may be construed as most directly accessing a conception belonging to only one mental space, such as the speaker's view of reality.

   A similar phenomenon is involved in many POV constructions, where two or more mental spaces are involved. (4a) can be characterized in terms of mental spaces as in Figure 8.2. The embedded clause *that Jim might have AIDS* is represented in two mental spaces, one which corresponds to the speaker's conception of reality (or the "reality" of a narrative situation, etc.) and one which corresponds to Jim's own

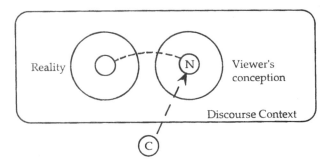

Figure 8.2   Accessing a conception within a viewer's dominion

thoughts. Both spaces have a conception of the referent known as *Jim;* the dotted line linking the two entities indicates that they correspond. The critical issue is which space the name *Jim* pertains to or, in other words, which mental space is the **focus space** (in the sense of Dinsmore [1991]), the space which is most centrally in the conceptualizer's awareness and which the expression directly applies to.

For speakers who find (4a) acceptable, we can assume that the name *Jim* applies directly to the conception of the referent in the speaker's view of reality, that is, Jim as seen from the speaker's perspective. This conception corresponds to the conception in the mental space representing Jim's thoughts, but there is no conflict, because the name *Jim* does not apply directly to that space. Intuitively speaking, there is no notion that Jim's own conception includes thinking of himself by name, as *Jim*. For speakers who find (4a) unacceptable, the name *Jim* applies directly to the conception of Jim's own thoughts, which is considered to be the focus space. The name is taken as a description of Jim's own thoughts, and since he would not think of himself using a low-accessibility nominal like *Jim*, the sentence is anomalous.

The question then becomes, What determines which mental space is construed as the focus space? The same basic notions that have applied throughout the reference point model apply here as well. Prominence, conceptual connectivity, and linear order are the key factors. The reason for the significantly greater variability of judgments with POV effects, as compared with the central anaphora data (the data traditionally accounted for by c-command, explained here in terms of the complement chain), is that the viewing relationship between the POV and the material conceived within its dominion is generally not explicitly coded, and

so is unprofiled and significantly less prominent than the profiled semantic connections making up the complement chain. There is much
greater freedom for the conceptualizer to construe a different mental
space as the most salient, and therefore as the focus space.

The appearance of a particular nominal form itself promotes construal of a particular mental space as focus space. The very fact that a
full noun phrase is present is one cue (in the sense of Bates and
MacWhinney [1987]) signaling that the referent of the nominal expression is not the person from whose POV the conception is to be construed, and that the mental space representing someone else's conception must be the focus space. There is evidence that speakers expect
nominal forms to be congruent with the focus space which they elaborate (i.e., they expect the nominal description to be appropriate to the
focus space), and that they use the choice of a particular nominal form
to signal a particular choice of focus space. In §3.1.1, I discussed two
examples where speakers referred to themselves with nominal descriptions from a third-person perspective; the examples are repeated here.

(7)   a.   "While reporters were talking about how Ollie North sodomized
             goats on the South Lawn of the White House, or how Ollie North
             was selling White House china to fund the Contras. . . ." (Oliver
             North interview in *TV Guide* 12/28/91)
       b.   Sometimes he can't believe what an idiot his father is. (Dave
             Barry, *Dave Barry's Greatest Hits*, p. 74; 'his father' refers to Dave
             Barry)

The speakers in each case (Ollie North in [7a], Dave Barry in [7b]) use
third-person forms for self-reference to promote a *de dicto* reading of the
clause. These examples work precisely because speakers expect nominal
forms to be congruent with the focus space which they apply to; an
unexpected choice of nominal form serves as a signal of a shift in focus
space. We can assume that the same principle is at work in less-dramatic
examples such as (4a), and that speakers take the appearance of a full
noun phrase as one cue signaling that the conception is not to be viewed
from that referent's perspective.

One may ask why we cannot simply place full nominals anywhere,
if the full nominal itself serves as a cue to the construal of the context;
this would seem to imply that there would be no anaphora constraints
at all if speakers simply shifted the focus space to accommodate whatever nominal is there. The answer is that these shifts are not possible
when other factors unequivocally signal a particular construal of the

context. The relations which make up the complement chain are explicitly coded and therefore highly salient, outweighing other considerations. A conceptualizer will not conclude from the appearance of a full nominal in an unexpected position that the relation coded by the verb, for example, is not to be construed as prominent.[2] The variability in judgments with sentences like (4a) indicates that speakers differ in the weight they assign to different factors in determining the choice of focus space.

If we tip the balance of prominence, POV effects can become much less slippery or variable and more like classic anaphora-constraint data. In (8), the placement of the embedded-clause material within a particular mental space is explicitly coded by the construction. Speakers seem to agree unanimously on the unacceptability of coreference in these cases. Note that the c-command constraint on coreference would not account for these data without significant reanalysis of the tree structure (I am not aware of any attempts to account for these data in terms of c-command).

(8)   a. *His worst fear is that Jim might have AIDS.
       b. *Her secret belief is that Sally should be in charge of the project.

(9) provides evidence that POV is at issue, and not just linear order (or any tree-structural relation). Speakers judge these constructions significantly more acceptable than (8).

(9)   a. His doctor's worst fear is that Jim might have AIDS.
       b. Her boss's secret belief is that Sally should be in charge of the project.

Linear order, specifically the temporal sequence in which mental spaces are accessed, also plays a role (see §4.3). Speakers find the sentences in (10) relatively improved as compared with (8), presumably because the clause is accessed before the mental space representing the referent's POV has been explicitly set up. It is reasonable to assume that speakers contextualize the clause first within conceived reality; the other mental space is set up later, and has less chance to be construed as the focus space (Dinsmore [1991] also notes that linear order plays a role in determining the focus space).

(10) a. %That Jim might have AIDS is his worst fear.
      b. %That Sally should be in charge of this project is her secret belief.

A different class of examples further illustrates the point that POV effects can be quite robust even where a c-command analysis (or the

other prominence and connectivity factors which define the complement chain) would predict that coreference should be acceptable. In
(11b) and (11d), coreference is ruled out because the main clause is construed as a description of the subject's thoughts. The examples have
been deliberately constructed to promote construing the main clause as
an assessment from the character's POV; syntactically parallel examples
worded differently could be construed from an external, narrator's perspective (e.g., [11e]). This is precisely the point: A syntactic structural
analysis would have difficulty accounting for these examples not only
because the pronoun fails to c-command the name in all of these examples but also because the same structures with different words would
produce different grammaticality judgments.

(11) a. When *John* thought about it, *he* didn't seem like such a loser after
          all.
      b. *When *he* thought about it, *John* didn't seem like such a loser after
          all.
      c. If *John* stopped to consider, *he* was a pretty OK guy, all in all.
      d. *If *he* stopped to consider, *John* was a pretty OK guy, all in all.
      e. When *he* had made a decision about it, *John* went right to work.

The sentences in (12) provide further illustration of the same phenomenon.

(12) a. *When *he* thought about it, *John* had done the best he could.
      b. *When *he* reflected, it was clear that *Ralph* needed to find a new
          job.

Examples like (8) and (11–12) illustrate the point that POV effects
are not always subtle. If POV phenomena have been tacitly considered
marginal, it is in part because some of the well-known examples allow
for variability in judgments (for reasons explained above), and in part
because less effort has been expended on constructing examples of robust POV effects which cannot be attributed to structural relations.

8.2 POV DOMINIONS

I am claiming that examples like (10) frequently get mixed or uncertain
judgments because it is not unambiguously clear which mental space
should be selected as the focus space, and that factors which influence
the relative prominence of the spaces will have an impact on the acceptability of coreference. In constructions which describe an experiencer's

reaction (such as [10]), one factor which may raise the salience of the space representing the speaker's conception of reality (or some other "external" viewer's conception) is the very fact that the experiencer's reaction is being described, implying an outside observer's perspective. Some speakers find examples like (10) unacceptable, presumably because they construe the embedded clause from the perspective of the experiencer. Speakers who find (10) acceptable may construe the entire construction as an external description of the impact of the event on the experiencer.

Evidence for this analysis comes from constructions in which the experiencer is not described "from the outside" at all, in which there is no overt pronominal reference to the experiencer. Since there is no overt nominal coding the experiencer, these sentences have to be set in a discourse context to make clear the intended construal (which means that the intended POV has to be set up in the preceding context rather than appear for the first time in the sentence in question; nevertheless it is possible to see differences between constructions which maintain that POV and constructions which are interpreted by some speakers as involving a switch in POV). In (13), the crucial sentence is the last one in each paragraph. Speakers I consulted were asked to read each paragraph as if it were an excerpt from a novel, and give a judgment on the felicity of the last sentence in the context of the paragraph.

(13) a. Sandy went into the bathroom and shut the door behind her. There was no one home, but you couldn't be too careful. She took the test kit out of the brown paper bag and read the directions. A few minutes later she sat down to wait for the results. Soon it would all be over. Maybe. The possibility that Sandy might be pregnant was frightening.

      b. John took a moment to gather his nerve before opening the envelope from the testing center. This had been the longest week of his life, but now, with the results in hand, he found it easy to wait a few more minutes before finding out. The idea that John might have AIDS was terrifying.

Each paragraph was constructed with three alternate endings: the endings shown in (13), an "external description" ending (*The possibility that Sandy might be pregnant frightened her; The idea that John might have AIDS terrified him*), and an ending with a pronoun in the embedded clause (*The possibility that she might be pregnant was terrifying*, etc.). I have found that while speakers disagree about the grammaticality of sentences like

(10) above (the "external description" sentences), there is agreement among all speakers I have consulted (over a dozen) that the final sentence of each of the paragraphs in (13) is unacceptable. In other words, variability and slipperiness of judgments seem to disappear when the construction is worded in such a way as to reduce drastically the plausibility of an external description reading (as compared with the near-equivalent construction involving an overt pronoun).

Interestingly, even with the heavily slanted viewpoint context set up in the paragraphs in (13), some speakers find the external description sentences acceptable. They reported that *The possibility that Sandy might be pregnant frightened her* and *The idea that Jim might have AIDS terrified him* read like narrator's descriptions of the characters' states, and that coreference was perfectly acceptable. The external description of the experiencer can be construed as part of an outside observer's (or narrator's) view, thereby enhancing the salience of that mental space and making it more likely to be taken as the focus space for the embedded clause overall. As has long been noted (though not in these theoretical terms), the likelihood that that mental space will be construed as focus space is variable across speakers, and no doubt interacts with a number of other contextual factors which have not been addressed here.

The degree of conceptual connectivity between a POV and a nominal conception depends in part upon the extent to which the nominal conception is conceived as accessible within a mental space other than the dominion of the POV. To put it another way, if the nominal describes part of a conception which is construed as solely a representation of the viewer's thoughts or perceptions, and not as part of "reality" or any other context which is separate from the viewer's awareness, then the nominal tends strongly to be construed in relation to the viewer. If the nominal can be construed as accessing a conception within a different mental space, such as conceived reality, it is less likely to be construed as viewed by the POV.

A great many data supporting this contention are available in the anaphora literature, though they have not previously been analyzed in precisely this way. Ross (1967) and Kuno (1987) have pointed out that viewing-based restrictions on the use of full noun phrases tend to disappear when it is possible to construe the full nominal as part of "objective reality" and as accessible to people in general rather than to think of it exclusively as a representation of the viewer's thoughts. Ross gives the examples in (14), in which both forward and backwards anaphora are possible:

(14) a. That *he* was blond worried *John*.
 b. That *John* was blond worried *him*.
 c. That *he* was unpopular didn't disturb *Oscar* at all.
 d. That *Oscar* was unpopular didn't disturb *him* at all.

In each of these sentences, the sentential subject describes a situation which can be considered common knowledge, construable as an objective fact rather than a representation of John's or Oscar's subjective thoughts. The full noun phrase in (14b) and (14d) can therefore be accessed within conceived reality rather than within the mental space representing the experiencer's thoughts. This is parallel to Fauconnier's analysis of (6) above, *Pope John Paul hopes a former quarterback will adopt needy children*. Kuno (1987:113–16) gives a number of examples as contrasts to these sentences, including the following:

(15) a. ?That *John* was always unhappy worried *him*.
 b. That *he* was always unhappy worried *John*.
 c. ?That *John* felt hungry all the time worried *him*.
 d. That *he* felt hungry all the time worried *John*.

In each of these examples, unlike (14) above, there is a strong tendency to construe the sentential subject as a representation of John's private thoughts, not directly accessible to anyone else and therefore not represented as part of reality as experienced by the speaker (or John as observed by a narrator). The lack of external access promotes construing the POV's thoughts as the focus space, making coreference anomalous.

As noted by Ross and Kuno, adverbs also have an effect on the judgments, as in (16a–b). The adverbs in question promote an outside observer's construal of the overall situation, thereby raising the salience of the observer's conceived perceptions and the likelihood that the embedded clause will be construed from the observer's POV.

(16) a. ?That John was sick worried him.
 b. That John was sick apparently / evidently / obviously worried him.

Bolinger (1979) provides another set which illustrates essentially the same point. Bolinger credits Lakoff (1976) for (17a), which is correctly predicted to be ungrammatical by Reinhart's c-command analysis (1981: 621). Noting that (17a) "tries to read John's mind," Bolinger gives the examples in (17b–c) as illustration of the effects of paraphrasing in promoting an external perspective. I disagree with Bolinger's judgment of these sentences as fully acceptable, but it does seem that they are improved relative to (17a).

(17)   a.   *It surprises *him* that *John* is so well liked.
       b.   It obviously surprises *him* that *John* is so well liked.
       c.   Does it surprise *him* that *John* is so well liked?

The larger point here is that, just as in the rest of the reference point model, the critical issue is the relative salience of the possible contexts in which the nominal is to be construed. POV phenomena seem to involve much more slippery judgments only because there are usually few overt clues about the intended construal of context as compared with the relatively unambiguous contexts defined by the complement chain.

8.3 VIEWING WITHIN THE COMPLEMENT CHAIN

As discussed in §3.4, the complement chain is a series of mental spaces which may be thought of metaphorically as a line of sight extending from the offstage region into the clause (see Langacker 1996). The role of conceived viewers in the complement chain is particularly interesting in this regard. The tendency for the subject to be construed as a POV is well known (DeLancey 1981; Kuno 1987). Although I have assumed that the primary landmark is a reference point within the complement chain solely because of its prominence, there is some evidence that its role as a reference point is partly dependent upon its being construed as a POV. Bolinger (1979) points out examples such as (18), in which the primary landmark of the verb is not construed as a co-conceptualizer or viewer of the conception expressed by the embedded clause. It would still be more natural to use forward anaphora in these cases, but coreference is in any event more acceptable than it would be if a verb such as *reassure* were used, as in (18c).

(18)   a.   I was glad for *him* that *John* was able to do it.
       b.   I pity *him* that *John* can't express his feelings.
       c.   *I reassured *him* that *John* was able to do it.

Even where the verb is one which normally portrays the primary landmark as a co-conceptualizer of something expressed as an embedded clause, it is in some cases possible to provide an alternate construal of the embedded clause, outside the landmark's dominion. Note first that where the verb profiles such a viewing relationship involving a conceived speaker and addressee, we find the same sharp, reliable judgments as with other connective relations that are made explicit by a verb—an argument of the matrix verb (a conceived 'viewer' of the conception in the embedded clause) cannot correspond to the referent of a full nominal in the embedded clause. This is exemplified by the sentences in (19).

(19) a. *I told *her* that *Sue*'s father was a Nazi war criminal.
     b. *John persuaded *him* that *Ralph* should look for a new job.

Merely negating the matrix verb is insufficient to salvage coreference, as expected under the assumption that a negated conception has all the internal semantic structure of its positive counterpart (Givón 1978, 1979a). A sentence which asserts that the discourse did not occur, as in (20), would still conceptually include the viewing relationship coded by the verb, and the viewer would still serve as a reference point in relationship to the embedded clause. Coreference is therefore predicted to be impossible, a prediction borne out by the data in (20). (Note that a nonsemantic interpretation of the grammatical relations hierarchy and of the head/complement relationships would also predict that coreference would be ruled out regardless of negation.)

(20) a. *I didn't tell *her* that *Sue*'s father was a Nazi war criminal.
     b. *John didn't persuade *him* that *Ralph* should look for a new job.

In §8.1.3 it was argued that the mental space set up by an implicit viewing relationship may, under some circumstances, be construed as less salient than the speaker's conception of reality, making the use of a full noun phrase acceptable. Where the viewing relationship is not implicit but is explicitly coded by a verb such as *tell*, the fact that the embedded clause may be construed as part of the speaker's reality is not sufficient to circumvent the explicit conceptual connection between the embedded clausal conception and the conceived viewer. But when negation of the viewing relationship is combined with the clear implication that the embedded-clause conception can be accessed as part of conceived reality, the combination of factors makes it more or less possible for the conceptualizer to construe the nominal as representing the speaker's view of the referent. Coreference is then acceptable, or at least improved. The examples in (21–22), from Brugman and Lakoff (1987), illustrate this point.

(21) a. *With no help, I convinced *her* that *Sue* needed a lawyer.
     b. Under no circumstances could I convince *her* that *Sue* needed a lawyer.

(22) a. *John forced himself to tell *her* that the lawyer *Louise* hired was a shyster.

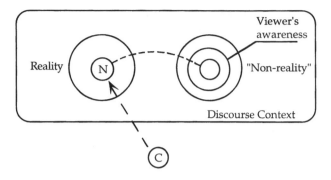

Figure 8.3   Access bypassing a potential POV

    b.   No one could bring himself to tell *her* that the lawyer *Louise* hired was a shyster.

    The diagram in Figure 8.3 illustrates the relevant facets of the conceptual organization of (21b) and (22b). The full nominal (*Sue* or *Louise*) is embedded in a clause describing part of a viewing relationship which did not take place. The conceived viewing relationship is embedded in some conception of nonreality. At the same time, the conception encoded by the embedded clause is construed as having an independent existence as part of (the speaker's conception of) reality. The full nominal may therefore be construed as accessing a conception within the speaker's description of reality rather than within the referent's view of herself. The speaker's perspective becomes the primary context within which the nominal is construed.[3]

    The sentences in (23) illustrate the same phenomenon.

(23) a.   There was just no reasonable way to tell *her* that *Rachel*'s stocks were now worthless.
      b.   It would've taken someone braver than me to inform *her* that *Rachel* was now the proud owner of 50,000 hula hoops.
      c.   No way will I be the one to break it to *him* that *Sam* is actually the illegitimate son of a trapeze artist.

In each of these examples, the embedded clause describes a conception which is construed as part of reality (or the "reality" of a narrative), a point which is underscored by the use of the word *now* in (23a–b) and *actually* in (23c). The conception can therefore be accessed within conceived reality rather than within the conception of the putative addressee's awareness.

The same effect can be seen with pairs of near-identical sentences which, insofar as phonological form is concerned, differ only in stress and intonation (indicated by boldface type). The majority of speakers I have consulted find (24b), with stress on "told," to be noticeably more acceptable than (24a), with stress on "never" (a few speakers accept [24b] completely while rejecting [24a]; most speakers report that [24b] is marginal and [24a] unacceptable). Speakers also report a clear contrast in *de dicto* versus *de re* readings (this contrast is even more reliable than the contrast in acceptability of coreference; while a few speakers feel no difference in the acceptability of coreference for this pair, all of the speakers I have consulted—eighteen in all—report that [24a] is more likely to be given a *de dicto* reading, and [24b] a *de re* reading).[4] Again the fact that the embedded clausal conception can be accessed within conceived reality, combined with the negation of the relation *tell*, promotes construing the nominal *Sue* as applying to the speaker's conceived reality rather than the mental space representing Sue's perspective.

(24)   a.   *I **never** told *her* that *Sue*'s father was a Nazi war criminal. (*De dicto* reading)
       b.   ?I never **told** *her* that *Sue*'s father was a Nazi war criminal. (*De re* reading)

A similar distinction is illustrated by (25).

(25)   a.   ***No one** told *her* that *Rachel*'s family was getting ripped off.
       b.   ?No one **told** *her* that *Rachel*'s family was getting ripped off.
       c.   No one could bring himself to break it to *her* that *Rachel*'s family was getting ripped off.

Effects of this type are more easily obtained when the pronoun corresponds to an object rather than to the subject of the clause (a fact also noted by Brugman and Lakoff [1987]). In examples such as (26), the effects seen above do not seem to occur.

(26)   a.   *She* never had any idea that *Sue*'s father was a Nazi war criminal.
       b.   *He* never suspected that *Ralph*'s stocks were actually worthless.

Presumably the difficulty in obtaining these effects with pronominal subjects is due to the greater salience of the subject, that is, its role as the most prominent reference point in the clause. Objects are less prominent and therefore less unambiguously construed as reference points; manipulations in conceptual connectivity and the salience of mental spaces may have a more noticeable effect.

In §3.4 it was noted that the explicit introduction of a POV may disrupt the conceptual connections between participants, enabling a full nominal to 'escape' the dominion of a pronoun. Combining negation-of-viewing with the POV-introducing devices discussed there results in examples which are nearly perfectly acceptable:

(27) a.   No one ever **told** *her* that the people who I guess worked with *Rachel*'s dad were in fact escaped war criminals.
      b.   I wasn't going to be the one to tell *her* that those guys who I think are from *Sue*'s hometown are here now looking for her.

The data presented in this section are significant in that they indicate that a clean separation between a completely predictive syntactic account of the "core data" and a separate, pragmatic account of the "peripheral data" cannot be maintained (see §3.4). It further indicates that the complement chain is, as has been claimed here, a semantic construct and hence sensitive (to some extent) to semantic manipulations, rather than operating as an insulated, autonomous syntactic construct.

8.4 SHIFTING BETWEEN SPACES

Despite the importance of taking POV factors into account, it should be pointed out here that it is potentially misleading to refer to these phenomena as POV shift. The critical issue in each case is not whether a different person's conceived POV is adopted; rather it is the shift of focus to a different mental space (which may represent the perceptions of a new POV). Even where there is arguably only one person in the conceived situation whose POV could be adopted, so that there can be no POV shift in an obvious sense, a shift from focus on one mental space to another has an impact on coreference possibilities. In a sense this brings us full circle, in that we return to the point that the critical issue is conceptual contexts, of which the dominions set up by a conceived POV are just one kind.

This point can be illustrated with an example from Malone (1993), who notes that there is some difficulty in analyzing it because both the main and subordinate clauses are construed from the POV of the speaker/narrator. Malone accounts for this example by proposing that the effects of introducing a new subject-of-consciousness have to some extent become structuralized.

(28)   She said so many dreadful things that in that moment I realized (although her teasing never makes me angry) that everything Mrs.

Thayer says about everyone else, except Jack, is something mean.
(She = Mrs. Thayer)

While the main clause sets up the conception of a single event in the past, the embedded clause *everything Mrs. Thayer says . . .* is construed within a different mental space, the conception of current reality (as indicated by the shift from past to present tense). The use of the full nominal underscores the speaker's intention of providing a general characterization of the referent rather than describing the referent only within the context of the event profiled by the main clause. The nominal is therefore contextualized directly in conceived reality (or the reality set up within the novel) rather than within the mental space corresponding to the conceived scene.

The contrast in (29), from Bolinger (1979, examples [30] and [32]), further illustrates this point. Bolinger points out that in (29a) but not (29b), *what John always does* is construed as a representation of John's usual behavior distinct from the conception of the one event described by the main clause. This can be characterized as a shift in focus to a mental space representing the conception of reality in general to describe John's usual behavior. Arguably, the conception of reality in general is not subsumed as a subcomponent in the conception of the specific event (as an embedded clause is frequently construed as a description of a component in the larger conception described by the entire sentence); rather it is an external mental space. (29b) contrasts with (29a) in that it is not quite as clear that the embedded clause is intended as a description of reality in general.

(29) a. What did John do?—*He* did what *John* always does—he complained.
      b. What did John do? **He* did what *John* does—he complained.

This analysis holds regardless of whether we analyze the subject, corresponding to the pronoun *he*, as the POV from which the clause is construed (in which case the shift to the speaker's description of reality would be a genuine POV shift in a traditional sense). It seems intuitively more likely that the entire sentence is construed from the speaker's POV, as an external description of John's behavior. Although no POV shift in the usual sense is involved, the shift from one focus space to another is sufficient to improve the possibility for coreference in (29a). (29a) is an example for which coreference would otherwise be predicted to be completely unacceptable given the model of reference points defined in the preceding sections. Examples like this underscore the point that the complement chain is not an autonomous syntactic construct, insulated from semantic considerations such as shifts in focus. (Analyses based on c-command would also predict coreference to be unacceptable in [29a] given standard assumptions about the tree structure representation of such sentences.)

Similar remarks apply to (30) (Bolinger 1979, his example [31]). Again the entire sentence is presumably construed from the speaker's POV, yet the shift in focus space from the specific event to a larger assessment of the surrounding circumstances provides a conceptual break between the subject of the main clause and the full nominal conception, and so makes coreference more or less acceptable.

(30) What did John know about it?—*He* knew what *John* alone could know—that there had been a secret agreement.

In each case, the full nominal occurs as part of a modifier attached to a complement of the main verb. Although modifiers tend to be construed within the same dominion(s) as the heads to which they are attached, they are not quite as strongly connected with the larger relation (e.g., the profiled process) as is the head itself, which corresponds to a participant in that relation (see §2.1.4). This may partially explain why descriptions of the speaker's (or some other viewer's) assessment tend to be expressed as modifiers rather than complements within the clause.

8.5 SUMMARY

The notion of POV plays a central role in the reference point model, although the full extent of its import is difficult to pin down owing to the possibility that POV considerations are involved even with data which can be explained by other factors. Within the reference point model, the notion of viewing also serves the same functions for which some researchers have invoked the idea of a theta role hierarchy (Jackendoff 1972, 1992; Bresnan 1995; see §7.5, §7.6.1). I have argued here that POV effects are best captured in terms of mental spaces, and that the marked variability of judgments concerning POV effects can be explained by the inexplicitness of most viewing relations and the interaction of a number of factors which promote the salience of one mental space or another. The interactions between POV considerations and the complement chain indicate, however, that POV effects are not a separate, peripheral module operating outside the core anaphora principles; rather we are dealing with a single, unified system.

NINE

CONCLUSION

This work has presented a model of anaphora constraints which accounts for the coreference patterns in terms of semantic notions, and without autonomous-syntactic constructs such as tree structures. The analysis has a number of implications for semantic and grammatical theory not only in its support for central claims of the theory of Cognitive Grammar but also in the claims it makes concerning the function of such notions as prominence and semantic connectivity. Here I briefly restate the major points of the model, and then discuss some of their implications.

9.1 GUIDING ASSUMPTIONS

The analysis takes as one starting point the basic assumptions of Accessibility theory (e.g., Givón 1989; Ariel 1988, 1990), most centrally the notion that different nominal categories (pronouns, full noun phrases, etc.) have different contextual requirements with respect to the status of their referents. Full noun phrases portray their referents as having relatively low accessibility, and so are appropriately used in contexts in which their referents are not highly salient. Embedding a full noun phrase in a context in which its referent is currently salient results in a semantic anomaly, that is, a judgment of unacceptability.

The critical question is how to determine which elements in a sentence set up the contexts within which other elements are interpreted. It has long been recognized that linear word order alone is inadequate, as it is frequently possible for a pronoun to precede a coreferential full noun phrase (as in *Near him, Dan saw a snake* [Lakoff 1968]). In this study

I have proposed a model of **conceptual reference points**, entities which define the contexts within which other nominals are interpreted. The organization of reference points is defined largely by prominence and semantic connectivity. A conception tends to be construed as a reference point to the extent that it is prominent (as determined by prominence notions which have been independently established in CG, specifically the profile/base distinction and figure/ground alignment), and other entities tend to be construed as belonging to the dominion of the reference point to the extent that they are semantically connected with that reference point (e.g., by participation in an interconnecting relation such as that designated by a verb).

In this view, the anaphora constraints are not distinct principles which must be independently listed in the grammar; rather they emerge from the nature of linguistic semantic organization in general and nominal semantics in particular. Nor are the sentence-internal constraints seen as separate from discourse-level phenomena, despite the apparent disparity in the sharpness and reliability of judgments at the intrasentential and intersentential levels. In accordance with general principles of CG, in which syntax and discourse form a continuum, the "syntactic" anaphora data—the data which are traditionally explained by specific syntactic principles based on c-command—are here viewed as a subset of a larger system which encompasses discourse-level coreference, point-of-view effects, backwards anaphora patterns, and so on.

The lack of separation between syntactic and discourse anaphora principles is one of the most significant points of difference between this analysis and generative analyses, both those based on c-command and the more recent o-command model of Pollard and Sag (1993). The following points, discussed in more detail below, also represent significant differences between the reference point model and generative accounts.

1. Nominal semantics plays a central role in explaining the constraints on anaphora. The various nominal categories differ systematically in their portrayal of a referent, and ungrammaticality is captured as semantic incompatibility between a nominal and the context in which it is embedded.

2. The theoretical machinery underlying grammaticality judgments involves the interaction of schemas, that is, constructional templates, which are entrenched to varying degrees. One result is that variability and fuzziness in grammaticality judgments are viewed as entirely nor-

mal and as data to be accounted for in their own right rather than as "noise" in the system.

3. The representations on which the anaphora constraints are defined are determined by semantic notions of prominence and connectivity in interaction with linear word order as well as point of view. None of these factors is relegated to a separate, extragrammatical component or domain of inquiry.

9.2 NOMINAL SEMANTICS

The analysis proposed here claims that different nominal categories vary subtly in their portrayal of a referent vis-à-vis the surrounding context. Calling a person *John* does not convey precisely the same nuance as calling him *he*. The difference has been described in terms of accessibility (e.g., Givón 1989; Ariel 1988, 1990) and in terms of the conceptual distance or degree of objectivity with which the referent is "viewed." Reference via name implies greater distance between the conceived referent and the discourse participants, and a correspondingly more objective conception of the referent. A pronoun portrays the referent as conceptually closer to the discourse participants, and correspondingly as more subjectively construed (in the sense of Langacker [1985]).

Contextual information is thus regarded as part of the meaning of the nominal. At the semantic pole a nominal expression includes, as an unprofiled part of its base, a schematic representation of the type of context in which it canonically appears, including information about the relative accessibility of its referent. Such a schema can be acquired through exposure to actual occurrences of nominals in context. A speaker's knowledge of nominal forms would include schematic representations of the contexts for each of the nominal categories—full noun phrase, pronoun, reflexive, null pronoun (i.e., no phonological content), and so on. Analyzing the anaphora facts in terms of nominal semantics represents a conceptual shift from the traditional view of syntactic anaphora constraints. Rather than ask only whether the placement of a certain nominal violates a constraint, we can ask how that nominal contributes to the construal of the context in which it is embedded.

This view has played a role at several points in the model. In the discussion of POV effects in the preceding chapter, it was noted that speakers may interpret a full noun phrase or a pronoun as a cue which promotes a particular construal of the context, as in constructions like *The idea that Jim might have AIDS worried him*, where the name *Jim* may itself signal that the embedded clause is not to be viewed from Jim's POV. In Chapter 7 I argued that reflexives which take a POV as their antecedent serve to heighten the salience of an implicit viewing relationship (as in *Somebody like yourself might like this*). The use of a pronoun where a reflexive would otherwise be expected (as in *I like me*) also conveys a special construal of the referent and of the construction overall. Backwards anaphora appears to be used as a way of signaling heightened focus on a conception (§5.2.2). As noted by Fox (1987b), full nominals may also serve as signals of discourse unit boundaries in some contexts (§5.6.3).

The overall point which emerges is that speakers do not merely assess the grammatical acceptability of nominal forms within syntactic contexts but also construe particular nominal forms as elements which contribute to a semantically coherent conception. I have listed here only a few examples of nominal choices influencing the construal of a construction or larger context; these are no doubt the tip of the iceberg. Within the reference point model, these considerations are not peripheral, nor are they relegated to a separate domain of inquiry from that of the anaphora constraints. Rather they are manifestations of the same principles which explain the constraints.

9.3 INTERACTION OF SCHEMAS

CG characterizes grammatical conventions as constructional patterns or schemas which speakers acquire through exposure to actually occurring expressions. The analysis developed here characterizes nominal construction types (e.g., forward anaphora, backwards anaphora, reflexive constructions, etc.) via these constructional schemas, which may be relatively specific or global and highly schematic. For expository purposes, it has frequently been easier to present only the most schematic characterization of a construction type. Forward anaphora has been described in terms of the schematic specification that the pronoun have an accessible referent in the immediate context. For some construction types, it is more revealing to analyze the data through a network of specific schemas organized around a prototype or a small cluster of semiprototypical constructional schemas. Backwards anaphora, discussed in Chapter 5, is one such case; the array of schemas for reflexive constructions described in Chapter 7 provides a different example. Presumably there is a network of entrenched conventional schemas for forward-anaphora constructions as well, but it has not been necessary to focus on that aspect of forward anaphora in order to explain the facts.

Grammaticality judgments are captured as judgments of the compatibility between a particular construction and the specifications of an entrenched schema. A minor discrepancy between the construction and the schema may pass unnoticed or be perceived as a mild innovation, but a more significant discrepancy will produce a judgment of unacceptability. Grammaticality is thus a matter of degree, and depends upon the inventory of schemas which are entrenched for a particular speaker.

This approach predicts some variation in judgments between speakers, as each speaker's inventory of schemas will be slightly different from those of all others. It also predicts less-clear judgments in cases involving moderate degrees of discrepancy between a particular construction and the schema against which it is compared, a prediction which seems likely to be correct. It is widely known that some constructions are readily accepted by all (or almost all) speakers, while others produce mixed judgments. Traditional accounts of the anaphora constraints have often been forced to ignore this difference, or to categorize the marginal cases as either fully grammatical or ungrammatical.

This is a vast area which remains to be researched in more depth. This study has presented one illustration of the kind of work that can be done in analyzing variable judgments, in the analysis of backwards anaphora in Chapter 5. To take one example, the c-command model (without augmentation from discourse principles) predicts that both of the sentences in (1) will be judged grammatical. But, in fact, speakers readily accept (1a) while giving mixed judgments on (1b).

(1)   a.   In *his* recent letter, *John Smith* argued for lowered property taxes.
      b.   *His* mother loves *John*.

The difference in acceptability is attributed to the greater entrenchment of the schema which sanctions (1a) as compared with the rarely activated schema which sanctions (1b). (There are additional differences as well: [1b] does not have a strong prominence asymmetry between the pronoun and the full noun phrase. Also, to the extent that the pattern exemplified by [1b] is entrenched at all, it may be conventionally established as a pattern for repeat identification rather than genuine backwards anaphora.)

Schema competition also provides a natural account for the fact (noted by Zribi-Hertz 1989; Pollard and Sag 1993; Reinhart and Reuland 1993) that reflexives anteceded by a POV cannot appear in positions such as direct object position, where the reflexive would typically be anteceded by the subject of the clause. As noted in Chapter 7, the appearance of the reflexive as direct object would strongly activate the schema for the reflexive prototype, which would therefore be invoked to categorize the construction as anomalous, since the subject of the clause is not the antecedent as specified by the schema. Although there is presumably a schema for POV reflexives which could in theory sanction the appearance of the reflexive, the reflexive prototype schema is more strongly activated, both because the construction matches it so exactly and because of the strength of connectivity between the reflexive-coded nominal conception and the subject as compared with the weak semantic connection between the reflexive and the implied POV (see below and Chap. 7).

Within the generative literature, at least one counterargument has been presented to this kind of approach. Lasnik (1989) has argued against a particular pragmatic account of the anaphora constraints which partially resembles the schema-competition account developed here. He addresses the question of whether Binding Condition B (Chomsky 1981:188), which forces the use of a reflexive when there is a c-commanding antecedent within some local domain, could be replaced by a pragmatic principle which would disallow a pronoun in any context in which a reflexive was possible—presumably on the grounds that a reflexive would be more explicit, less ambiguous, and so on. Such a principle would explain why coreference is not allowed in a sentence like *John likes him* without requiring an explicit statement in the grammar such as Binding Condition B, which says that a pronoun cannot have "too close" an antecedent (specifically, that it cannot be c-commanded by a coreferential noun phrase within its governing category).

Lasnik's putative pragmatic account is reminiscent of the CG schema-competition account, in which the use of the pronoun is judged anomalous because the construction strongly activates a schema for reflexive constructions, which becomes the **categorizing schema.** The construction using a pronoun conflicts with that schema in one crucial respect (a pronoun appears where a reflexive is expected), and so it is judged anomalous. At first glance, this appears to be the same as Lasnik's hypothetical analysis, which says that a pronoun cannot be used where a reflexive could appear. But Lasnik points out that such an approach would fail to account for data such as the following.

(2)   a.   *We like me / myself.

      b.   *_John_ and Mary like _him / himself._

In each case, neither a reflexive nor a pronoun is acceptable, so these data cannot be explained by the principle that a pronoun may not be used wherever a reflexive can appear. These data raise the important question of whether and how the schema-competition model could account for sentences in which neither a reflexive nor a pronoun is acceptable.

Recall that the schema used to evaluate an expression (the categorizing schema) is selected through competition among the various schemas that are activated by the expression. The relative activation of schemas is determined by the extent to which the expression matches the various schemas, and the extent to which schemas are entrenched (through repeated activation) and hence readily activated.

The more properties are shared between the expression and the schema, and the more salient those properties are, the more the schema is activated. The exact workings of the system depend on the schemas posited, the weight given to the schemas (i.e., how entrenched they are), and the weight given to the various factors which can activate a schema—that is, which factors contribute the most to making a construction similar to a particular schema. Since we do not know all of those details with any precision, it is not possible to predict every last bit of data; however, we can describe what the system would do with a particular construction given certain assumptions about the inventory of schemas and the weight given to different factors.

First, consider the reflexive schema. It will be strongly activated by constructions such as (2), which match it in a number of respects—there is correspondence between one of the participants elaborating the trajector of the process and the landmark of that process. The two corresponding participants are also connected by a viewing or cognizing relation (this is made explicit by the verb _like,_ though I have suggested that most processes involving an agent or experiencer include some conception of a viewing relation). The reflexive schema will therefore become highly active, and could be selected as the categorizing schema—in which case the construction would be judged anomalous, since there is correspondence between only _part_ of the trajector and the landmark. The correspondence between participants would be sufficient to activate the schema, but the lack of correspondence between participants would conflict with that schema.

Now consider the pronominal schema(s). Defining the complete in-

ventory of pronominal schemas for English, and the degree of entrenchment of the various schemas for typical speakers, is of course not possible. But we can safely assume for certain highly frequent patterns that
there is a specific, entrenched schema. One such schema captures the
typical pattern for direct object pronouns. Speakers are exposed to hundreds of thousands of examples of constructions involving direct object
pronouns, which should be more than adequate for the development
of a schema, and in fact in many languages the direct object pronoun
takes a different form (accusative case) from that of pronominal objects
of prepositions—indicating that speakers certainly have adequate exposure to the pattern to extract the necessary schemas. We can safely assume therefore that English speakers have acquired a schema for the
use of direct object pronouns. Such a schema would include the specification that the profile of the direct object pronoun correspond to some
nominal which is not part of the profile of the clause which includes
the direct object.

The presence of the pronoun in a construction such as *We like me* or
John and Mary like him would strongly invoke the direct object pronoun
schema. But the construction would conflict with the schema, since the
pronoun corresponds with one of the participants which is "upstream"
in the action chain. If the direct object pronoun schema is selected as the
categorizing schema, the construction is judged anomalous. No matter
which schema is selected, the reflexive direct object schema or the pronominal direct object schema, and no matter whether a pronoun or a
reflexive marker is used, the construction will conflict with the schema.
This explains (in fact, predicts) Lasnik's observation that neither the
reflexive nor the pronoun is acceptable. Essentially, it falls out from
local patterns of usage for pronouns and reflexives in direct object position rather than being derived directly from a maximally general statement of anaphoric principles.

A possible question is why the constructions in (2) cannot be sanctioned by a more general pronominal schema rather than a direct object
pronoun schema. We can assume that speakers have a representation
of English pronouns which includes merely the conception that the pronoun corresponds with some kind of an antecedent (with differentiation
for person, number, and gender, of course). Such a schema would not
conflict with the constructions in (2), and so it would seem as if it should
be chosen as the categorizing schema, and sanction the pronominal version of each sentence.

The reason this would not happen is that such a nonspecific pronominal schema would have to be so highly schematic that it could not compete successfully. For a schema to be selected as the categorizing schema, it is not sufficient for it to have no conflict with the construction in question. The outcome of the competition also depends on how closely the construction matches—and thereby activates—each schema. If a pronoun is used in a construction like (2), the maximally vague pronoun schema cannot compete successfully against the direct object pronoun schema, because the latter is far more specific and matches the construction in too many respects. By the same token, the most schematic pronoun schema cannot compete successfully against the reflexive schema, which also matches the construction in far too many specifics, regardless of whether a reflexive is used.

One might suppose that the categorizing schema should be the schema which conflicts with the construction as little as possible. This hypothesis is termed by Langacker (1987a:431) the "minimal deviance principle." He points out that under that hypothesis, nothing should ever be judged ungrammatical, since some schema could always be found that would not conflict with the construction in question. As a worst-case scenario, the schematic conception of an utterance, consisting of some phonological form paired with some semantic form, could be selected as the categorizing schema. The minimal deviance hypothesis is therefore untenable, and the actual work of categorizing constructions must be done by lower-level, more-specific schemas which are activated by constructions which match them with respect to specific characteristics.

This view of the mechanisms underlying the anaphora constraints is consistent with Langacker's (1988b) characterization of CG as a "usage-based model," one which emphasizes local patterns which are instantiated by actually occurring expressions rather than high-level generalizations. While some of the anaphora patterns can be explained by maximally general statements, many of the details are better explained by considering the more local schemas which capture frequent patterns of usage.

9.4 CONCEPTUAL FACTORS IN REFERENCE POINT ORGANIZATION

One goal of this study has been to ground the analysis of anaphora constraints in semantic notions and, ultimately, in more general principles of cognition. The factors used to define the organization of reference points and dominions are prominence, connectivity, linear order, and POV. The central role which these independently developed CG constructs play in the analysis of the anaphora constraints provides indirect support for their validity in much the same way that the successful predictions made by the c-command model have provided indirect support for the correctness of certain syntactic tree structures, and for the necessity of tree structures in general. At the same time, a number of new directions are suggested for further investigating these constructs.

CG posits two main manifestations of the notion of prominence. The grammatical relations hierarchy SU > DO > OBL is interpreted specifically as a hierarchy of prominence, involving figure/ground asymmetry (Langacker 1987a). The profile/base distinction is also a prominence asymmetry which figures in the distinction between complements and modifiers. Complements, which are incorporated into the profile of the head, are more prominent than modifiers, which are not profiled within the composite conception.

In this model, prominence hierarchies cover much of the same territory as structural relations in c-command-based models (e.g., the subject c-commands more of the clause than does the object; complements of the verb c-command more of the clause than do elements embedded within modifying relations). Data from outside the domains traditionally examined in generative analyses provide supporting evidence for the claim that prominence (rather than structural superiority) is the relevant factor. The backwards anaphora patterns observed in actual usage (Chap. 5) are explained largely by the requirement that the antecedent be significantly more prominent than the pronoun. The patterns for introducing and maintaining referents across discourse (discussed in Chap. 5) also support the claim that certain elements in the clause have greater semantic prominence.

A different manifestation of the requirement of prominence for reference points was discussed in the study of bound anaphora in Chapter 6. There it was argued that nominal conceptions which are contained in modifying phrases are typically not salient enough to serve as antecedents (i.e., reference points) for bound anaphora except under certain circumstances where the nature of the modifying relation is such that it promotes the salience of the nominal in question. This area needs to be explored further, but it appears that a number of seemingly disparate facts can be unified under the requirement that an intended antecedent be sufficiently prominent to function as a reference point.

Prominence also plays a significant role in connectivity. While a great deal remains to be discovered about semantic connectivity, in both its role in language and its cognitive underpinnings, this study has made two specific claims about its nature: first, that connectivity is a matter of degree and can be described as a continuum; second, that the strongest connectivity involves semantic overlap (i.e., correspondences) between explicitly coded (i.e., profiled) entities—in other words, that prominence in the form of profiling plays an essential role here as well.

The continuum of connectivity ranges from the strongest connectivity, which is provided by explicitly coded semantic interconnections, to the weakest connectivity, in which two entities (e.g., two nominal conceptions) are separated by a conceptual break or disjuncture of some kind, such as a change in topic, focus, a change of scene (in narrative), or a narrative event juncture (such as Fox's [1987b] development structures). The intermediate level of connectivity is that in which two entities are co-contained in some local linguistic unit (such as a sentence or a discourse paragraph) without any explicit interconnection between them.

The importance of linear order is in inverse proportion to the strength of the connection between two entities. Where two elements are strongly interconnected, as in (3a–b), in which both nominals elaborate complements of the verb, a change in linear word order does not suffice to remove the less-prominent entity (coded by the name) from the dominion of the subject; coreference is therefore unacceptable.

(3)   a.   *He* placed a deck of cards in front of *John*.
      b.   *In front of *John*, *he* placed a deck of cards.
      c.   *He*'ll have to pay his bills if *John* comes back.
      d.   If *John* comes back, *he*'ll have to pay his bills.

In (3c–d), the modifier is more loosely connected with the conception coded by the verb and its complements, and so preposing the modifier permits the modifier and the nominal within it to "escape" the dominion of the main-clause subject; coreference in (3d) is therefore grammatical. Coreference in (3c) is ungrammatical because the modifier follows the clause in the linear string without an obvious conceptual break, and so it is construed within the dominion of the main-clause subject.

The strongest connectivity is provided by explicitly coded interconnecting relations, as when two nominals function as complements of the same verb so that the profiled process conception contributed by the verb links the nominals together. Most of the cases of obligatory non-coreference covered by Reinhart's c-command analysis involve this kind of strong connectivity. Weaker connectivity, as is typical in cross-sentential contexts and some sentential modifier constructions, gives rise to more variable, less-robust judgments. From the perspective of the reference point model, the c-command approach designates one portion of the continuum of connectivity as a special domain, subject to syntactic restrictions, while relegating the rest to some sort of discourse component. I have argued in Chapters 4 and 5 that this compartmentalization of the data is not necessary, nor is it supported by the facts, which clearly indicate that we are dealing with a continuum (see also Bolinger 1977, 1979).

As argued in Chapter 8, this analysis also accounts for the relative variability of judgments involving POV effects. Where the viewing relation is not explicitly coded—that is, not profiled—it is more easily disregarded than in constructions where the main verb (e.g., *see*, *think*, *tell*, etc.) profiles the viewing relationship (or its metaphorical equivalent, a construal relationship). POV therefore need not be relegated to a separate component of the grammar, and preliminary evidence discussed in Chapter 8 supports the position that POV considerations are more tightly integrated with other factors than has been suggested by generative accounts.

In sum, this model claims that rather than a proliferation of subsystems to account for syntactic anaphora data, POV effects, cross-linguistic coreference, and so on, we are in fact dealing with one system, in which strength of connectivity, as determined by the prominence of conceptual interconnections, plays a critical role.

9.5 CROSS-LINGUISTIC APPLICABILITY

This study has focused entirely on English, leaving open thus far the question of how the reference point model would apply to other languages. The answer comes in two parts. First, the basic components of the reference point model—prominence, semantic connectivity, and linear order—are posited as cognitive and linguistic universals, which leads us to predict that the claims made for English will be largely applicable to other languages. Second, the specifics of reference point organization for English involve conventional patterns, captured as networks of entrenched schemas. While the schematic patterns in other languages should be motivated by the same principles of reference point organization used for English, the development of particular constructions is in

part a matter of historical accident, and may therefore vary considerably; indeed, there is variation even among speakers of English.

Cross-linguistic variation will presumably be of two types: variation in the positioning of nominals along the accessibility scale, and
variation in the inventory of specific constructional schemas which have
become entrenched within a language.

Differences in the Accessibility of Nominals. Ariel (1990:89–92) reports
on a range of literature documenting differences in the Accessibility
Scale across languages (see, in particular, Givón 1983b, 1989; and additional references cited in Ariel). While it appears that languages universally categorize certain nominal forms as higher accessibility markers
than others (e.g., null pronouns represent higher accessibility than overt
pronouns, which represent higher accessibility than full nominals),
equivalent forms in different languages do not necessarily represent the
same degree of accessibility. Languages such as Spanish, Japanese, and
American Sign Language use null pronouns to access referents which
in English would be coded by unstressed overt pronouns; overt pronouns in those languages correspond more or less to English stressed
pronouns.

Ariel (1990:198–206) points out that certain nominal forms may take
on additional connotations which are not described solely by their positioning on the Accessibility Scale. To take one example, in English, the
demonstrative *this* is frequently used as a marker of emotional involve-
ment on the part of the speaker or for intensification in a narrative,
providing a "close-up view" of the referent, as in *It was hysterical to see
this cat perched on top of all these books.* In Japanese, overt pronouns imply
"a personal connection between the speaker and the referent" (Ariel
1990:90; Hinds 1978), with the result that the distribution of overt pronouns is more restricted than in English, and even more restricted than
one would predict solely on the basis of accessibility. These kinds of
considerations will of course affect the cross-linguistic applicability of
any account of nominal coreference constraints.

Differences in the Inventory of Constructional Schemas. The array of
conventional schemas can be expected to vary considerably across languages, but also to reflect universal patterns based on the principles of
accessibility and reference point organization developed here. Backwards anaphora provides one preliminary example. The specific inventory of acceptable backwards anaphora constructions differs from language to language. Hendrick (1990) reports that in Breton the
equivalent of *His mother loves John* is ungrammatical with coreference,

while the equivalent of *Her father told me that Mona drinks* is grammatical. In English, the first sentence is marginal, while the second one is more widely accepted, for the reasons given in Chapter 5, namely that the antecedent is more prominent relative to the pronoun in the second sentence. Assuming the judgments Hendrick reports are typical for Breton speakers, this indicates that a schema which is only marginally included in the inventory of constructional schemas for English speakers is not present in the inventory for Breton speakers.

While cross-linguistic research on the inventories of constructional schemas is only in its infancy, we can make certain predictions about what will be found. The networks of schemas that are entrenched in a given language will have developed in accordance with the general principles of reference point organization laid out here, specifically that nominals tend to be construed as reference points to the extent that they are prominent, and in relationship to nominals with which they are closely connected. We can therefore predict that certain kinds of networks either will not be found or will be exceedingly rare, such as networks of constructional schemas in which nominals coded via a reflexive tend to be associated with more loosely connected entities rather than more strongly connected ones, or conventional patterns of backwards anaphora in which a relatively nonprominent nominal functions as antecedent, while more prominent nominals cannot.

We can also expect to find that in many cases, the same general principles will be manifested in different specific inventories of constructional schemas. This raises questions of how to conceptualize systematic differences in schematic inventories across languages. American Sign Language, for example, seems not to allow backwards anaphora (as determined by consultation with several informants); in other languages, backwards anaphora may be attested but much more restricted than in English. This could be captured by saying that some languages assign more "weight" to linear order than do other languages, but this raises the question of what it means for a certain factor to be accorded greater weight or significance in the determination of reference point organization.[1]

We can also expect differences in the schemas involving connectivity. It was noted in Chapter 5 that different written genres in English conventionally take certain unit boundaries as representing closure of a previously established dominion. While this is motivated by general principles of semantic connectivity, the particular conventions (such as renaming characters after a development structure boundary) are no doubt not only language specific but also genre specific. We can reasonably expect that there will be considerable cross-linguistic variation with respect to these kinds of conventions, capturable by differing inventories of schematic discourse units.

9.6 APPLICATIONS BEYOND ANAPHORA

One of the most impressive attributes of the c-command analysis of the anaphora constraints is the applicability of the c-command construct to a wide range of syntactic issues beyond the original question of the pronominal anaphora constraints. C-command is central to generative syntactic accounts of constraints on wh-question formation (Chomsky 1981; Aoun 1985), negative polarity (Progovac 1994), and quantifier scope (May 1985), among other things. The present study explains the success of the c-command notion in terms of the observation that tree structures (perhaps inadvertently) capture certain facets of semantic structure which are significant for reference point organization. More-prominent nominals, as defined by the CG notions used here, c-command more of the tree structure than less-prominent nominals.

Although I will not attempt to demonstrate this here, I believe that the reference point model can be applied to phenomena such as restrictions on wh-question formation, negative polarity, and quantifier scope. The foundation for a CG analysis of quantifier scope has been laid by Langacker (1991:125–41) and van Hoek (1996a), and in Chapter 6 of the present work. For a quantifier to take scope over some portion of a sentence means essentially that that portion of the sentence is construed within the mental space set up by the quantifier. Langacker notes that a quantifier is apt to be construed as setting up such a context to the extent that it is prominent within the sentence. In van Hoek (1996a) and in Chapter 6 I argue that the same prominence notions used elsewhere in the reference point model—profiling and figure/ground organization, also known as the complement/modifier asymmetry and the grammatical relations hierarchy—are relevant in determining the prominence of quantifiers and their ability to take scope over other conceptions. In van Hoek (1996b) I argue that the reference point/dominion construct accounts for the relationship between a negative polarity item and negative polarity *any* (as in *He didn't know I knew anyone*).

The constraints on wh-question formation have traditionally been formulated in terms of a complex set of principles which include requirements that the wh-word c-command the site to which it is anaphorically related (i.e., the "gap"), and that certain kinds of syntactic structures cannot intervene between the wh-word and the gap (the island constraints which restrict the kinds of structures from which the wh-word can be extracted). In terms of the reference point model of sentential semantics, we can assume that the wh-word functions as a topic, that is, a reference point, with the gap in its dominion. Deane's (1991) analysis of extraction constraints draws on very similar notions, using prominence and semantic connectivity to describe the relationship between a wh-word and the gap. Kluender (1992) develops a somewhat similar proposal cast in terms of predication theory.

While I have not attempted here to provide detailed analyses of phenomena outside the domain of pronominal anaphora constraints, it seems quite likely that the semantic relationships which underlie the reference point model will be shown to be applicable to a range of additional phenomena, just as c-command has been. This is of course only to be expected under the view that c-command partially captures semantic relationships which are crucial to the conceptual organization of the sentence.

9.7 SUMMARY

I have argued that the constraints on pronominal coreference can be accounted for without appeal to autonomous-syntactic notions such as tree structures or c-command, but rather in terms of semantic constructs posited in CG. This approach enables us to unify the account of sentence-internal constraints with cross-sentential, discourse principles. Perhaps the most significant result of the analysis is its claims concerning the fundamental role of prominence and conceptual connectivity, two notions which are arguably rooted in nonlinguistic cognition. The investigation of pronominal anaphora constraints, which have long been a central concern for syntactic analysis, points toward cognitive underpinnings of grammar which are not unique to grammar itself. In that respect, the analysis of pronominal anaphora has profound implications for our conception of the nature of syntax.

CHAPTER ONE

1. The c-command relation has undergone a number of refinements and redefinitions; here I am citing one of the simplest definitions. The precise relationship between c-command restrictions on coindexing of nominals and restrictions on coreference has also been reconsidered at various points; see §1.3 and see Reinhart (1983) and Grodzinsky and Reinhart (1993).

2. I use "referent" and "coreferential" as convenient terms, without thereby adopting or implying an analysis involving real-world objects. For my purposes, a referent is a conceptual entity, and coreference is correspondence between two such conceptions, i.e., a construal of the two conceptions as being in some sense the same.

3. It is unclear whether the reference points proposed here are precisely identical to the starting points discussed by Chafe and MacWhinney, as neither of those researchers develops a detailed model of clause-internal starting points or the principles by which they would be selected. I believe, however, that the model developed here is entirely congruent with Chafe's Information Flow model; see §3.2.3.

4. The extrasyntactic status of linear order is to some extent controversial; see Carden (1986), Solan (1983), Lust (1986:26), and Barss and Lasnik (1986) for discussion.

5. But see Belletti and Rizzi (1988) for a movement analysis of psych verbs, in which the semantic link between experiencer and theme is reflected by a c-command relationship which holds in D-structure. Their analysis, with covert c-command, which is not observable in the surface representation, can serve to bring some kinds of point-of-view data under the scope of the c-command model, but does not apply to all of the examples I will discuss.

CHAPTER TWO

1. For additional illustration of the application of CG to a range of issues, see Tuggy (1981), Vandeloise (1984), Rice (1987), Cook (1988), Hawkins (1984), Lindner (1981), Rubba (1993), Manney (1993).

2. In its reduction of levels of representation to semantic and phonological poles, CG could perhaps be said to anticipate recent developments in the Minimalist Program (Chomsky 1995). The CG conception of semantics and of the nature of the symbolization relationship between semantic and phonological poles is quite different, however.

3. The mere fact that a syntactic convention is idiosyncratic or arbitrary does not constitute proof that a special syntactic component is required in order

to characterize it. Arguments for autonomous syntax based on the seeming arbitrariness or nonpredictability of syntactic patterns (see Newmeyer 1983:9–11 for examples) are flawed by what Langacker (1991:517) calls the **type/predictability fallacy:** confusing the two distinct issues of what *kinds* of linguistic units there are and the *predictability* of their behavior.

4. CG defines the meaning of an expression in terms of activation of concepts, not in terms of reference in the sense of correspondence between words and real-world entities.

5. The profile/base distinction is also similar (though not identical) to Fillmore's (1977) distinction between a frame and a perspective on a frame. The verbs *give* and *receive* invoke the same frame or, in CG terms, the same base, but impose different profiles on the base.

6. The use of iconic notation is intended only as a heuristic; it does not entail any theoretical claim. It should not be construed as a claim that semantic representations consist solely of visual images.

7. The distinction between trajector and landmark is conceptually similar to Talmy's (1978) distinction between Figure and Ground, but the CG notions trajector and landmark are applied more narrowly. Talmy's notion Figure would sometimes pick out the entity which in CG is identified as the trajector, but in some contexts it would pick out the entity which would be identified in CG as the profile. In CG the two different kinds of prominence are considered distinct.

8. Langacker's (1987a:306) notion of dependence is distinct from "dependency" as that term is used by other researchers (e.g., Hudson 1976).

9. Processes are characterized by sequential scanning (sequential activation of their component states), as opposed to the summary scanning (simultaneous activation of components) characteristic of nouns and nonprocessual relations (Langacker 1987a, 1987b).

10. The same general observation applies to Reinhart's (1983) reformulation of the constraints as a pragmatic coreference condition overlaid on a syntactic binding constraint. The binding constraint is still formulated in terms of tree structures which have neither semantic nor phonological content, and the constraint essentially filters out binding configurations which do not fit the specifications.

11. This study focuses only on English, but I assume that the same general Accessibility principles lead to similar (though not necessarily identical) coreference patterns in other languages (see §9.5, and see Ariel 1988, 1990).

12. While the term **ground** is commonly used in CG to refer to facets of the discourse situation (cf. Langacker 1978, 1985), it should not be confused with the distinct notion **figure/ground.**

13. Here as elsewhere in this work, I use the term "referent" to mean a conception within a speaker's or addressee's mind, not the real-world entity (if any) to which it corresponds.

14. Ariel (1990) argues that different kinds of full noun phrases differ with respect to accessibility; e.g., a full name indicates lower accessibility than a first name by itself. In this study I will not be concerned with differentiating degrees of accessibility among full noun phrases.

15. This is not to say that full noun phrases do not invoke the conception of the offstage region at all. All complete nominals (i.e., complete NPs) include some conception of the relationship between the profiled nominal instance and the speech-event context (as in the definite / indefinite distinction). But the "type description" invoked by a full noun phrase is not nearly so tied to the offstage region as that invoked by a pronoun. A pronoun identifies its referent *primarily* in terms of its role in the discourse (as speaker, addressee, topic of discourse, etc.). A full noun phrase invokes a type conception, then includes as a relatively extrinsic component a conception of the relationship between the nominal instance and the discourse context.

16. The same processes would apply when a speaker formulates a sentence. We can assume that production of an utterance begins with the activation of some conception to be encoded, which would immediately begin activating candidate lexical items and grammatical structures to be used in the linguistic encoding. These items would compete for activation, with activation stimulated by their degree of 'fit' with the conception and with the other linguistic items which have already been selected for the encoding. As the linguistic predication becomes more fully defined, it may include reference point / dominion patterns; correspondence between a reference point and a nominal conception in its dominion would tend to activate a schema which would sanction the use of a pronoun, which will then suppress any schemas which might sanction the use of a full noun phrase. The speaker will then use a pronoun rather than a full noun phrase.

CHAPTER THREE

1. This is a matter of language-specific convention. In American Sign Language, the addressee's name is never used for direct address, even to get the addressee's attention or to offer reassurance (as reported to me by several deaf native signers). The use of the addressee's name in those specific contexts in English is therefore not *predicted*, but is motivated by the viewpoint considerations.

2. Similar effects of POV adoption have been discussed, though within a different context and with different emphases, in studies of written narrative; see, e.g., Wiebe 1995; Hewitt 1995; Bruder and Wiebe 1995.

3. I use the terms "point of view" and "viewer" interchangeably as equivalents to the notion which Zribi-Hertz (1989) and others have termed "subject-of-consciousness."

4. I do not wish to claim that there is necessarily a temporal sequence in processing reference points and dominions (though there may be), but only that the reference point plays two roles—as a salient entity in the focus of awareness, as one makes mental contact with it, and as a subjective background conception which is used to shape and construe the conceptual material in its dominion.

5. One possible difference between the notions "starting point" and "reference point" is that a reference point must be construed as still active in some sense and as a central, significant part of the background context in relation to which subsequent material is construed. Not all starting points would be

considered reference points, if starting point includes elements which come first on some natural path (such as the linear string) but which are not necessarily construed as salient or active in relation to following material. The first word of a sentence is a starting point, but in a sentence like *His mother loves John*, I claim that the possessive pronoun need not be construed as a reference point in relation to the rest of the clause, as it is not particularly salient within the clause (though linear precedence *encourages* construing a particular element as a reference point). Coreference is therefore possible between the pronoun and full noun phrase.

6. Chafe (1994 and references there) develops a detailed model of intonation units, to which I am not attempting to do justice here.

7. The trajector of a relation is *always* a reference point in relationship to any landmarks of that same relation owing to the close connection between the trajector and the landmark. The trajector (i.e., figure) of a relation tends to function as a reference point for other conceptions which are more or less loosely associated with the relation. But the landmarks of a relation are not more or less loosely associated, but instead are strongly connected with the trajector by virtue of participating in (i.e., elaborating) an overt, profiled relation.

8. Langacker (1991:436) defines a subordinate clause as one whose profile is overridden by that of another clause—either because the subordinate clause is subsumed as a complement of the main-clause verb or because the subordinate clause is in some way attached to the main clause as a modifier.

9. This does not contradict the earlier claim that modifiers of a nominal are construed within the same context as the overall nominal to which they are attached (e.g., *John* in *John's mother*). Two different notions are involved; here we are considering the question of whether a nominal is prominent enough that it is obligatorily construed as a reference point, while previously we were addressing the question of whether a nominal is construed within the dominion of another reference point. With respect to the former question, nominals in modifiers behave differently from nominals which correspond to profiled arguments of the verb; with respect to the latter question, all of the components of a nominal—head, modifier(s), and / or complement(s)—are construed in the dominion of any preceding reference point(s).

10. I say that the conceptualizer need not take the possessor as a reference point in relation to the rest of the clause, rather than does not, because almost any nominal could potentially be construed as a reference point inasmuch as it becomes part of the evolving discourse context and may be construed as "still active" in relation to following material. In the case of possessive pronouns, prominence relations within the complement chain do not contribute to making the possessor a reference point, but nothing prevents the speaker from using that slot to introduce a new referent, which then functions as an antecedent for a pronoun, as in *John's mother loves him*.

11. Lakoff (1968) notes that while some speakers find this type of construction grammatical, he himself rejects it; Roberts (1987:85–86) observes that it is acceptable only as an instance of repeat identification of a previously mentioned referent, and not as genuine backwards anaphora.

12. This example is taken from a posting on the Internet. This is an instance

of genuine backwards anaphora, as the story "Cindy's Torment" had not been mentioned previously.

13. If POV factors rendered sentences unacceptable which were predicted, by the complement chain, to be acceptable, then one might still claim that the complement chain is really an autonomous syntactic construct and that POV effects operate at a different level. The data discussed below are of the opposite kind, however: POV effects can make sentences acceptable which would otherwise be predicted to be unacceptable. This would be problematic for a c-command based account (Malone 1993), as well as for an interpretation of the complement chain as a notational variant of c-command.

CHAPTER FOUR

1. This level of connectivity appears to be equivalent to Ariel's (1990) notion of Unity.

2. Linear order appears to have an effect even in constructions involving strong connectivity, but it is not the sole—or even primary—determinant of grammaticality. Speakers report, for example, that *Near Dan, he saw a snake* is, if not entirely acceptable, more nearly acceptable than *He saw a snake near Dan* (under the coreferential reading). The impact of linear order in these cases may best be measured in terms of reaction times or rankings of relative acceptability rather than absolute grammaticality judgments.

3. Linear precedence is a **primacy relation** in Langacker's model, and Langacker notes that "when *A* bears one or both primacy relations to *B*, *A* tends to act as a nucleus while *B* tends to assume the status of a satellite" (1969:169). The model developed here attempts to capture essentially the same intuitions which Langacker stated as primacy relations, expressed here in terms of the interaction of linear precedence and prominence asymmetries.

4. Reinhart does not develop this discourse principle in any detail, and so it is unclear, for example, why sentences such as *Near him, Dan saw a snake* would not similarly be judged unacceptable at the discourse level.

5. This distinction is similar to Foley and Van Valin's (1984) distinction between the **core,** which is the verb and its arguments, and the **periphery,** which may include other nominals, the spatial and temporal setting, and so forth. However, I differentiate between degrees of extrinsicness or peripherality which are not distinguished in Foley and Van Valin's model.

6. Although I term the distinction process internal and process external, analogous remarks may be made concerning modifiers of categories other than clauses, e.g., modifiers of deverbal nouns.

7. There is some ambiguity to modifiers describing the spatial or temporal setting for an event; depending on context and word order (and intonation), they may be construed as process-internal spatial-temporal settings or as more abstract "conceptual settings." This variability in construal becomes more of an issue when these modifiers are preposed; when they follow the clause, they are usually construed as part of the spatial-temporal setting, and hence as internal to the process conception. Bolinger (1977) has described this tendency with the idea that the VP "captures" the modifier.

8. I am grateful to an anonymous reviewer for pointing out (17a).

9. Linear order appears to have an effect even in constructions involving strong connectivity, but it is not the sole—or even primary—determinant of grammaticality. Speakers report, e.g., that *Near Dan, he saw a snake* is, if not entirely acceptable, more nearly acceptable than *He saw a snake near Dan* (under the coreferential reading). The impact of linear order in these cases may best be measured by reaction times or rankings of relative acceptability rather than absolute grammaticality judgments.

10. For detailed analysis of the different construals given to modifiers which incorporate a subordinate clause (e.g., *if* and *when* adverbials) when they appear sentence-initially or sentence-finally, see Chafe (1984), Ramsay (1987), Matthiesen and Thompson (1988). (Matthiesen and Thompson point out, however, that it is in some ways misleading to describe these constructions as involving modification of one clause by another.)

CHAPTER FIVE

1. Similar observations have been made by McCray (1980) and by Mittwoch (1983), both of whom based their claims on invented examples and restricted their attention to a small range of construction types.

2. I excluded examples in which the pronominal referent could have been recovered from the context without the full noun phrase, but where the resulting construction would have been stylistically awkward. Some of those examples may have been genuine backwards anaphora, but I did not want to impose my own stylistic preferences for reidentification of a referent, and so I limited the corpus to those examples in which it was truly implausible that the pronoun could find its antecedent in the preceding context.

3. As elsewhere in this study, I use the term "preposed" as convenient shorthand for "modifier attached to the beginning of the clause," without adopting any notion of a movement transformation.

4. Matthiesen and Thompson (1988) term such constructions "hypotactic clause combinations," and note that it can be quite misleading to refer to them as involving clausal adverbials or subordinate clauses. I use the term "modifier" for convenience here.

5. (19a) is well known for producing mixed judgments. Lakoff (1968) notes that he himself rejects it, though other speakers accept it. Roberts (1987:85–86) notes that it is acceptable only as an instance of repeat identification of a previously established discourse referent, and not as genuine backwards anaphora.

6. A particularly awkward example of this "compact backwards anaphora" style is this sentence, the complete text of a picture caption: "The standardised script introduced throughout his empire by Charlemagne" (James Burke, *The Day the Universe Changed*, p.25). Although this construction is quite unusual as an example of backwards anaphora, it is in a sense typical as an example of the compact writing style found in picture captions and other one-line texts.

7. Note that it is the entire preposed phrase which sets the scene for the subject. The pronoun alone could not function as a topic or reference point in relation to the subject, as that would violate the principle that full noun phrases

do not appear in the dominion of a corresponding reference point. Since the pronoun is not profiled in the composite conception (it is contained in a modifier), it need not be construed as a reference point.

8. The texts used were popular magazines (mostly *Reader's Digest*) and popular science fiction novels.

9. The reference point model thus avoids the pitfalls of an anaphora-constraint analysis stated in terms of "given" versus "new" information, pitfalls such as those pointed out by Reinhart (1983:94–101), who notes that manipulating the given versus new status of nominals within a clause does not significantly affect coreference possibilities.

10. Ariel (1990:98) notes that it should, in principle, be possible to reinterpret the Binding Conditions as a set of Accessibility principles, but does not develop a specific proposal.

CHAPTER SIX

1. A different kind of focus shift is seen when a speaker establishes a correspondence between the profile of a pronoun and the conception of an entire group which is invoked by a quantifier expression. Examples of this are discussed by Heim (1990), who notes that it is problematic for her analysis. Her example (79) is *Every student turned in a paper. They were all identical*, where *they* corresponds to the conception of the group of papers that were turned in, though there is no plural antecedent in the preceding sentence. Heim notes that one might perhaps claim that "those papers have somehow been made salient by the previous discourse" (1990:172), but rejects this analysis as incompatible with the rest of her model. I would claim that the replicate process conception sets up the conception of a group of papers, which can then be accessed via a pronoun.

2. For ease of exposition, I use the term "replicate construal" to refer to the special construal invoked by a quantifier, though this is intended to cover negative constructions (such as *No one loves his mother*) as well.

3. Roberts (1987) captures this observation in terms of the notion that the possessor always takes wide scope over the NP of which it is a part. Here this scope behavior is attributed to its status as a grounding predication.

4. Heim (1982:201–4) also develops the idea that the quantifier in this type of construction cannot get scope outside the immediate clause containing it. Unlike the analysis here, which is based on principles governing the spread of a replicate construal, her analysis is based on a c-command-based definition of scope and on NP adjunction which is limited to the immediate clause containing the quantifier phrase.

5. The sentences were presented in writing, without the underlining of antecedent and pronoun. Speakers were first given sample sentences such as *Everyone loves his mother* and *Every man who owns a donkey beats it* in order to ascertain that they understood the relevant (bound) readings and that they rejected clearly ungrammatical examples (such as *His mother loves everyone*).

6. Several speakers felt strongly that "his or her" should be substituted for "his," but otherwise accepted the construction.

7. May (1985) also analyzes sentences like those in (10), and proposes a c-command-based account involving NP movement and adjunction and a significantly revised definition of c-command.

8. Reinhart (1987) argues that the constraints on backwards bound anaphora do not in fact have to do with linear order, but rather pertain to the requirement that the quantifier phrase c-command the pronoun.

9. The parallelism between bound anaphora and anaphora involving nonspecific antecedents has been noted by a number of researchers, using various terminologies and theoretical frameworks. Kamp (1984:37–38) analyzes ungrammatical backwards bound anaphora as an instantiation of the same principles by which he rules out backwards anaphora involving nonspecific antecedents in conditional constructions. Heim (1982:210–20) also points out the parallels between restrictions on these two construction types, though her account is couched in terms of tree structural representations in Logical Form.

10. Constructions of the type in (21a) were first pointed out by Higginbotham (1980), those of the type in (21b) by Geach (1962).

11. It is possible to form closely related paraphrases, such as *the lid that goes to that jar*; however such paraphrases involve additional conceptual content contributed by the verb within the relative clause. The unacceptable relative clause constructions are those based solely on a prepositional phrase which describes a relation wholly intrinsic to the meaning of the head noun.

12. In earlier versions of this work, I argued that relative clauses were used for relatively extrinsic modifying relations, and prepositional phrases for more intrinsic ones. But there are counterexamples: The preposition *with* in the sense of ownership cannot be used in a relative clause construction—*a man who is with a donkey* is not at all equivalent to *a man who has a donkey* (this was pointed out by a reviewer). It still appears to be true that the relative clause describes a somewhat more temporary situation than the bare prepositional phrase; in this case the relative clause implies a more temporary association than ownership. I have no explanation for the awkwardness of a quantified version of this expression—e.g., *every person who is with a donkey/an escort/a date*, all of which seem unacceptable aside from any question of using them in a bound anaphora construction.

13. As discussed in Chapter 3, nominal conceptions introduced in modifiers are not so prominent that they are obligatorily construed as reference points relative to subsequent material, but they are potentially *available* as reference points simply by virtue of having been recently mentioned. This is equivalent to what Roberts (1987) calls discourse anaphora as opposed to c-command anaphora; however I do not, of course, draw a sharp distinction between the two. "Discourse anaphora" means here simply that the nominal conception is accessible solely on the grounds of having been recently mentioned in the discourse rather than being elevated in prominence owing to profiling or figure / ground alignment within the clause.

14. Heim (1990:166) seems to come close to proposing this kind of analysis; she comments that the difference between *every man who has a wife*, in which *wife* can function as an antecedent for bound anaphora in a donkey-type construction, and *every married man*, which does not set up the conception of the

wife as a possible antecedent, may be that the former provides greater psychological salience to the conception of the wife than the latter. However, she does not pursue this line of reasoning in detail.

CHAPTER SEVEN

1. The original examples ended with the phrase *with the children placed behind them/themselves*. The addition of *placed* could bring in another vantage point—the conceived agent of *place*. The example was therefore reworded to remove ambiguity.

2. (8a) is ambiguous in the same way as (7a) above, owing to the notion that a house has an inherent front/back orientation.

3. The use of a pronoun does not necessarily signify an objective view from the perspective of all onstage participants: rather it marks the perspective of the viewer conceived as the closest. In some contexts the use of a reflexive would not be conventionally sanctioned (typically because the intended antecedent would not be the closest reference point), and so a pronoun is the only possible choice (as in *John believed that Mary loved him*). Here the referent of the pronoun is viewed objectively by the closest viewer (Mary) but semisubjectively by the more distant viewer; the pronoun marks the closer viewer's perception of the referent.

4. This notion of onstage correspondence may capture the intuition which Zribi-Hertz (1994) describes in terms of endophoricity.

5. Faltz (1985), Dalrymple (1993), and Reuland and Koster (1991), among others, note that constructions of this type are not permitted in all languages which have distinct reflexive markers; many languages require that the antecedent be the subject of its clause.

6. See Langacker (1986b) for discussion of the setting/participant distinction.

7. The Awareness Condition specifically states: Use of a picture noun reflexive is obligatory if the referent of the reflexive perceived/perceives/will perceive the referent of the picture noun as one that involves him. Use of a picture-noun nonreflexive pronoun is obligatory otherwise.

8. Alternatively, it is possible that these constructions merely instantiate an entrenched, highly specific constructional schema whose entrenchment was initially motivated by the possessor's status as the closest reference point in relation to the possessum. This possibility and the POV analysis are not mutually exclusive.

9. Baker cites the source for (31a) as *Jane Austen's Letters to Her Sister and Others*; Vol. 2, ed. R. W. Chapman (Oxford: Oxford University Press, 1932, p. 94). For (31b), the cited source is Jane Austen, *Sense and Sensibility* (London: Penguin, 1985, p. 282).

CHAPTER EIGHT

1. Kuno notes that the sentence *That he would be elected was anticipated by John* is also somewhat anomalous with coreference, suggesting that (2) has addi-

tional difficulties besides POV considerations. (2) is significantly worse, however, illustrating the contribution of the POV conflict.

2. Constructions of the kind discussed in Chap. 6 such as *I like me* may be considered an example of a situation in which an inappropriate nominal form *is* taken as a cue that a significant aspect of the conceptual organization of the clause (correspondence between trajector and landmark) is to be ignored. But note that these constructions are clearly recognized as deviating from the norm—the unusual choice of nominal form does not suffice to change the construal of head/complement structure and figure/ground organization; instead speakers construe the expression against the background of the usual, expected form (e.g., *I like myself*).

3. This is not strictly a binary opposition. Rather, the extent to which it is felt that a nominal must be semantically compatible with one context or another is a matter of degree.

4. To reduce the possibility of my inadvertently cuing subjects in their judgments, half of the subjects were given the sentences in writing and asked (also in writing) to read the sentences out loud with the two different stress patterns. Speakers who read the sentences to themselves were as likely to report the expected contrasts as speakers who heard the sentences read to them.

CHAPTER NINE

1. Bresnan (1995) has proposed an LFG account of cross-linguistic variation in weak crossover effects, similar in many respects to the reference point approach, which incorporates the notion of variable weighting of factors. The question of how to incorporate weighting of factors in CG, which of course does not permit either the constraints or their rankings to be listed as independent elements in the grammar, remains open.

Aoun, Joseph. 1985. *A Grammar of Anaphora*. Cambridge, MA: MIT Press.

Ariel, Mira. 1988. "Referring and Accessibility." *Journal of Linguistics* 24:65–87.

———. 1990. *Accessing Noun Phrase Antecedents*. New York: Routledge.

Baker, C. L. 1995. "Contrast, Discourse Prominence, and Intensification, with Special Reference to Locally Free Reflexives in British English." *Language* 71:63–101.

Bamberg, Michael. 1987. *The Acquisition of Narratives*. Berlin: Mouton de Gruyter.

Barss, Andrew, and Howard Lasnik. 1986. "A Note on Anaphora and Double Objects." *Linguistic Inquiry* 17:347–54.

Bartsch, R., and T. Vennemann. 1972. *Semantic Structures*. Frankfurt: Athenäum.

Bates, Elizabeth, and Brian MacWhinney. 1987. "Competition, Variation and Language Learning." In B. MacWhinney, ed., *Mechanisms of Language Acquisition*. Hillsdale, NJ: Erlbaum.

Belletti, Adriana, and Luigi Rizzi. 1988. "Psych-Verbs and (Theta-)Theory." *Natural Language and Linguistic Theory* 6(3): 291–352.

Bolinger, Dwight. 1977. "Pronouns and Repeated Nouns." Ms., Indiana University Linguistics Club, Bloomington.

———. 1979. "Pronouns in Discourse." In Givón 1979b.

Bosch, P. 1983. *Agreement and Anaphora*. New York: Academic Press.

Bresnan, Joan. 1978. "A Realistic Transformational Grammar." In M. Halle, J. Bresnan, and G. A. Miller, eds., *Linguistic Theory and Psychological Reality*. Cambridge, MA: MIT Press.

———. 1982. *The Mental Representation of Grammatical Relations*. Cambridge, MA: MIT Press.

———. 1995. "Morphology Competes with Syntax: Explaining Typological Variation in Weak Crossover Effects." Paper presented at the Optimality Workshop, MIT, April.

Broadbent, D. E. 1973. *In Defence of Empirical Psychology*. London: Methuen.

Brown, Cheryl. 1983. "Topic Continuity in Written English Narrative." In Givón 1979b.

Bruder, Gail A., and Janyce M. Wiebe. 1995. "Recognizing Subjectivity and Identifying Subjective Characters in Third-Person Fictional Narrative." In J. Duchan, Bruder, and Hewitt 1995.

Brugman, Claudia, and George Lakoff. 1987. "The Semantics of Aux-Inversion and Anaphora Constraints." Paper given at the Annual Meeting of the Linguistic Society of America, San Francisco.

Cantrall, William R. 1974. *Viewpoint, Reflexives, and the Nature of Noun Phrases*. The Hague: Mouton.

Carden, Guy. 1982. "Backwards Anaphora in Discourse Context." *Journal of Linguistics* 18:361–87.

———. 1986. "Blocked Forwards Coreference: Theoretical Implications of the Acquisition Data." In B. Lust, ed., *Studies in the Acquisition of Anaphora*. Vol. 1: *Defining the Constraints*. Dordrecht: D. Reidel.

Chafe, Wallace. 1976. "Givenness, Contrastiveness, Definiteness, Subjects, Topics, and Point of View." In C. Li, ed., *Subject and Topic*. New York: Academic Press.

———. 1979. "The Flow of Thought and the Flow of Language." In Givón 1979b.

———. 1984. "How People Use Adverbial Clauses." In C. Brugman and M. Macauley, eds., *Proceedings of the Tenth Annual Meeting of the Berkeley Linguistics Society*. Berkeley, CA: Berkeley Linguistics Society.

———. 1987. "Cognitive Constraints on Information Flow." In R. Tomlin (1987a).

———. 1991. "Grammatical Subjects in Speaking and Writing." *Text* 11:45–72.

———. 1994. *Discourse, Consciousness and Time*. Chicago: University of Chicago Press.

Chomsky, Noam. 1981. *Lectures on Government and Binding*. Dordrecht: Foris.

———. 1995. *The Minimalist Program*. Cambridge, MA: MIT Press.

Clancy, Patricia. 1980. "Referential Choice in English and Japanese Narrative Discourse." In W. Chafe, ed., *The Pear Stories: Cognitive, Cultural and Linguistics Aspects of Narrative Production*. Norwood, NJ: Ablex.

Cook, Kenneth. 1988. "A Cognitive Analysis of Grammatical Relations, Case and Transitivity." Ph.D. diss., University of California, San Diego.

Cooper, R. 1974. "Montague Semantic Theory of Adverbs and the VSO Hypothesis." In E. Kaisse and J. Hankamer, eds., *Papers from the Fifth Annual Meeting of the North Eastern Linguistic Society*.

Croft, William. 1991. *Syntactic Categories and Grammatical Relations*. Chicago: University of Chicago Press.

Dalrymple, Mary. 1993. *The Syntax of Anaphoric Binding*. Stanford, CA: Center for the Study of Language and Information.

Deane, Paul. 1987. "English Possessives, Topicality, and the Silverstein Hierarchy." *Proceedings of the Berkeley Linguistics Society* 13:65–76.

———. 1991. "Limits to Attention: A Cognitive Theory of Island Constraints." *Cognitive Linguistics* 2:1–63.

———. 1992. *Grammar in Mind and Brain: Explorations in Cognitive Science*. Berlin: Mouton de Gruyter.

DeLancey, Scott. 1981. "An Interpretation of Split Ergativity and Related Phenomena." *Language* 57:626–57.

Delisle, G. A. 1973. "Discourse and Backward Pronominalization." Ms., Bloomington: Indiana University Linguistics Club.

Dinsmore, John. 1989. "Foundations of Knowledge Partitioning." *SIU Computer Science Technical Report* 88-16.

———. 1991. *Partitioned Representations: A Study in Mental Representation, Language Understanding and Linguistic Structure*. Dordrecht: Kluwer.

Duchan, Judith F., Gail A. Bruder, and Lynne E. Hewitt, eds. 1995. *Deixis in Narrative: A Cognitive Science Perspective*. Hillsdale, NJ: Erlbaum.

Elman, Jeffrey L., and James L. McClelland. 1984. "Speech Perception as a Cognitive Process: The Interactive Activation Model." In N. Lass, ed., *Speech and Language*, Vol. 10. New York: Academic Press.

Erteschik, Nomi. 1973. "On the Nature of Island Constraints." Ms., Bloomington: Indiana University Linguistics Club.

Erteschik, Nomi, and Shalom Lappin. 1979. "Dominance and the Functional Explanation of Island Phenomena." *Theoretical Linguistics* 6:41–86.

Evans, G. 1982. *The Varieties of Reference*. Edited by J. McDowell. Oxford: Clarendon Press.

Faltz, Leonard. 1985. *Reflexivization: A Study in Universal Syntax*. New York: Garland.

Fauconnier, Gilles. 1985. *Mental Spaces: Aspects of Meaning Construction in Natural Language*. Cambridge, MA: MIT Press.

———. 1988. "Quantifications, Roles and Domains." In U. Eco, M. Santambrogio, and P. Violi, eds., *Meaning and Mental Representations*. Bloomington: Indiana University Press.

Fauconnier, Gilles, and Eve Sweetser. 1996. *Spaces, Worlds, and Grammars*. Chicago: University of Chicago Press.

Fillmore, Charles. "The Case for Case Reopened." In P. Cole and J. M. Sadock, eds., *Syntax and Semantics*, Vol. 8: *Grammatical Relations*. New York: Academic Press.

Fillmore, C., and P. Kay. 1993. "Construction Grammar." Ms., University of California, Berkeley.

Foley, William A., and Robert D. Van Valin, Jr. 1984. *Functional Syntax and Universal Grammar*. Cambridge: Cambridge University Press.

Fox, Barbara. 1987a. *Discourse Structure and Anaphora*. Cambridge: Cambridge University Press.

———. 1987b. "Anaphora in Popular Written English Narratives." In Tomlin 1987a.

Geach, Peter. 1962. *Reference and Generality*. Ithaca, NY: Cornell University Press.

Givón, Talmy. 1976. "Topic, Pronoun and Grammatical Agreement." In Li 1976.

———. 1978. "Negation in Language: Pragmatics, Function, Ontology." In P. Cole, ed., *Syntax and Semantics*. Vol. 9: *Pragmatics*. New York: Academic Press.

———. 1979a. *On Understanding Grammar*. New York: Academic Press.

———, ed. 1979b. *Syntax and Semantics*. Vol. 12: *Discourse and Syntax*. New York: Academic Press.

———, ed. 1983a. *Topic Continuity in Discourse: A Quantitative Cross-Language Study*. Amsterdam: John Benjamins.

———. 1983b. "Topic Continuity in Discourse: An Introduction." In Givón 1983a.

———. 1984. *Syntax: A Functional-Typological Introduction*, Vol. 1. Amsterdam: John Benjamins.

———. 1985. "The Pragmatics of Referentiality." In D. Schiffrin, ed., *Meaning, Form and Use in Context*. Washington, DC: Georgetown University Press.

———. 1989. "The Grammar of Referential Coherence as Mental Processing Instructions." Technical Report No. 89-7, Eugene: University of Oregon.

———. 1994. Introduction to T. Givón, ed., *Voice and Inversion*. Amsterdam: John Benjamins.

Goldberg, A. 1995. *Constructions*. Chicago: University of Chicago Press.

Grimes, J. 1975. *The Thread of Discourse*. The Hague: Mouton.

Grimshaw, Jane. 1990. *Argument Structure*. Cambridge, MA: MIT Press.

Grober, E. H., W. Beardsley, and A. Caramazza. 1978. "A Parallel Function Strategy in Pronoun Assignment." *Cognition* 6:117–33.

Grodzinsky, Yosef, and Tanya Reinhart. 1993. "The Innateness of Binding and Coreference." *Linguistic Inquiry* 24(1): 69–101.

Gruber, Jeffrey S. 1965. *Studies in Lexical Relations*. Bloomington: Indiana University Linguistics Club.

Gundel, Jeanette, Nancy Hedberg, and Ron Zacharski. 1993. "Cognitive Status and the Form of Referring Expressions in Discourse." *Language* 69:274–307.

Haïk, Isabel. 1984. "Indirect Binding." *Linguistic Inquiry* 2:185–223.

Hawkins, Bruce. 1984. "The Semantics of English Spatial Prepositions." Ph.D. diss., University of California, San Diego.

Hawkins, J. 1978. *Definiteness and Indefiniteness: A Study in Reference and Grammaticality Prediction*. London: Croom Helm.

Heim, Irene. 1982. "The Semantics of Definite and Indefinite Noun Phrases." Ph.D. diss., University of Massachusetts, Amherst.

———. 1990. "E-type Pronouns and Donkey Anaphora." *Linguistics and Philosophy* 13:137–77.

Hendrick, Randall. 1990. "Breton Pronominals, Binding, and Barriers." In R. Hendrick, ed., *Syntax and Semantics*. Vol. 23: *The Syntax of the Modern Celtic Languages*. San Diego: Academic Press.

Hewitt, Lynne E. 1995. "Anaphor in Subjective Contexts in Narrative Fiction." In Duchan, Bruder, and Hewitt 1995.

Higginbotham, James. 1980. "Pronouns and Bound Variables." *Linguistic Inquiry* 11(4): 679–708.

Hinds, John. 1978. "Anaphora in Japanese Conversation." In J. Hinds, ed., *Anaphora in Discourse*. Alberta: Linguistic Research.

———. 1979. Organizational Patterns in Discourse." In Givón 1979b.

Hirschberg, Julia, and Gregory Ward. 1991. "Accent and Bound Anaphora." *Cognitive Linguistics* 2(2): 101–21.

Hopper, Paul. 1979. "Aspect and Foregrounding in Discourse." In Givón 1979b.

Hudson, Richard. *Arguments for a Non-transformational Grammar*. Chicago: University of Chicago Press.

Jackendoff, Ray. 1972. *Semantic Interpretation in Generative Grammar*. Cambridge, MA: MIT Press.

———. 1977. *X-Bar Syntax: A Study of Phrase Structure*. Cambridge, MA: MIT Press.

———. 1992. "Mme. Tussaud Meets the Binding Theory." *Natural Language and Linguistic Theory* 10:1–31.

Kamp, Hans. 1984. "A Theory of Truth and Semantic Representation." In J. Groenendijk, T. M. V. Janssen, and M. Stokhof, eds., *Truth, Interpretation and Information: Selected Papers from the Third Amsterdam Colloquium*. Dordrecht: Foris.

Karmiloff-Smith, Annette. 1981. "The Grammatical Marking of Thematic Structure in the Development of Language Production." In W. Deutsch, ed., *The Child's Construction of Language*. London: Academic Press.

———. 1985. "Language and Cognitive Processes from a Developmental Perspective." *Language and Cognitive Processes* 1:61–85.

Karttunen, Lauri. 1968. "Coreference and Discourse." Paper presented at the Annual Meeting of the Linguistic Society of America, New York.

———. 1976. "Discourse Referents." In J. McCawley 1976.

Kasher, A. 1976. "Conversational Maxims and Rationality." In A. Kasher, ed., *Language in Focus*. Dordrecht: Reidel.

Keenan, Edward L., and Bernard Comrie. 1977. "Noun Phrase Accessibility and Universal Grammar." *Linguistic Inquiry* 8:63–99.

Kemmer, Suzanne. 1993. *The Middle Voice*. Amsterdam: John Benjamins.

Kluender, Robert. 1992. "Deriving Island Constraints from Principles of Predication." In H. Goodluck and M. Rochemont, eds., *Island Constraints: Theory, Acquisition and Processing*. Dordrecht: Kluwer.

Koster, Jan, and Eric Reuland, eds. 1991. *Long-Distance Anaphora*. Cambridge: Cambridge University Press.

Kuno, Susumu. 1972. "Functional Sentence Perspective: A Case Study from Japanese and English." *Linguistic Inquiry* 3:269–320.

———. 1975. "Three Perspectives in the Functional Approach to Syntax." In R. E. Grossman, L. J. San, and T. J. Vance, eds., *Papers from the Parasession on Functionalism*, Vol. II. Chicago: Chicago Linguistic Society.

———. 1987. *Functional Syntax: Anaphora, Discourse and Empathy*. Chicago: University of Chicago Press.

Lakoff, George. 1968. "Pronouns and Reference." In McCawley 1976.

———. 1971. "Presupposition and Relative Well-Formedness." In D. D. Steinberg and L. A. Jakobovits, eds., *Semantics: An Interdisciplinary Reader in Philosophy, Linguistics and Psychology*. Cambridge: Cambridge University Press.

———. 1976. "Pronouns and Reference." In McCawley 1976.

———. 1987. *Women, Fire, and Dangerous Things: What Categories Reveal about the Mind*. Chicago: University of Chicago Press.

Lakoff, George, and John Ross. 1972. "A Note on Anaphoric Islands and Causatives." *Linguistic Inquiry* 3:121–25.

Langacker, Ronald W. 1969. "Pronominalization and the Chain of Command." In Schane and Reibel, eds. *Modern Studies in English*. Englewood Cliff, NJ: Prentice-Hall.

———. 1978. "The Form and Meaning of the English Auxiliary." *Language* 54: 853–82.

————. 1982. "Space Grammar, Analysability, and the English Passive." *Language* 58:22–80.

————. 1985. "Observations and Speculations on Subjectivity." in J. Haiman, ed., *Iconicity in Syntax*. Amsterdam: John Benjamins.

————. 1986a. "An Introduction to Cognitive Grammar." *Cognitive Science* 10: 1–40.

————. 1986b. "Settings, Participants and Grammatical Relations." In S. De-Lancey and R. Tomlin, eds., *Proceedings of the Second Annual Meeting of the Pacific Linguistics Conference*. University of Oregon, Dept. of Linguistics.

————. 1987a. *Foundations of Cognitive Grammar*. Vol. 1: *Theoretical Prerequisites*. Stanford: Stanford University Press.

————. 1987b. "Nouns and Verbs." *Language* 63:53–94.

————. 1987c. "Grammatical Ramifications of the Setting / Participant Distinction." *BLS* 13:383–94.

————. 1988a. "Autonomy, Agreement and Cognitive Grammar." *Proceedings of the Chicago Linguistic Society* 24:147–80.

————. 1988b. "A Usage-based Model." In B. Rudzka-Ostyn, ed., *Topics in Cognitive Linguistics*. Amsterdam: John Benjamins.

————. 1990. "Subjectification." *Cognitive Linguistics* 1:5–38.

————. 1991. *Foundations of Cognitive Grammar*. Vol. 2: *Descriptive Application*. Stanford: Stanford University Press.

————. 1992. "The Meaning of *of* and *of*-periphrasis." In M. Pütz, ed., *Thirty Years of Linguistic Evolution: Studies in Honor of René Dirven on the Occasion of His 60th Birthday*. Philadelphia: John Benjamins.

————. 1993. "Reference-Point Constructions." *Cognitive Linguistics* 4:1–38.

————. 1995. "Viewing in Grammar and Cognition." In P. W. Davis, ed., *Alternative Linguistics: Descriptive and Theoretical Models*. Amsterdam: John Benjamins.

————. Forthcoming. "A Dynamic Usage-based Model."

Larson, Richard. 1985. "Quantifying into NP." Ms., Philadelphia: University of Pennsylvania.

Lasnik, Howard 1986. "On the Necessity of Binding Conditions." Reprinted in Lasnik 1989.

————. 1989. *Essays on Anaphora*. Dordrecht Kluwer.

Lees, Robert, and Edward S. Klima. 1963. "Rules for English Pronominalization." *Language* 39:17–28.

Levy, E. 1982. "Toward an Objective Definition of 'Discourse Topic.'" In K. Tuite, R. Schneider, and R. Chametzky, eds., *Papers from the Eighteenth Regional Meeting of the Chicago Linguistic Society*. Chicago: Chicago Linguistic Society.

Li, Charles, ed. 1976. *Subject and Topic*. New York: Academic Press.

Lindner, Susan. 1981. "A Lexico-Semantic Analysis of English Verb-Particle Constructions with "Up" and "Out". Ph.D. diss., University of California, San Diego.

Longacre, R. 1979. "The Paragraph as a Grammatical Unit." In Givón 1979b.

Longacre, Robert, and Sandra A. Thompson. 1985. "Adverbial Clauses." In T.

Shopen, ed., *Language Typology and Linguistic Description*. Cambridge: Cambridge University Press.

Lust, Barbara. 1986. Introduction to B. Lust, ed., *Studies in the Acquisition of Anaphora*. Vol. 1: *Defining the Constraints*. Dordrecht: D. Reidel.

MacWhinney, Brian. 1977. "Starting Points." *Language* 53:152–68.

McCawley, James, ed. 1976. *Syntax and Semantics*. Vol. 7: *Notes from the Linguistic Underground*. New York: Academic Press.

McCray, A. 1980. "The Semantics of Backwards Anaphora." In J. Jensen, ed., *Proceedings of the Tenth Annual Meeting of the North Eastern Linguistic Society*. Ottawa: University of Ottawa.

McGann, William, and Arthur Schwartz. 1988. "Main Character in Children's Narratives." *Linguistics* 26:215–33.

McKeown, K. 1982. "Generating Natural Language Text in Response to Questions about Database Structure." Ph.D. diss. University of Pennsylvania.

Malone, Joseph. 1993. "Referring Expressions in Bound Position: Infraction of Principle C of the Binding Theory." *General Linguistics* 33:1–55.

Mann, W., C. Matthiessen, and S. Thompson. 1982. "Rhetorical Structure Theory: Toward a Functional Theory of Text Organization." *Text* 8(3): 243–81.

Manney, Linda. 1993. "Middle Voice in Modern Greek." Ph.D. diss., University of California, San Diego.

Matthiessen, Christian, and Sandra A. Thompson. 1988. "The Structure of Discourse and 'Subordination.'" In J. Haiman and S. A. Thompson, eds., *Clause Combining in Grammar and Discourse*. Amsterdam: John Benjamins.

May, Robert. 1985. *Logical Form: Its Structure and Derivation*. Cambridge, MA: MIT Press.

Mittwoch, Anita. 1983. "Backward Anaphora and Discourse Structure." *Journal of Pragmatics* 7:129–39.

Morrow, Daniel. 1985. "Prominent Characters and Events Organize Narrative Understanding." *Journal of Memory and Language* 24:304–19.

Newmeyer, Frederick J. 1983. *Grammatical Theory: Its Limits and Possibilities*. Chicago: University of Chicago Press.

Perlmutter, David, and Paul Postal. 1983. "Towards a Universal Characterization of Passivization." In D. M. Perlmutter, ed., *Studies in Relational Grammar*, Vol. 1. Chicago: University of Chicago Press.

Perlmutter, David, and Carol Rosen. 1984. *Studies in Relational Grammar*, Vol. 2. Chicago: University of Chicago Press.

Planck, Frans. 1979. "Exklusivierung, Reflexivierung, Identifizierung, Relationale Auszeichnung: Variationen zu einem semantisch-pragmatischen Thema." In I. Rosen, ed., *Sprache und Pragmatik*. Lund: Gleerup.

Pollard, Carl, and Ivan Sag. 1992. "Anaphors in English and the Scope of Binding Theory." *Linguistic Inquiry* 23:261–303.

———. 1993. *Head-driven Phrase Structure Grammar*. Chicago: University of Chicago Press.

Postal, Paul. 1969. "Anaphoric Islands." *Proceedings of the Annual Meeting of the Chicago Linguistic Society* 5:205–39.

———. *Crossover Phenomena*. New York: Holt, Rinehart & Winston.

Progovac, Lillian. 1994. *Negative and Positive Polarity: A Binding Approach.* Cambridge: Cambridge University Press.

Ramsay, Violeta. 1987. "Preposed and Postposed 'If' and 'When' Clauses." In R. Tomlin, ed., *Coherence and Grounding in Discourse.* Amsterdam: John Benjamins.

Redeker, G. 1985. "References to Story Characters in Interactive and Noninteractive Narration." Paper presented at the International Pragmatics Conference, Viareggio, Italy.

Reinhart, Tanya. 1976. "The Syntactic Domain of Anaphora." Ph.D. diss., MIT.

———. 1981. "Definite NP Anaphora and C-Command Domains." *Linguistic Inquiry* 12:605–36.

———. 1983. *Anaphora and Semantic Interpretation.* Chicago: University of Chicago Press.

———. 1986. "Center and Periphery in the Grammar of Anaphora." In B. Lust, ed., *Studies in the Acquisition of Anaphora,* Vol. 1. Dordrecht: D. Reidel.

———. 1987. "Specifier and Operator Binding." In E. J. Reuland and A. G. B. ter Meuten, eds., *The Representation of (In)definiteness.* Cambridge, MA: MIT Press.

Reinhart, Tanya, and Eric Reuland. 1991. "Anaphors and Logophors: An Argument Structure Perspective. In J. Koster and E. Reuland, eds., *Long-Distance Anaphora.* Cambridge: Cambridge University Press.

———. 1993. "Reflexivity." *Linguistic Inquiry* 24:657–720.

Rice, Sally. 1987. "Towards a Cognitive Model of Transitivity." Ph.D. diss., University of California, San Diego.

Riddle, Elizabeth. 1984. "The English Possessives as Topic-Focus Structures." Paper presented at the Annual Meeting of the Linguistics Society of America, Baltimore.

Roberts, Craige. 1987. "Modal Subordination, Distributivity and Anaphora." Ph.D. diss., University of Massachusetts, Amherst.

Ross, John. 1967. *Constraints on Variables in Syntax.* Ph.D. diss., MIT.

———. 1970. "On Declarative Sentences." In R. A. Jacobs and P. S. Rossenbaum, eds., *Readings in English Transformational Grammar.* Waltham, MA: Ginn.

Rubba, Johanna. 1993. "Discontinuous Morphology in Modern Aramaic." Ph.D. diss., University of California, San Diego.

Sanford, A., and S. Garrod. 1981. *Understanding Written Language.* Chichester: John Wiley.

Solan, Larry. 1983. *Pronominal Reference: Child Language and the Theory of Grammar.* Dordrecht: D. Reidel.

Sperber, D., and D. Wilson. 1986. *Relevance.* Oxford: Blackwell.

Sproat, Richard, and Gregory Ward. 1987. "Pragmatic Considerations in Anaphoric Island Phenomena." In. B. Need, E. Schiller, and A. Bosch, eds., *Papers from the twenty-third Annual Regional Meeting of the Chicago Linguistic Society.* I: Pt. 1: *General Session.* Chicago: Chicago Linguistic Society.

Sweetser, Eve. 1984. "Semantic Structure and Semantic Change: A Cognitive Linguistic Study of Modality, Perception, Speech Acts, and Logical Relations." Ph.D. diss., University of California, Berkeley.

Talmy, Leonard. 1978. "Figure and Ground in Complex Sentences." In J.

Greenberg, ed., *Universals of Human Language,* Vol. 4. Stanford: Stanford University Press.

———. 1995. "The Windowing of Attention in Language." Ms., State University of New York, Buffalo, Center for Cognitive Science.

Taylor, John R. 1989. *Linguistic Categorization: Prototypes in Linguistic Theory.* Oxford: Oxford University Press.

———. 1994a " 'Subjective' and 'Objective' Readings of Possessor Nominals." *Cognitive Linguistics* 5(3): 201–42.

———. 1994b. "Possessives and Topicality." *Functions of Language* 1(1): 67–94.

———. Forthcoming. *Possessives as Topics.*

Thomason, Richmond, and Robert Stalnaker. 1973. "A Semantic Theory of Adverbs." *Linguistic Inquiry* 2:195–220.

Tomlin, Russell S. 1983. "On the Interaction of Syntactic Subject, Thematic Information, and Agent in English." *Journal of Pragmatics* 7:411–32.

———. 1984. "The Identification of Foreground-Background Information in On-Line Descriptive Discourse." Ms., University of Oregon, Dept. of Linguistics.

———, ed. 1987a. *Coherence and Grounding in Discourse.* Amsterdam: John Benjamins.

———. 1987b. "Linguistic Reflections of Cognitive Events." In Tomlin 1987a.

Tuggy, David. 1981. "The Transitivity-Related Morphology of Tetelcingo Nahuatl: An Exploration in Space Grammar." Ph.D. diss., University of California, San Diego.

van Dijk, T., and W. Kintsch. 1983. *Strategies of Discourse Comprehension.* New York: Academic Press.

van Hoek, Karen. 1992. "Paths through Conceptual Structure: Constraints on Pronominal Anaphora." Ph.D. diss., University of California, San Diego.

———. 1993. "Conceptual Connectivity and Constraints on Anaphora." In *Chicago Linguistics Society Parasession* 29:363–75.

———. 1995a. Conceptual Reference Points: A Cognitive Grammar Account of Pronominal Anaphora Constraints." *Language* 71(2): 310–40.

———. 1995b. "Reflexives from a Subjective Point of View." Paper presented at the Fourth Meeting of the International Cognitive Linguistics Association, Albuquerque, NM, July.

——— 1996a. "Quantifiers as Starting Points." Paper presented at the Conference on Functionalism and Formalism in Linguistics, Milwaukee, April.

———. 1996b. "Negative Polarity 'Any': A Mental Spaces Account." Paper presented at the Conference on Conceptual Structure and Discourse; Buffalo, April.

Vandeloise, Claude. 1984. "Description of Space in French." Ph.D. diss., University of California, San Diego.

Vendler, Zeno. 1967. *Linguistics in Philosophy.* Ithaca, NY: Cornell University Press.

Ward, Gregory. 1983. "On Non-reflexive Pronouns in Reflexive Environments." *University of Pennsylvania Review of Linguistics,* pp. 12–19.

Ward, Gregory, Richard Sproat, and Gail McKoon. 1991. "A Pragmatic Analysis of So-called Anaphoric Islands." *Language* 67: 439–74.

Wiebe, Janyce M. 1995. "References in Narrative Texts." In Duchan et al. 1995.

Williams, Edwin. 1977. "Discourse and Logical Form." *Linguistic Inquiry* 8(1): 101–39.

———. 1994. *Thematic Structure in Syntax*. Cambridge, MA: MIT Press.

Zribi-Hertz, Anne. 1989. "Anaphor Binding and Narrative Point of View: English Reflexive Pronouns in Sentence and Discourse." *Language* 65:695–727.

———. 1994. "Emphatic or Reflexive? On the Endophoric Character of French *lui-même* and Similar Complex Pronouns." Ms., University of Paris, Dept. of Language Sciences.

Ziv, Yael. 1994. "Pronominal Reference to Inferred Antecedents." Paper presented at the Conference on Anaphoric Relations and (In)coherence, Antwerp, December.